MW01054420

RECOVERY ZONE Volume 1

Other books by Patrick Carnes, Ph.D.

Out of Shadows: Understanding Sexual Addiction

A Gentle Path Through the Twelve Steps: A Guidebook for All People in the Process of Recovery

A Gentle Path Through the Twelve Principles: Living the Values Behind the Steps

Contrary to Love: Helping the Sexual Addict

Don't Call It Love: Recovery from Sexual Addiction

Sexual Anorexia: Overcoming Sexual Self-Hatred

The Betrayal Bond: Breaking Free of Exploitive Relationships

Open Hearts: Renewing Relationships with Recovery, Romance & Reality

Facing the Shadow: Starting Sexual and Relationship Recovery

In the Shadows of the Net: Breaking Free of Compulsive Online Sexual Behavior

Clinical Management of Sex Addiction

Recovery Start Kit: The First 130 Days

Facing Addiction: Starting Recovery from Alcohol and Drugs

RECOVERY ZONE Volume 1

Making Changes that Last: The Internal Tasks

Patrick J. Carnes, Ph.D.

Gentle Path
PRESS

Carefree, Arizona

Gentle Path
P R E S S

Gentle Path Press
PO Box 3172
Carefree, Arizona 85377
gentlepath.com

First Edition: November 2009
Second Printing: March 2012
Third Printing: August 2013

For more information regarding our publications,
please contact Gentle Path Press at
1-800-708-1796 (toll-free U.S. only).

ISBN-10: 0-977-44001-X

ISBN-13: 978-0-977-44001-6

Table of Contents

Introduction

Here is the truth: There is no overnight fix for recovery. For those who enter recovery, it is a truth no one wants to tell us for fear we will not do the work. Reflect back on your first days of recovery. For most of us, people had to work desperately hard to get us to realize that on our own we were self-destructing. We were destroying ourselves, our relationships, and all that we held most dear. Consider the pain, losses, consequences, failures, arguments, and lies revealed—all that had to happen before we finally accepted we had a problem. The word *recovery* was used. Then we learned that it was more than a problem, it was an illness. That fact alone was hard to stomach. Then words like *sobriety*, *letting go*, and *surrender* were used. Stopping the swirl was agony. So much was wrong.

So the people helping us—if they knew at all—did not tell us this truth for fear that knowing it would send us back to the maelstrom. It would be parallel to parents not fully realizing the pain and sacrifice of raising a child at the moment of conception. Some of us would not have had children, but almost all of us who have children are grateful for every moment of child-raising after they leave (an awareness we typically do not fully realize until we see our child have a child). But at the time of sex and romance, the reality would be overwhelming compared to the reward. Similarly, our helpers told us the goal was to get to a meeting, to get to therapy, or to get to treatment. Everything would get better if we just did that.

The truth is the same for everyone, whether he or she is an addict or codependent, trauma survivor or adult child, adolescent or elderly, or a combination of all of these. At this point we know no exceptions. And the truth is, to establish a viable recovery process takes at least three and a half years and for most up to five years. To say that you will work on this the rest of your life understates the agony of that three- to five-year period. It is harder than establishing sobriety. Going through that agony causes many to relapse. Becoming sober is not the hardest part. Staying sober is. Making changes in our lives halts the pain. Keeping the changes is what saves our lives. Like sex and kids, if you knew what the sacrifices were going to cost, you would evaluate the orgasm differently.

But like raising children, or achieving successful relationships, or reaching other big goals, you would not trade the rewards of recovery for anything. You now know too much. The price is worth the knowledge recovery gives. Nothing compares to the quality of life that recovery provides.

Deep gratitude exists for the day we walked into a meeting or the door to treatment. Most of us do not believe all the good things that would be in store that fateful day we started. Yet every fellowship, starting with Alcoholics Anonymous, talks of "promises."

This book is designed to help you find the richness of recovery. It should take you at least eighteen months to implement what you find here. A good strategy is to read through it now. Then with others in your groups and support meetings, take time to work through the tasks outlined for you. I remember a physician who was a superb student and very accustomed to pulling "all nighters." Upon entering treatment he read a book called the *Gentle Path Through the Twelve Steps*, and stayed up two nights completing all the exercises and formulas in the book. Then the next morning, as a very tired patient, he stood up and announced that he had completed everything and was ready to return to work. He was stunned at the friendly laughter of the other patients and staff. To this day he tells the tale about himself to make the point. Filling in the blanks is not the same as doing the work.

Doing the work is like unraveling a very large ball of string. Each tug brings more into view. If you are like most of us, we find ourselves taking the threads and weaving them into a tapestry which is the story of our lives. For me it started almost four decades ago with Al-Anon when my father returned to drinking after thirty years of abstinence. I had to face issues about being an "adult child." Then I examined the threads of addictions and deprivations in my life which wove their way across food, sex, work, money, and chemicals. Finally, I had to explore the deep issues of anxiety, anger, shame, and grief that were the background for the chaos of my life. After almost forty years, I still am learning from it all.

And it is reasonable to do so. If you look at my family of origin, these themes of addiction and codependency have generations of power behind them. A complex mosaic appeared that took decades for me to live through and decades for me to work through. At the time I did not know there was a faster, more focused way to sort all this out. Today we do. As a result, it has been my goal for some time to distill what actually has been proven to work for people and make it accessible. We call it the Recovery Zone.

Recovery Zone is built on the following truths:

- Addicts and codependents have a complex set of neural networks in their brains causing them to behave in self-destructive and dysfunctional patterns even though they at times know better. The behaviors have become compulsive and addictive. It now is biological.

- In most cases they have more than one of these patterns. No amount of willpower will work. Decision making has become impaired.

- It takes weeks to clear the brain of destructive behavior. It takes months to gain focus to do the necessary work to make the change permanent. It takes years for the brain to heal. Like all of our organs, the brain wants to be fully functional but it takes time.

- In order to change we must understand and face the underlying factors to destructive patterns. These factors include early childhood trauma, family genetics, grief, anxiety, and not the least, brain damage.
- There is a clear recipe that helps to restore what was lost.
- The recipe works best if done in a focused, systematic way.

Put another way, you do not have to wander through decades of your life working through problem after problem as you become aware and as you discover resources. This wastes opportunities, creates relapses, and requires some luck. There is a real possibility of making decisions (or sometimes avoiding them) which some of us spend much of our remaining lives untangling. However, there is a proven path which requires a great deal of effort now. It requires focus, study, and time. And, of course, courage.

The results are extraordinary. I learned this first hand by following one thousand addicts and their families for seven years. Most of the addicts and their partners had layers of dysfunction, compulsion, and addiction. Seven of us researchers labored carefully to isolate what made the difference for successful recovery. When we finished, we broke down the recipe into concrete ingredients and actions. We called them tasks. There were thirty of them. Then we broke the tasks down into specific "performables." These were activities that most people could do. We further verified the process by following people and measuring their progress. We found very little relapse. We realized that to really finish this story, we needed to teach the process to many therapists. And now we need to measure what happens.

The result is what you see here in this book, *Recovery Zone,* and its future companion volumes. Literally thousands of people have helped to create this recipe. Therapists have been trained in it across North America and many foreign countries. Details about the thirty tasks, resources available, and accessing trained therapists are presented in the appendix.

The Tasks One through Seven concentrate on stopping behavior and creating sufficient progress to establish recovery. *Recovery Zone: Making Changes that Last* focuses on Tasks Eight through Thirteen. These tasks all relate to creating a platform for healthy recovery. Our future volume, *Recovery Zone: Achieving Balance in Your Life,* will relate to taking your recovery and incorporating it into all facets of your life. Tasks Nineteen through Thirty relate to what has to happen for couples and families. Those tasks will be described in a future series called *Family Zone: Creating Family Recovery.* More than likely you will be using all the Recovery Zone books since many of us have to work on our own recoveries while attending to life issues at the same time. To have clarity about this book, look at **Figure 1**, on page 4, which helps indicate our place on the path we have described.

We assume you have either completed the first seven tasks or have established three to six months of recovery. You have decided to keep what you have and now know that recovery is more than just changing some behaviors. Now you are willing to do the deep work necessary to make

You Are Here

Tasks 1–7

1. Break through denial
2. Understand addiction
3. Surrender
4. Limit damage
5. Establish sobriety
6. Physical integrity
7. Culture of support

Facing the Shadow

Tasks 8–13

8. Multiple addictions
9. Cycles of abuse
10. Reduce shame
11. Grieve losses
12. Closure to shame
13. Relationship with self

Recovery Zone: Volume 1
Making Changes that Last:
The Internal Tasks

Tasks 14–19

14. Financial viability
15. Meaningful work
16. Lifestyle balance
17. Building support
18. Exercise and nutrition
19. Spiritual life

Recovery Zone: Volume 2
Achieving Balance in Your Life:
The External Tasks

Tasks 19–30

19. Spiritual life
20. Resolve conflicts
21. Restore healthy sexuality
22. Family therapy
23. Family relationships
24. Recovery commitment
25. Issues with children
26. Extended family
27. Differentiation
28. Primary relationship
29. Coupleship
30. Primary intimacy

Family Zone:
Creating Family Recovery

Figure 1

the shift. Doing the deep work will mean dramatic changes to your relationships, career, finances, and lifestyle. Remember it is more than filling in the blanks. To do the tasks requires time and effort. You will feel pulled by work, kids, and life's complications, so you will need structure and support in order to do it most effectively. Remember it is best to do the work in a period of eighteen months to two years. Nav 12 - 2022

Therefore, you must have a good therapist. Hopefully you have found one who is trained in the task-centered methodology. However, any good addiction oriented therapist will be able to help you with these materials. This work requires a long term relationship with a competent therapist who serves as a flight tower so you do not lose your way on the path. Also, group psychotherapy is a critical element in the recipe upon which the path is based. We found the optimum to be about 175 hours.

Historically many people have gone to treatment in a residential program. They are then referred to "aftercare." The term "aftercare" was built on the core assumption that treatment and stopping your addictive behaviors was the goal. The main work was done in rehab. Unfortunately, many people relapse (some within days of leaving), and they are viewed as "not getting it" in treatment. The real problem is the need for continuing the momentum into deeper work. Most professionals now understand the need for residential facilities because many people cannot get sober any other way. The reality is, residential programs only open the door to the critical underlying effort that must now take place. Addiction is a serious biological and psychological problem which requires much more than we have ever understood.

With advances in neuroscience (which have shaped much of the work you will see here), we now know more than ever how critical the long term effort is. We know so much more now about why psychotherapy works. And why it takes time. We have to grow new neural networks in our brains. Brief approaches, while convenient to our health care system, do not address the underlying causes of addictive behavior and the realities of our synaptic connections. This does not happen in thirty days of residential treatment or ten sessions of outpatient treatment. In short, find a good therapist. Better still, find a therapist who understands trauma and addiction. Best, find someone who is certified to work with the content presented in this book.

The other critical part is that you must participate in a Twelve Step Program. The people who do that have success. In one of our early outcome studies, we found that only twenty-three percent of our patients completed Steps One through Nine in eighteen months. Of those who did, there was almost no relapse. The bottom line is that you have to build momentum, keep it going, and follow the recipe. It depends on how much you do and how focused you are when you do it. To piecemeal the work, put things off until you have time, and wait until things come up put all your efforts in jeopardy. Twelve Step programs serve people who have problems with alcohol, drugs, sex, food, gambling, high risk experiences, codependency (compulsive attachment), or money.

And they all ultimately bring us to the core issues. *Recovery Zone* is designed to work with the Twelve Steps no matter what brought you to the table.

Finally, another core resource is recoveryzone.com. Along with your therapist, the recoveryzone.com website will help with resources, pacing, and structuring your efforts. Your computer can help you with the exercises in this book. For those of you who found the computer was part of your problem, our experience is that you can work out safe ways for you to access this website. Recoveryzone.com has a whole section dedicated to assist you with this challenge. Also, consult with your therapist, your group, and family about how you utilize the web to help.

When we followed the original one thousand families in which this recipe first emerged, we noticed that there were predictable stages that both addicts and their family members would go through. It was basically a seven-year process, with the first two years focused on realizing there was a problem. Six distinct phases or stages were identified:

- **The Developing Stage** in which they start to understand that addiction is present in themselves or a loved one and that something has to be done. They may have made half-hearted efforts to change by going to a meeting, a therapist, or to treatment, but really they are not ready yet.
- **The Crisis Decision Stage** in which they realize they simply can no longer tolerate the problem. Something forces them to realize they can no longer live like this. So they commit no matter what the cost.
- **The Shock Stage** in which they absorb the reality of how bad things have gotten and deeply engage in therapy to change it.
- **The Grief Stage** in which they profoundly understand their losses and pain throughout life and specifically how their behaviors fit larger patterns. These patterns need to be understood, and then new effective processes adopted.
- **The Repair Stage** in which they reconstruct their lives and work. Core to the repair work, they change how they interact with themselves and those around them.
- **The Growth Stage** in which they experience a new depth in their relationships and a new level of openness and effectiveness.

Figure 2, on page 7, presents a timeline of how the stages occurred over time.

The Course of Recovery Over Time

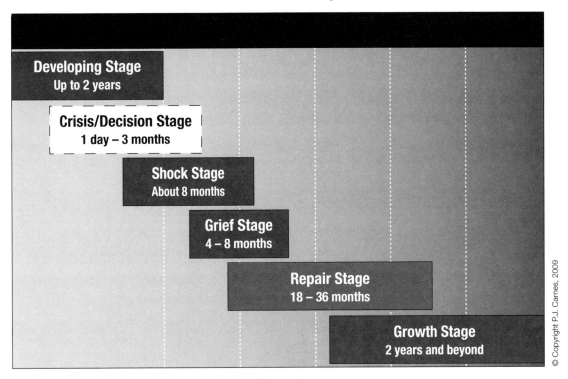

Figure 2

At the time we were researching this pattern, Joseph Campbell's work on the hero's story was coming into popular awareness. Campbell carefully examined myths and stories from all cultures and times. He made the case that heroes and heroines basically share the same story:

- The heroes at first are innocent. They do not know what they do not know, nor are they aware that they need to know.

- Then they have a growing awareness that something is not right. There are signs and disconcerting developments. Or there is a hunger for better. (For example, Bilbo Baggins did not want to accept his challenge in *The Hobbit*.)

- Something happens that forces them into action. They do not know how they will do it, but they accept the call. And he or she knows there is no going back. (Luke Skywalker's family is killed in *Star Wars*.)

- Things become desperate and grim. (It parallels driving at night in a storm. You may know where you are going, but you can only see what is in the headlights.) Fortunately, guides emerge. Often the guides provide gifts and tools critical to the quest. New skills and abilities are developed. The first conflicts initiate the journey. The first wounds and scars portend how difficult it will all be. There is no going back now.

- There is usually an ordeal in a series of challenges. (I remember as a child, while watching Saturday matinees that this occurred every ninety seconds.) These are dark times in which the heroes confront the demons. They have no security, allies show up; there are worthy companions who offer humorous wisdom and in battle they offer protection. This is the dark night of the soul (Jacob wrestling with the angel). Usually there are great losses and suffering. Almost always essential tasks appear, as when Ulysses had to find his way home. Tasks are always important in the heroic journey.
- Forged in great difficulty, heroes and heroines find a deep resolve which brings them to a breakthrough. With the breakthrough, they are transformed. Everything in their lives changes, which may take a while to make happen. (For example, Harry Potter pieces together the mystery of Lord Voldemort.)
- They reflect on their losses and what they have learned. Suffering is channeled into new creativity. The warrior princess becomes the healer or medicine woman. (Think of the *The Mists of Avalon* or author Patricia Cornwell's heroine in several books, Dr. Kay Scarpetta. Or, remember how Daedalus serves his countryman after losing his son.)

Figure 3 is a diagram which summarizes the heroic journey.

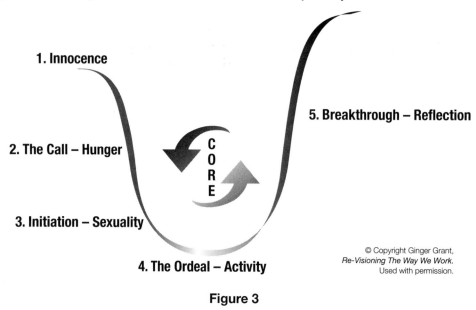

1. Innocence

2. The Call – Hunger

3. Initiation – Sexuality

4. The Ordeal – Activity

CORE

5. Breakthrough – Reflection

© Copyright Ginger Grant,
Re-Visioning The Way We Work.
Used with permission.

Figure 3

The story of the hero or heroine is the story of all of us. As we reflected on all the stories and data that went into the tasks of recovery, we saw great parallels in the heroic journey. Campbell's work informed us of the significance of what emerged in our research. Most recovering people did not want to start the sobriety process but they were thrust into it. The journey involved overwhelming challenges and profoundly painful realizations. There were mentors and new skills. Allies showed up. Transformation occurs. But when it starts you have no idea. Kind of like having kids. When it starts you have no idea.

Figure 4 compares the stages of recovery with the heroic journey. It also helps to illustrate how the tasks fit into the whole process. We make the comparison for a number of reasons. First, it helps to get through the process if you can see that it taps into the deeper rhythms of being human. Plus, there are important lessons that will help you. We will make them explicit as you go through this process. And we wish for you to see the inevitability of the work you must do. Compare it to the last weeks of pregnancy. No matter what pain is coming, it will require all of your attention and it will bring some of the greatest joy you will know.

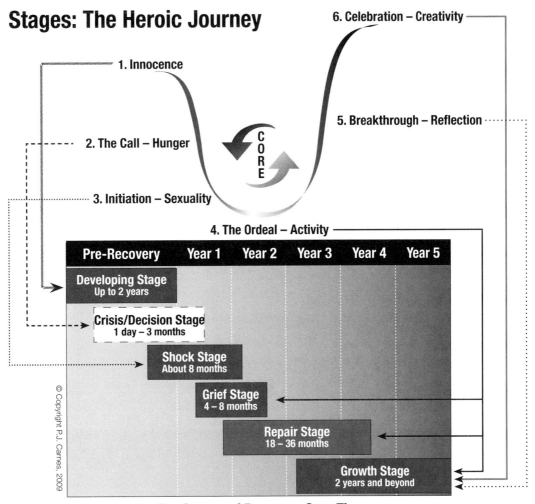

Stages: The Heroic Journey

1. Innocence
2. The Call – Hunger
3. Initiation – Sexuality
4. The Ordeal – Activity
5. Breakthrough – Reflection
6. Celebration – Creativity

CORE

| Pre-Recovery | Year 1 | Year 2 | Year 3 | Year 4 | Year 5 |

Developing Stage Up to 2 years

Crisis/Decision Stage 1 day – 3 months

Shock Stage About 8 months

Grief Stage 4 – 8 months

Repair Stage 18 – 36 months

Growth Stage 2 years and beyond

© Copyright P.J. Carnes, 2009

The Course of Recovery Over Time

Figure 4

This book is organized as a journey to guide you through the internal tasks (8–13). **Part One** describes three tools you will need to meet your recovery challenges: the Decision Table, so you do not lose sight of all that troubles you; the Recovery Zone, so you will know your strengths; and a map to navigate addiction and codependency (or what we will call compulsive attachment).

Part Two is the dark night of the soul, which we recommend as a process that occurs over two hundred days (just short of thirty weeks). Anger, shame, grief, and trauma—these are the primary ingredients of human suffering. Learning to make yourself do what you do not wish to do creates a whole new way to take your hurt and transform it into doing only that which matters. Going through the pain will provide a new compass for your life. Once you have reclaimed your compass, you will realize how much has to change. *Recovery Zone, Volume 2: Achieving Balance in Your Life*, the sequel to this volume, will become your next companion on your journey. To help reorient yourself, you will need what we call the Vision Table. In addition, you will have to rid yourself of some baggage. We call this a closure process. Finally, you will need a way to discover new allies. Then follows the deep focus work of changing relationships, money and work habits, and how you care for yourself and your body. In that focus, however, a most profound spiritual shift occurs.

At this point it may seem complex, but it is a proven recipe. If you follow the steps and the timing—just like making bread—you should have a predictable result. Once again, I strongly recommend that you read the book once through before starting your work. Your therapist will help you integrate the work into your therapy and will have other tools for you to use. Like all good stories, it does make sense at the end.

At the beginning, though, there usually is a "MacGuffin." This term was first used by Alfred Hitchcock to describe how good stories work. It has been talked about by some of our most outstanding movie producers, including George Lucas and Steven Spielberg. Basically, a MacGuffin is something that occurs which forces the hero/heroine into the adventure. It is that which starts the whole process, maybe giving it meaning, and bringing the character into something extraordinary in scale. The journey is always much, much more than the MacGuffin that starts it. Addiction is a MacGuffin that starts the recovery journey. However, recovery turns out to be much bigger than just ceasing the addictive behavior. Generations of recycled pain are stopped. In a sense the addictions become almost incidental. A whole new level of being present to life can result with recovery. Life is never the same. There is no going back. *Consider yourself called.*

Patrick Carnes

Recovery Zone **Part One**

Chapter 1 **The Decision Table**

We have all seen it. We know someone who has a problem. In fact everyone around that person more or less sees the problem clearly. The person who has the problem knows it and can describe it in detail. Friends and family may become exasperated by hearing the story of the problem. Ironically, the person can talk about what has to happen to fix it. Yet no action happens. The problem persists or even becomes worse. The worst situation, of course, is when that person is yourself.

Imagine a table in front of each of us. On it are decisions we know we should make. Every one of us has choices that, if made, would make our lives remarkable. These choices include diet, weight, career, relationships, and unfinished tasks. These are tasks we wish we would simply do, but do not; statements we wish we would say, but leave unsaid; and habits and addictions we hope we could stop, but persist in. Add in the projects we started but never finished and the creative ideas thought about but never completed. In short, it is the life we want but do not have.

These decisions wait on the table until we pick them up and act on them. We may even imagine what it would be like to have what we want and take comfort in that fantasy. But that is all the comfort we allow ourselves. We may torture ourselves with "shoulds" and perceive ourselves as lazy or worthless. Perhaps we convince ourselves that the timing is not right, or that other priorities must prevail. When that happens we have entered what we will call the "deferred living" plan. Often people postpone what they wish for to enjoy life until some later point, such as retirement. In deferred living we put things off until it is too late. We banish our most important agendas to a province called "someday." The net result is: what we clearly see needs to be done for our well-being stays on the table.

Our life changes when we understand the "decision table." At any point in our lives there are decisions to be made. Some need to be made now; some need to be thought about. The critical issue is to recognize the nature of our choices and that they have to be made. People have trouble when they do not see that a choice has to be made and they ignore the realities on their table, or they agonize about them, and in effect postpone them. In more than thirty years of doing therapy, I have come to the conclusion that making choices is an essential life skill. Much of therapy is really about helping people face choices. Most people would not have to go to therapy or treatment if they were willing to face the realities presented by their choices.

Recovering people understand that decision making is a core recovery skill. The Big Book of *Alcoholics Anonymous* sets the tone in the Third Step, which starts off with "Made a decision." The Third Step asks for a commitment to the program, as the way alcoholics can heal their lives. This decision is, in effect, to trust a Higher Power—even though the new member does not yet know where this will all lead. Not knowing the outcome is one of the critical risks of change. Throughout the Big Book there is the constant request for commitment that forces us to look for the courage to decide to do something on our own behalf. Bill W. writes that if you are not in the solution, you are still in the problem. Bill W. also wrote about the "willingness to go to any lengths."

The commitment to change or decide on your own behalf is echoed throughout all the recovery groups and self-help programs. A constant theme in Al-Anon is that, in your decisions, you get to decide "how important your serenity is." Sex addicts talk about the sobriety imperative. One of the traditional closings of a Twelve Step meeting, after the recitation of the Serenity Prayer, is "keep coming back—it works if you work it—and take action." Most addicts and codependents have problems because of inaction. They are not facing the decisions on the table.

They are not alone. In one of the classic lines in self-improvement literature, M. Scott Peck wrote that "mental health is dedication to reality at all costs." The basis of all reality is to know what your choices are. The problem for most of us is that no one taught us about the essentials of decision making. We learned by absorbing what happened in our families, by watching what happened in school, or by learning in business or career. If we were lucky we had mentors who coached us. The first critical component to effective change is to master the essentials of decision making.

Essential One: You have to decide

I learned an incredibly important lesson about decisions from my youngest daughter, Erin. For ten years, I was a single parent with four children. During the first three years I did not date anyone. When I started to date I was, at best, tentative. I met a woman named Paulette whom I dated for about six weeks. When I woke up on a Thursday morning, having been out with Paulette the night before, I realized that I had feelings that I had not experienced in a long time. I had learned in my own therapy not to sit on my reactions. I called her to tell her that I had crossed the line from dating to something more serious. Paulette responded by saying that the same thing had been happening to her. She also wanted me to know something had just happened which altered the whole picture for her. I could tell that the moment of romance had evaporated into something much more difficult.

In a halting and sad voice her story came out. Paulette was also a single parent with three children. Three years prior she had met a man about whom she became very serious. After two years of being together she could see that he was commitment aversive. He was not willing to go to the next level. She was very disappointed because she really cared for him and could see how difficult it was for him. She also realized that she had to leave, no matter how painful it was, because there was no future for her and her children. She did not date for about a year and a half. Shortly after she started dating again, she met me. On this morning she realized, as I had, that there was some extraordinary potential for both of us. She was just about to call me when the phone rang. It was this man who called to tell her that he was now ready and he asked her to marry him.[1]

Paulette now had a choice. She told me that she had found things with me she had never had with him. On the other hand, she had two years invested in someone who was very dear to her. I invited her over for supper so we could talk. The truth was, I was hoping to influence her decision. That evening we sat on my deck after dinner, and Paulette shared how difficult the situation was for her. My eight-year-old daughter, Erin, came out and noticed that Paulette was crying. She later cornered me in the living room and asked why Paulette had been crying. I responded by saying that Paulette had a difficult choice to make, that she was going to be all right, and that Erin need not worry about it. I also asked her to go bed so I could tuck her in.

When I walked in to Erin's room, she was propped up on her pillows with her arms folded in what I like to call her "announcement" position. She said, "Dad, I want you to give Paulette a message for me. If she has a difficult choice to make—like she is in love with two men at the same time—first, she has to accept that she does have to decide. Once she realizes that she has to choose, she will know who it is." I walked downstairs and said to Paulette, "You are not going to believe the message I have for you from Erin." Two days later Paulette called. She told me to thank Erin because it was exactly what she needed to hear. She realized that no matter what choice she made there would be a painful loss and she did not want to face it. She had made her choice and it was not me. I was sad, but I learned so much from this experience.[2]

I think of this story often because this is where many of us get stuck. We cannot resolve things because we have not accepted that we have to decide. Any time you decide something, you give up something. Decisions become paralyzing because of our unwillingness to sustain the grief. The word *decision*—like the word *incision*—comes from the Latin *to cut*. Basically to decide is to cut away something. When the choice is made to enter recovery you often have to give up things. If you are an addict, giving up the addiction is hard because the addiction has been like a comforting friend during some desperate moments. The codependent has to give up certain relationship styles and obsessions and maybe some relationships that seem indispensable. The survivors of abuse have to give up dreams and trust because reality was not what they were told. The depressed person gives up the relief of doing nothing. Ironically, to postpone decisions in any of these cases often creates more hurt and harm.

That is why the metaphor of the decision table is so helpful. Later in this chapter we will help you with your own decision table. You will learn that there are issues in front of you that you must assess and prioritize so you can have an optimum life. Second, by laying your decisions out you begin to see patterns in yourself. Identifying these patterns becomes important in making significant systematic change in how you conduct your life. If therapy is about facing choices, the essence of therapy is learning how to do it effectively and how to do it ineffectively. You can also see how one decision affects another, which improves your problem-solving skills. Finally, having a decision table brings into focus that which you have to decide. Acceptance brings us to the second essential: courage.

Essential Two: Most critical decisions are made without knowing what the outcome will be

Our myths and stories help us understand ourselves. Joseph Campbell, in his studies of the stories of thousands of cultures, found that all heroes and heroines go through the same process that addicts do. First of all, they did not want to go on adventures or accept challenges. They found themselves thrust into situations in which they had a choice of doing something or being defeated by despairing circumstances. Invariably, the choice to do something meant embarking on a quest without knowledge of how it would end. Bilbo Baggins in *The Hobbit* wanted to remain in the Shire. Luke Skywalker in *Star Wars* did not want to go, but preferred to stay with his aunt and uncle on their farm on Tatooine. Harry Potter had no clue about his exceptional future as he struggled with his Muggle family. In the Greek stories, Oedipus, Medea, and Atreus all are thrust into circumstances beyond their control. As these characters encounter challenges they are refined and become stronger and more discerning. They confront demons in various forms and are transformed into exceptional human beings. Usually they have the help of others, including wise guides such as Gandalf, Obi-Wan Kenobi, or Albus Dumbledore. Essentially our stories help us grow personally and teach us about the courage it takes to be human beings.[3]

No better example of deciding without knowing where it leads can be found than in J.R.R. Tolkien's *Lord of the Rings* series. We are introduced to the tale in *The Hobbit* where we learn about the wonderful human-like characters who are about half the size of men. Hobbits are distinguished by their simplicity and their attention to creature comforts, including food, sleep, gardening, and more food. The hero, Bilbo Baggins, is thrust into an adventure in which he finds a ring of great power crafted by the most powerful of the dark lords, Sauron. Bilbo manages to thwart Sauron's plan for domination of Middle Earth by keeping the ring and hiding it.

This tale is followed by *The Fellowship of the Ring* in which Frodo Baggins, Bilbo's nephew, has to destroy the powerful ring given to him by his uncle. To do this he must take it into the very heart of the Land of Mordor where Sauron, the evil wizard, is mustering his legions of demons. We watch as Sauron expands his dark powers in all directions. The hobbit and his fellows make it all the way to Rivendell, the land of Elrond, the elfin king who still holds on to his power. Frodo had hopes that his job was over. There is a council of elves, dwarves, men, and hobbits from all the corners of middle earth. As each shares what they have learned, the dark machinations of Sauron become painfully clear to all. The Council resolves that the ring must be destroyed in the place where it was made by Sauron. The problem is that the ring is dangerous to its bearer. One by one, candidates for carrying it have to be eliminated. Tolkien describes the scene:

> The noon bell rang. Still no one spoke. Frodo glanced at all the faces, but they were not turned to him. All the Council sat with downcast eyes, as if in deep thought. A great dread fell on him, as if he was awaiting the pronouncement of some doom that he had long foreseen and vainly hoped might after all never be spoken. An overwhelming longing to rest and remain at peace by Bilbo's side in Rivendell filled all his heart. At last with an effort he spoke, and wondered to hear his own words, as if some other will was using his small voice. "I will take the Ring," he said, "'though I do not know the way."

Heroes and heroines are reluctant and almost always do not know the way.

Decisions require courage because we do not know the outcome. In the Twelve Step fellowships, the phrase that honors this moment in people's lives is "some of us cried out, it is too great a task." Significant change usually means facing an uncertain end and a profound desire to "rest and remain at peace." Deciding to make the commitment leads to other decisions—so the process of facing our fears goes on for some time. One change requires another. Suddenly all of life becomes different with all the changes. More importantly, there is transformation. That is the grand design of being human. Life is a refining process that calls us to be better people—unless we avoid making the necessary decisions.

So it is with recovery. Most of us did not want to start the process. When we did, we just wanted to fix the part that was the problem. Once started, however, it led to a whole series of events and efforts we had not planned. In order to stay in recovery the changes we make will be many. We must continue to find the courage to make the decisions that the process demands of us. That is why this book is constructed the way it is. The book helps structure decisions in a recovery context, and we need to understand the essentials at the beginning of the process. The tasks of recovery are a demanding quest, and it helps to understand that it is not the easier, softer way. To use M. Scott Peck's phrase, it is truly the road "less traveled," and it often means not knowing where that road leads.

Essential Three: True decisions require that we do all that we can to make them happen

I propose a decision index that will indicate the level of our courage. It starts off with "wishing." We will hear statements like, "I wish I could give up cigarettes" or "I wish we could communicate better." It escalates to "hoping" with phrases like, "I hope I can start losing weight" or "I hope I can find more rewarding work." Then comes a higher level of energy in which people really "want" to be better. They may be very emphatic to indicate how serious they are. "I really want to do something about our marriage" or "I really want to change my career." Yet in the very structure of their language you can tell that it is not going to happen. As long as they use words like *hoping*, *wishing*, or *wanting*, one can simply add "but I am not ready yet."

Listen for "whethering." Listening to oneself or others, one can usually hear whether the task will be done or not. Hear the difference in the following statements:

- "I am giving up cigarettes. I have had my last one. Ever."
- "I am going to communicate differently with you from here on out. I will not leave you guessing what I want or feel any more."
- "I am done being overweight. I will lose 60 pounds by the end of the year."
- "I am changing my career. I have resigned and am starting my own business."
- "Our marriage is the most important thing in my life. I am staying for the duration and I will do whatever it takes to make it rewarding for both of us."

Implicit in each of these statements is the fact that a decision is also a commitment. It is not about a preference or a leaning or a testing of the waters—although each of those stances have their uses. The person makes a commitment and is now dedicated to change, wherever that leads.

There is a well-known scene in the *Star Wars* saga where Luke Skywalker notices that his X-wing fighter is sinking into the swamp. He is being coached by Yoda, the short green Jedi master who seems to be the most improbable of teachers. Luke becomes visibly frustrated while Yoda is coaching him to use the Force to extract his fighter. Luke says, "All right! I'll give it a try." To which Yoda replies, "No! Try not! Do, or do not. There is no try."

The same sentiment appears in our Twelve Step heritage when the phrase "going to any lengths" is used. There is a stage beyond "whethering" in which any means possible will be used to effect profound, deep commitment and change. I watched this happen with a man named Ray. He had reached hard times. He was having a hard time achieving sobriety in both his sex addiction and alcoholism. He went to his Twelve Step group and said he had no money for treatment. In fact he was living in his old Ford van and doing temporary work. He was willing to do whatever it would take and he asked the group for help. He went to meetings every day and sometimes twice a day. Group members in the early weeks were in touch with him around the clock. They worked in shifts supporting him and joining him at meetings. He stabilized, started to earn an income, and got into therapy. As of this writing he is seven years sober from all of his addictions and doing well financially. Consider his progress given that he started as homeless, destitute, and possessing only the commitment to go to any lengths.

I often think of that story as I listen to clients who talk of missed opportunities and how fortune has not gone their way. Rarely does the quality of life just happen. We can and must choose to be our best. We need to raise our standards from "shoulds" to "musts." As we progress in this book, we will see that optimum performance and addiction have a very similar internal architecture. Put another way, being our best, pursuing excellence, and doing all that we can do draw upon the same physiological and psychological processes as do addictions and compulsions. From that perspective, being at our best and being at our worst have significant parallels. So, what Yoda was teaching Luke and what Ray did in putting his life together make the case for believing in the possible and going to any length to make it happen. To summarize, the decision index looks like this:

- **hoping**—beginning to desire to change
- **wishing**   having a moderate desire to change
- **wanting**—having a high desire to change
- **whethering**—committing to make it happen
- **going to any length**—using every possible advantage for success

As we return to the decision table, we need to understand that these key decisions will depend upon where we are on the decision index.

Essential Four: The critical decision in life is to decide to come to your own assistance

Sooner or later in life one has to make a core decision about oneself—am I worthwhile enough to fight for? It is a choice that is revisited many times in one's life. It is much more than the will to survive. It is even more than a positive self-concept. In recovery it is the decision to heal. In its most robust form it is the decision to thrive. As a clinician I am often asked to make a prognosis—that is, whether the patient is going to get better, stay sober, or not hurt anyone. Almost always my prognosis is based on the motivation of the patient and their willingness to come to their own assistance. Everything turns on it.

Imagine that you were given the opportunity to clone yourself. Suddenly you had a little baby that was the absolute re-creation of yourself. How would you treat the baby? In what ways would you make sure that the child was not hurt or abused? What would you make sure happened to maximize the child's opportunities? How would you go out of your way to help the child?

In therapy and recovery we frequently use "healing the child within" as a metaphor to help people get in touch with an essential compassion for themselves. Charles L. Whitfield, M.D., and

John Bradshaw did much to crystallize the concept of the child within in the 1980s and 1990s.[4] Pia Mellody wrote about the "permission to be precious."[5] The metaphor of healing the child within allows for deep compassion and appreciation for the impact of trauma, addiction, and neglect on ourselves. I think, ultimately, to heal at a profound level calls for something more. We have to act on our own behalf over and over again.

For example, I am a grandfather to ten children whom I love dearly. If I saw harm coming their way, without hesitation, I would put my body in between them and that harm—even if it meant my life. I would also do that for my grown children. Chances are, if it was a child I did not know, and I saw harm coming, I would step in harm's way. My guess is that you would, too. So why would you not have that level of commitment to yourself? Why not put everything on the line to make your
life better?

There are many reasons why people do not intercede on their own behalf. They have family messages that told them what they could not do or what they could not be. Or they have some loyalty to the family to be unsuccessful. As long as they keep having problems, they fulfill the family scripting and the prophecies of failure. Some seek comfort in their dreams rather than gain satisfaction through their accomplishments. Or they are paralyzed by fear and, therefore, the worst comes to pass. Or they wither under their own perfectionism. Whatever the path, they ignore the obvious and live in the improbable. The only way out is to cultivate the willingness to come to their own assistance. Not deciding simply creates suffering, prolongs agony, squanders opportunity and talent, and makes for vulnerability to addiction and depression. Life is hard enough without adding unfulfilled goals.

Making Change

A simple formula exists for understanding how change occurs or does not occur:

$$A + B + C = \textbf{Change when:}$$
$$A = \text{A model of the world}$$
$$B = \text{A decision to come to your assistance}$$
$$C = \text{A plan with concrete steps}$$

These three elements have to be present for significant change.

The model of the world is our internal paradigm, our belief system and our perceptions of the world. You must start with what it is you wish to change or some task you wish to do. This motivation can come in a number of forms. You are changing:

- because what you are doing does not work for you or for others
- because what you are doing works but is not honorable—that is, it is inconsistent with who you are

- because you have discovered new ways of doing things that will make your life better
- because you want to be the best you can be
- because of others who matter to you
- because change will be meaningful to you

In other words, change is about your core values, or your core sense of yourself (reclaiming or discovering who you are), or your relationships, or an image of what you can be. You know that you cannot continue life in the same manner. Most of us in recovery tap into all or almost all of the above. When this happens it is called a "paradigm shift," meaning we seek new options or a more congruent fit between what we believe and how we live. Stephen Covey observes that if you focus on behavior you will get modest change, but if you change the paradigm—your internal programming—the change will be significant.

Change also involves a plan with concrete steps for making a change. Breaking it down into component parts that are not overwhelming is critical. No act of creativity just happens. The author or artist thinks through the project and has clear steps and order to accomplishing the tasks. Sometimes people think of creativity as being simply spontaneous. Real genius couples vision with discipline and focus. The truth is, recovery does the same thing—breaking things down to a day or a moment at a time.

When I was in graduate school I was so focused on my studies that I neglected exercise, and compulsive eating was a way to cope with my anxiety. I went from 165 pounds to 280 pounds. I ended up wearing a forty-eight long coat whereas normal was a forty. My waist went from thirty inches to forty-two inches. I joined a psychotherapy group who, on the first night, asked me why I was there. I told them I was there because I wanted to do something about my weight. They asked how I was going to do that. (I already knew I was not going to like this.) I suggested that I needed to exercise since diets did not work for me. That position was a testimony to my delusion about portion control and food choices. At that time in my life I was telling myself that bones in the human male become more dense and heavier. Thus, I had a case of "heavy bones."

The group members then asked what kind of exercise I would do. I responded by saying that I had wrestled in college so maybe I would take up some form of martial art. They asked which one. I said that I noticed a judo school in a nearby city so maybe I would go there. The group said that was great and then asked when I would start. (By this point I really did not like the process.) I said I would start the next week. They asked what night I was going to go.

I went on a Wednesday night. When I first walked out on a judo mat it was exhilarating. The mat felt spongy, almost springing me into action. I noted that I was about the biggest person there. While people were warming up and practicing, a tiny woman came up to me. Unaware that it was my first night, she asked if I would like to *randori*. Not wanting to admit that I did not know what that was, I said, "Sure." In a matter of three seconds I was flat on my back looking at the ceiling. I later found out she was the Grand National champion that year at 102 pounds and under.

I had a sudden paradigm shift. Winning is not about how big or strong a person is, but rather it is about skill, timing, and leverage. Thus began a whole journey for me in which I learned more about myself than anything else I had ever done. And I lost weight. Some of the longest moments of my life, however, were spent on a judo mat looking up.

Note that what I set out to do was to lose weight. Notice also that I ended up learning things about which I had no concept. The role of the group was to harness my motivation to determine concrete steps so I could start the journey. That is how all change works. You have to have a model of what you want, make a decision to commit, and have concrete steps to get there. And you can almost count on more changes than you expect. The hardest part is the initial decision to make your life different.

Making Decisions

Most people reading this book have initiated extraordinary change. They have decided to confront addiction and codependency in their lives. Invariably, this also means confronting trauma, depression, and the family you came from. In order to do that work, core perceptions in your life have to change, which will manifest in many ways if change is to be permanent, and if it is truly the transformation you want. To make the change permanent you have to see the whole package. That does not mean you get it all changed in short order. You already know this is a major personal project. Yet it must be your priority and if you truly make it so, your recovery will become this extraordinary treasure trove that will mean more to you than anything else you have done.

The following exercises will help you begin to scope out what remains to be done and to assist you in the "whethering" process. The first exercise looks at your history to give you a sense of your own power in making decisions. The second exercise brings you to your own decision table. On that table are the decisions and commitments you know you need to make. Recording them will build momentum in your transformation process.

A word of caution: *do not do this work alone*. These exercises and this book work best if you share them with others. Minimally, you should be in therapy and your therapist will help you in your process. If you need a therapist please go to the Recovery Zone website (www.recoveryzone.com) and find one in your area who knows about task-centered therapy and the Recovery Zone. If you are in a Twelve Step group, members and sponsors should know about your work as you go through the process in this book. Some groups actually use this book as part of regular meetings to advance their recoveries. Finally, these exercises have been shared by couples with success. So, if you have a partner, share your work with each other. Start with your decision tables.

Your Decision History
Coming to Your Own Assistance

Reflect now on your own history and identify positive decisions you made to help yourself. Remember commitments you made and followed through on that have affected your life. List them in the table below, list the time you did it, what actions you took, the long-term impact, and your most important learnings. As you record these choices, notice any patterns that emerge.

Key Positive Decision	Time	Specific Steps	Long-Term Impact	Most Important Learnings
1.				
2.				
3.				
4.				
5.				

Exercise 1.1

Your Decision History continued
Coming to Your Own Assistance

Key Positive Decision	Time	Specific Steps	Long-Term Impact	Most Important Learnings
6.				
7.				
8.				
9.				
10.				

Exercise 1.1

© Copyright P.J. Carnes, 2009

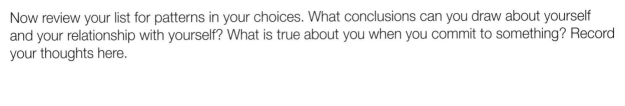

Your Decision History continued

Now review your list for patterns in your choices. What conclusions can you draw about yourself and your relationship with yourself? What is true about you when you commit to something? Record your thoughts here.

As you look back at these key decisions, did you find that once you started you went further than you ever imagined? Did you achieve things beyond your original intention? What does that tell you about starting toward a goal even though you "know not the way"? Note your reflections here.

Exercise 1.1

The Decision Table

At the beginning of this chapter you were asked to imagine a table upon which were key decisions waiting for you to pick them up and take action. On the charts on pages 27 and 28 list the decisions you already know you need to make in your life. In what ways are you on the "deferred living" plan? After each decision you list, make a brief list of steps you will have to take. Record what you now believe would happen to your life. Then assess your own "courage index" by placing a number one to five to indicate your readiness to make the choice using the following scale:

1	**2**	**3**	**4**	**5**
Hoping	**Wishing**	**Wanting**	**Whethering**	**Go to any lengths**

After assessing your courage, rank how important this issue would be in improving your life as a way of establishing priorities. Rank it by using the following scale:

1	**2**	**3**	**4**	**5**
Minimal Importance	**Some Importance**	**Important**	**Very Important**	**Critical Importance**

We have included some examples to demonstrate how your decision table might look. It is critical to notice how the numbers align. Notice gaps such as a one in courage and a five in your ranking. Take time with your "guides" and talk through the list. Use their feedback as you think about the work you must do. Journal and reflect as you move to the next chapter.

Decisions to Make	Steps to Take	Impact My Life	Courage Index	Rank
1. **Lose 75 pounds**	• start OA • do exercise program • buy scale	Feel better, live longer, start dating, depression lifts, face sexual trauma	3	4
2. **Finish my Master's thesis**	• call advisor • register at school	Higher pay immediately, feel better about self, opens career opportunity, stop feeling guilty	4	3
3. **Tell spouse about how unhappy I am sexually in our relationship and why**	• call therapist • journal about why • talk to sponsor	Sex would improve, marriage would improve, stop carrying anger around	1	5
4. **Complete 8th and 9th step**	• call sponsor • locate guide • read about it • talk to therapist	Resolve outstanding issues, bring closure, stop agonizing about past	5	3
5. **Check out pain in chest which comes and goes**	• make appointment • talk to doctor by phone	Prevent early death, take care of myself, reduce stress about it	5	5

Exercise 1.2

Be as thorough as you can. You are laying the foundation of "areas of work" that will be central to progressing through this book. You will have the opportunity to revisit, revise, and think about the decisions on your table.

Decisions to Make	Steps to Take	Impact My Life	Courage Index	Rank
1.				
2.				
3.				
4.				
5.				
6.				
7.				
8.				
9.				
10.				

Exercise 1.2

The Decision Table continued

Decisions to Make	Steps to Take	Impact My Life	Courage Index	Rank
11.				
12.				
13.				
14.				
15.				
16.				
17.				
18.				
19.				
20.				

Exercise 1.2

Chapter 2 **The Recovery Zone**

I can feel it when it happens. A day of counseling that goes well, or better than most. A speech that brings out things in me I did not know I had. Writing a book that just flows from some space inside and I know it is working. A special connection somehow brings out the best in me. For a long time I looked at these as aberrations. They were eddies of excellence which I could deny because of ancient voices telling me to not expect too much of myself. Such little dust ups of ability should not be taken seriously. Now I know those moments are the portals to excellence that make recovery work. No longer do I take them for granted.

We all have such moments that bring out the best in us. I was flying from Tulsa to Dallas. As I stepped on the plane and headed toward my seat, I noted a flight attendant standing in front of where I thought my seat was. When I arrived, I saw that my seat was a middle seat which I hate. Sitting in the window seat was a six-year-old girl. The flight attendant looked at me and said with pleading in her voice, "Sir, she is traveling alone. Can you watch over her for us?" As a father of four, and grandfather of six at the time, being with a young person was not intimidating. I took a breath and said that I would. A sign of my own travel fatigue (and maybe a lack of consciousness) was that I was more concerned about middle seats being a challenge given my height. A kid, I figured, I could handle.

I introduced myself to Lucy. She quickly told me her story. Her parents were divorced. She had been living with her dad, and now it was time to live with her mom for a while. Then I told her a little about me, that I had children and grandchildren, and that I had been giving a talk that day. The airplane took off, Lucy took some toys out of her backpack, and I started reading my novel.

After we had been in the air about a half hour, I looked over at Lucy and noticed tears making tracks down her face. I asked, "Honey, what is the matter?" She looked at me with tears brimming in her eyes, and responded. "My dog died. Somebody poisoned him." Haltingly, she told me that she talked to her mom on her dad's cell phone before getting on the plane. Her mom had told her about this family tragedy. Finally, she broke down and cried. I put my arm around her and she started to sob. I said, "Honey, feelings are like lemon drops. Crunching them really does not work. You suck on them until they go away. So cry as hard as you want." And she did. Amidst the tears, a deeper truth emerged. It was not just the dog. In her little heart she had finally admitted that no matter where she was she would miss a parent. When with her dad, she missed her mom.

When with mom, she missed her dad. Another death had occurred. The loss of the intact family is truly sadness beyond measure.

I remember thinking about how hard we as adults work to access this level of feeling. And then I looked up and saw that all the adults within earshot had tears in their eyes. The woman in the outside seat was passing Kleenex to me to give to Lucy. Two flight attendants were standing in the aisle listening to a six-year-old's confession of pain. Not one of us would have hesitated to do whatever we could to ease her grief. All we could do was listen. It took about half an hour for Lucy to finish and collect herself. I imagined it was a gathering of a tribe. The elders had stood in witness of a youngling's initiation to the world of grief and suffering.

As we walked off the plane, the woman who had sat next to me whispered, "I am so glad it was you." I protested that I had not done anything, I just listened. She smiled knowingly, and ran to catch her connection. The truth was I did just listen. The further reality was that I had just spent an hour being totally present to a six-year-old. Not just another stranger. But a six-year-old child. Then I thought of my own grandchildren whom I love so much. Had I ever been as present for as long in the same way to them? For sure, my own children did not have as much of that experience with me. For starters I did not know how when they were that young. And as a single parent, working full time, and trying to hold things together, the truth was there often was not much left over. So I resolved to be more present to all my kids and their kids. If I could do it with Lucy, I could do it with those in my family.

I know how I felt, how I responded, and what I said. I realized if I worked at it, I could do this. Like when I run. I have been a runner since I was nineteen. Some days things come together. I have a rhythm, a stride, and a coordination so that hips, shoulders, breathing—everything works. The synchronicity of it makes me feel like I am effortlessly floating. On days that are hard, I feel awkward and uncoordinated. If I focus, I can get the rhythm back, recapture the ease of a good run. The more I concentrate the more time I can spend in that zone. Or consider public speaking. I am in general a good speaker. With the right audience and the right situation, I can be a great speaker. I can even give the same speech to different audiences, but there are certain times when I really nail it. Other times, my presentation is not as strong. However, I know what it feels like when I have really connected with the audience. I know what has to happen, and I know when I have hit the groove. If I focus, I can do better speeches and all my abilities can reach a higher level. The point is, I must focus.

When we achieve those moments of being better than usual, we can first acknowledge that we have abilities. Once we accept that we are, in fact, capable, we can concentrate and spend more time in the zone. Everything gets better. We use phrases like *being in the zone*, *in the groove*, *getting it together*, and *in the spirit*. We all have those moments when we hit it exactly right. And in the synchronicity of that moment, we attempt to describe it using terms such as *Tao*, *Enlightenment*, and *Spiritual Connection*. By focusing, the brain integrates our efforts and we do better without having to think about it. And the reward centers of the brain are deeply satisfied by our successful efforts. The brain takes challenge very seriously and saves its best for when we attempt our best.

Psychologist Mihaly Csikszentmihalyi calls this synchronicity, *flow*. He pointed to more than 180 studies of people who made achievement effortless. Diverse ways humans could be challenged were studied; those studied included scientists, actors, mountain climbers, athletes, and factory workers. Whether it was a physician doing surgery or an assembly line worker making a game out of beating production targets, certain characteristics emerged beyond focus and reward. These are people who thrived by setting and exceeding goals they have set for themselves. They set aside anxiety and fear. They became oblivious to time passing. They entered a zone so rewarding, they could most be themselves. Whatever the activity, it became meaningful on its own. For example, surgeons start off wanting to help people. Eventually when they truly achieve excellence, the art of surgery assumes prominence and the great surgeons ask, "Can I be even better today than yesterday?"

Csikszentmihalyi also demonstrated that people who were addicted accessed their brains in much the same way as those who were able to achieve great things. Addicts turn focus into obsession. They become preoccupied with whatever they used as a rewarding activity. If you have a room full of addicts of any type, and you ask the question, were you "good" at being an addict, laughter ripples through the room along with a collective exchange of knowing glances. Every addict knows that feeling of being good at succeeding in their addictions! Whether it is scoring coke, pulling off another affair, or creating a brilliant solution to another self-made financial crisis, most addicts remember feeling that they were on top of things. So the ability to handle liquor, get sexual satisfaction whatever the cost, or keep the house of financial cards still standing was a challenge you met.

Outsiders, friends, and loved ones would be stunned at the risks taken. Like the surgeon who learns to ignore the possible death of the patient, or the mountain climber who casts aside the obvious precariousness of the challenge, the addict easily takes risks of disease, arrest, career disaster, and loss of loved ones. Also time passes. The jokes are many about real time and "addict time." When the addict is engaged all worries disappear. The anxieties of life are suspended on some neural shelf in the brain while addictive obsession absorbs the addict's awareness.

The addiction itself takes on meaning. In recovery circles, euphoric recall of being high reveals how meaningful the addictive experience was. Consider the alcoholics who will reminisce about a vodka gimlet, and a light appears in their eyes as if talking about an old lover. Or think of the compulsive eater who remembers wistfully binge eating in great detail. Their grief is real. What they share in common is a sense of nurturing that was gathered at the edge of human experience. Their addictions got them through difficult times. And often addiction masked truths unbearable to accept.

Bill W., the co-founder of Alcoholics Anonymous, had to face both financial and alcohol issues. He described those heady days of "pulling it off" like this:

> For the next few years fortune threw money and applause my way. I had arrived. My judgment and ideas were followed by many to the tune of paper millions. The great boom of the twenties was seething and swelling. Drink was taking an important and exhilarating part in my life. There was loud talk in the jazz places uptown. Everyone spent in thousands and chattered in millions. Scoffers could scoff and be damned. I made a host of fair-weather friends.

Like many addicts, Bill W. felt in control and unstoppable. He along with most of us who enter recovery later had to admit the great illusion of being in control. In Tom Wolfe's novel, *The Bonfire of the Vanities*, Sherman McCoy, a central character, perceives himself as a "Master of the Universe." He did not have to attend to the limits that others did. This character is a little further along in what Bill W. describes with his encountered problems. Here is McCoy's sexual logic:

> Sherman resumed his walk toward First Avenue in a state of agitation. It was in the air! It was a wave! Everywhere! Inescapable! … Sex! … There for the taking. It walked down the street, as bold as you please! … It was splashed all over the shops! If you were a young man and halfway alive, what chance did you have? … Technically, he had been unfaithful to his wife. Well, sure … but who could remain monogamous with this, this, this tidal wave of concupiscence rolling across the world? Christ Almighty! A Master of the Universe couldn't be a saint; after all … It was unavoidable. For Christ's sake, you can't dodge snowflakes, and this was a blizzard! He had merely been caught at it, that was all, or halfway caught at it. It meant nothing. It had no moral dimension. It was nothing more than getting soaking wet.

Bill W. eventually started to have "unhappy scenes" at home. Sooner or later it starts to impact others. Addicts rationalize their behavior. Recovery brings to all addicts the fundamental realization that while the addiction was taking hold they thought that they could handle it, deserved it and it was a choice. Unknowingly, they were making a bargain with chaos. (We will speak in much more detail about bargains with chaos.)

Ironically, family members and others close to addicts also take on the same features. Extreme living ripples through intimacy networks. Spouses, for example, take on the challenge of controlling the addict. In rooms of recovering codependents, if a speaker says, "I was a good codependent," the room is filled with laughter and nods of recognition. Family members become obsessed with reining in the addict's behavior. They become preoccupied and—in their own way—sneaky about showing the addict the errors of addictive ways. The challenges of controlling an addict increase, of course, requiring greater efforts with fewer results.

Family members, including children, start to take risks. These are risks that would cause others outside the family to shake their heads. No one should cover up bad behavior to such a degree that they compromise their health, work, finances, and sanity. But they do. In the drama of it all, time passes, and normal, real anxieties slip into the background. Family members compromise their values and agreements, and they too feel entitled.

One of the great stories of Al-Anon is about Lois W., the wife of Bill W. Her friend Elise had seen the chaos in which Lois was living with Bill's alcoholism. Lois was attempting to adopt a baby, and Elise knew that would be a bad idea. Elise intervened to stop the adoption process without her friend knowing. In effect, Elise betrayed her friend because she saw the peril she was persisting to live in. Eventually, Lois learned that her friend had blocked the adoption that she so desperately wanted. She perceived this lack of support by her friend as a deep betrayal of what Lois most wanted in life. When Lois was finally working a program for herself she realized that she needed to reframe her friend's betrayal. Although not having a family was one of the great pains of her life she had to admit that she was not seeing what her friend saw. Out of this came the Eighth Step of Al-Anon in which Lois made "amends" to her friend.

One of the real culprits is stress. Addiction always has a stress component in which high drama leads to incredible hormonal changes in the body. With the evolution of neuroscience we now know that when a therapist says "That man is your drug," it is the truth. Much of addiction and co-addiction is about the body's adaptation to a stressful way of life. The Big Book of *Adult Children of Alcoholics and Dysfunctional Families* describes it clearly in their famous Laundry List: *we became addicted to excitement*. As we explore the nature of addiction we will see how true that is.

So how do some people become achievers and some get lost in addictive disorders? Clearly both groups respond to challenge and stress. Yet there must be a way of contrasting the path to excellence and the path of addiction. On the following page, in **Figure 2.1** we summarize the characteristics of "flow" that Csikszentmihalyi describes. We contrast those characteristics with the basic elements of addiction and co-addiction. The goal is to provide a simple overview of how the two processes are parallel.

Recovery Zone: Flow vs. Addiction

Flow	vs.	Addiction
Task completion	vs.	Addiction objective
Focus	vs.	Obsession
Clear goals	vs.	Immediate purpose
Feedback	vs.	Reality distortion
Removes worries	vs.	Anxiety reduction
Sense of control	vs.	False empowerment
Stronger self-connection	vs.	Disintegration of self/relationships
Duration of time	vs.	Timeless
Meaning	vs.	Anomie (*meaningless*)

Figure 2.1

In his description of flow, Csikszentmihalyi makes the further observation that the brain is always trying to find order in the world. The brain thrives on the challenge of making order. Like a shark in the water that has to keep moving in order to breathe, the brain must have the next challenge. Addiction is really a problem of attention and focus. If there is not a healthy, conscious focus, the brain will find order in another way. Addiction is simply a way to put order in life. Another analogy is to think of it as the ultimate attention deficit disorder. It is attention gone awry.

Scientists and therapists use the term, the *hijacked brain*, to describe how addiction takes charge of the brain. Consider this experience most of us have had. You are driving down the freeway and are late to an appointment. As you drive by the exit to your home you automatically turn off the freeway as if you meant to go home. You become furious with yourself for being inattentive. Now you will be even later because it will take time to get back on the freeway. You were intending to go one way, but your brain had you go another. That in a nutshell is what addiction is. The addict intends to do one thing but ends up doing something else, because the brain is hijacked.

Your brain is remarkable in that it takes on challenges and tries to help you out. It streamlines the decisions necessary to live your life so you will not have to think about it. To give your focus more room, it takes the cues of coming up to your turn off the freeway and makes the whole decision-making process automatic. Then each time you come to that point you make the turn without giving it much thought. When you learned to ride a bike, it took all your concentration to make it successful. After awhile your brain's wonderful capacity to streamline those decisions made riding the bike automatic. The brain actually makes three billion decisions a second. So if we did not have the capacity to make things automatic, life would be much more challenging.

When we are most engaged in the ordering process we call it flow, Tao, in the groove, in the zone, genius or spiritual experience. We feel at one with creation, life has meaning and purpose, and we function at our optimum. We focus on our being our best. Addictions are phantom optimums. They ask the brain to perform many of the same functions such as focus, improved performance, overlooking risk, passing time, and being meaningful. In essence, it is akin to trying to "drink God from a bottle."

Csikszentmihalyi suggests that addictive disorders are really distortions of attention. He writes, "Almost any activity can become addictive in the sense that instead of being a conscious choice, it becomes a necessity that interferes with other activities." One becomes "captive to a certain kind of order." Alcohol, drugs, sex, gambling, and compulsive eating all become more than habitual. Domestic violence, codependency, traumatic bonding, and romance junkies are all part of what we term "compulsive attachment," which is another variant of addictive attention. Even violence, war, and criminal activity can be part of this process. But an addiction is not a simple matter of turning back on the freeway. Addiction constructs a complex array of profound neural pathways in the brain that access our deepest reward centers and that short circuit the brain's ability to make good decisions. In fact, with addiction, error codes cause terrible decision making which keeps addicts and their family members constantly at risk.

When addiction starts, however, the addict feels on top of things whether it be the sex addict ignoring emerging problems, the codependent overlooking relationship issues, or the cocaine addict neglecting work duties. The "bargain with chaos" is that the emerging addict starts to ignore reality. We call this denial. In Goethe's *Faust*, the story is about a man who sells his soul to the devil in order to have more advantages while alive on earth. The devil in the play is called Mephistopheles. When Faust asks Mephistopheles who he is, the devil responds, "I am the spirit who denies." By focusing on the immediate reward, the addict early on makes an unconscious bargain with denial. Addiction takes our greatest abilities and harnesses them to self-destructive patterns that are more powerful than will power. It is also why so many talented and gifted people end up with addictions. The brain hungers for focus.

The early choices are almost always about trade-offs or beliefs that the addict or coaddict can operate outside the rules that other people have to observe. This denial is almost always rooted in entitlement or what we will call a "grievance" story. There are significant rewards in the pleasure centers or the stress systems of the brain. The result is obsession which affects good judgment and the ability to stop addictive behaviors. What you think about is what the brain rehearses to do! Unmanageability of one's life and powerlessness over behavior generates cyclic self-repeating patterns. The hallmark of this process is being self-destructive even when at some level you know that is what is happening to you.

Most people think the goal of recovery is attaining some type of sobriety or change. Getting sober is easy compared to staying sober. The goal of recovery is to maintain the change. And permanent change will not happen unless you know where the optimum is. To make recovery work, you must focus on your excellence. You must have clarity about where you are at your best. Not doing this is why so many fail. The brain must make this shift in a conscious, determined way. This is, in part, why sustained recovery takes three years to achieve. You have to reengineer your life so that "automatic pilot" means working at being your best. "Reengineering" means growing new networks in your brain. The biological process of creating those new neurons in your brain and linking them takes time—and focus.

With more clear insight into how our brains function, we see why relapse is so common. Addiction and codependency treatment has been so directed toward preventing relapse we have failed to help recovering people appreciate the "reengineering" necessary. As a result, they do not realize how focusing on your optimum can make such a difference. A wise Buddhist aphorism applies here: "If you are going to say no to something, you must know what yes is."

An illustration will help. The following comes from Alan Alda's wonderful book, *Things I Overheard while Talking to Myself*. He describes what it feels like to be perfectly within the expression of his talent.

> Sometimes, standing on the stage, I have an experience of unusual awareness. I know I'm in a theater and that an audience is watching; and I know that the woman across from me is not really who she is claiming to be. And in spite of knowing we're in front of other people, I know we're alone in this room. I'm also aware of something much weirder than that. I'm aware that the two of us are other people, someplace else, arguing over something. We are so completely involved with this struggle, we could say almost anything at this moment. But we say the same thing we said last night. And I'm aware that this is because we are acting. It's like an endless arc of images in paired mirrors curving off into infinity. And when this moment is at its most intense, it's at its lightest. There is no strain; in fact, there is a feeling of floating. But, of course, I'm aware that, far from floating, I'm standing on a stage that's raked for the audience to see us better, and I have to be careful where I plant my feet or I'll lose my balance.

> This multiple awareness is for me the ecstasy of acting. When this happens, there doesn't seem to be any part of my brain that isn't working on something. The clock stops, and an intricate pas de deux takes place in slow motion. You choke with

emotion, yet you feel nothing. You know everything and nothing at once. You walk a narrow beam a hundred stories high, but your steps are as sure as on a sidewalk. Failure can't happen. Death is remote. There is no way to know what you'll say next; and then you say it. And you notice that you're saying it slightly differently from the last time you said it at exactly this moment.... Once you have tasted this beautiful madness, you want it again and again. It's delicious. And in that moment when nothing else exists but you and them, and yet everything exists, that's a moment when you know what it is to be alive.

Alan Alda makes the comparison that it is like being a sky diver—only as you leap you go up instead of down. Notice the themes: brain completely absorbed, risk, time passing, competence, anxiety delay, spiritual oneness, being most alive, and a "delicious madness" that you wish to repeat. It is an extraordinary description that fits Csikszentmihalyi's criteria of flow. Contrast Alda's description with this characterization written by Bill W. in the Big Book, or *Alcoholics Anonymous*:

More than most people the alcoholic leads a double life. He is very much the actor. To the outer world he presents his stage character. This is the one he likes his fellows to see. He wants to enjoy a certain reputation, but knows in his heart he doesn't deserve it. The inconsistency is made worse by the things he does on his sprees. Coming to his senses, he is revolted at certain episodes he vaguely remembers. These memories are a nightmare. He trembles to think someone might have observed him. As fast as he can, he pushes these memories far inside himself. He hopes they will never see the light of day. He is under constant fear and tension—that makes for more drinking.

So what is the difference between acting as an addict and acting as an authentic person? The answer is alignment. When we are at our optimum we feel at one with ourselves and those around us. Repeating behavior that achieves a sense of excellence adds to our lives and ironically reduces stress. We have a profound sense of achievement tempered by a keen sense of our own limits. Because of our positive efforts we become more conscious and present to life. There evolves an "inner observer" who reflects on the meaning and joy of being in synch with oneself and others. Most importantly, the pursuit of the optimum deepens the functioning of our brains by requiring the brain to grow more circuits of integration.

In many ways, Bill W. and Lois W., and early pioneers of AA, opened the door to this process. Very early they discovered that it took ninety days before a person could really start making progress. This discovery is the origin of the ninety days/ninety meetings process that has helped so many. Now modern neuroscience tells us that it takes ninety days for the brain to "reset" itself in order to begin momentum for change. The Twelve Steps were organized around "inventories" which basically require the brain to reflect on what is working and what is not. Fundamental to the whole process is bringing things in alignment. No more secrets or hiding things. We have to face the reality of how bad things are. Out of that congruency emerges a different vision of how things can be different. In almost all Twelve Step programs there is a version of "the promises" that point to the rewards of recovery.

The A.A. Promises

If we are painstaking about this phase of our development, we will be amazed before we are half way through. We are going to know a new freedom and a new happiness. We will not regret the past nor wish to shut the door on it. We will comprehend the word serenity and we will know peace. No matter how far down the scale we have gone, we will see how our experience can benefit others. That feeling of uselessness and self-pity will disappear. We will lose interest in selfish things and gain interest in our fellows. Self-seeking will slip away. Our whole attitude and outlook upon life will change. Fear of people and of economic insecurity will leave us. We will intuitively know how to handle situations which used to baffle us. We will suddenly realize that God is doing for us what we could not do for ourselves. Are these extravagant promises? We think not. They are being fulfilled among us—sometimes quickly, sometimes slowly. They will always materialize if we work for them.

Creating that "new freedom" requires that we identify that zone in which we are at our best. Having a vision of a different life is perhaps the most important tool for significant change. A vision only works when the image is clear in our minds. For every one of us that zone is known to us already. We have to access and articulate those areas of being at our best in order to make recovery work. That is why we call it the Recovery Zone. The decision table on pages 27 and 28 helps us see what is not working beyond our addictive or codependent behavior. The path to a different life means we must have a way of knowing when we are out of our optimum behavior. Whatever addiction brought you to this book, your life is now different from that of most people. There are certain things you know will bring you back to disaster. The key now is to know where your zone is. Then we can focus.

Best Moments: Finding Your Zone

As part of first step preparation, we ask patients to list their "worst moments." In preparing for recovery, we must focus on life's "best moments." Reflect on the best moments of your life—meaning those times when you truly were at your most effective, most accomplished, most honorable, or most who you are. These are times which stand out in your memory as "extraordinary" examples of who you can be. Please list them below with descriptive phrases about the impact of those moments.

Best Moment	Impact on Self and Others
Best Moment – Example A: **Completing my graduate degree with honors**	Proved I could do it. Opened my life professionally. Realized no one could take it away from me. Created better income, better life.
Best Moment – Example B: **Hung in my marriage when all was falling apart**	Learned a lot about self and intimacy. Saved kids heartache, plus was a good example for them. Feel secure and rewarded now.
Best Moment 1:	
Best Moment 2:	
Best Moment 3:	
Best Moment 4:	

Exercise 2.1

Best Moments: Finding Your Zone continued

Best Moment	Impact on Self and Others
Best Moment 5:	
Best Moment 6:	
Best Moment 7:	
Best Moment 8:	
Best Moment 9:	
Best Moment 10:	

Review your best moments and think of your skills, attributes and abilities. What emerges as a profile of you when you are at your best? Then reflect on what you do not like to do or those activities you do not feel competent with.

Exercise 2.1

Best Moments: Finding Your Zone continued

Make two lists: 1) A profile of when you are at your best or most yourself, and 2) when you are least effective or not yourself.

"Best" Qualities Profile
(feel most like myself)

Least Effective Profile
(not who I am)

_____

_____

_____

_____

_____

_____

_____

_____

_____

_____

Now think of the percentage of the time you are at your best:

_____ % of time doing activities in my best abilities and qualities

_____ % of time doing activities in my least effective abilities and qualities

Exercise 2.1

Targeting Your Recovery Zone

There will always be challenge in life. Our brain thrives on it. Yet too much challenge overwhelms our ability to respond, thus generating too much stress. We have already started to paint the picture of how stress is a major player in all addictions. As we have discussed, avoiding challenges creates a hunger for attainment and order and can lead to addiction and despair. Csikszentmihalyi's research on success and happiness found that people who have a sense of achievement and flow know how to tap into a zone in their lives. By targeting that zone we define the bedrock of recovery and further—and most importantly—start to map out a course of future challenges that can transform how we live.

The following tool is called the "recovery zone" and has helped many thousands of people redirect their lives and to keep their focus during the rocky road of recovery. In this book the tool is presented as one page since it is more complex than can be printed easily in a traditional book. You can use the tool on the one page. It is better on larger paper. Plus you will find that you will use this tool often throughout the book and in your recovery. So much change occurs it is important to keep your eye on your zone as it grows and defines itself. The Recovery Zone www.recoveryzone.com online community is your best way to stay current with innovations and advances in the process. Your task-centered certified therapist also will have various versions as part of treatment.

Here is how you use the tool. Always start in the middle where there is a list entitled "current optimums." Give yourself credit for where things are going well. If you are happy with your work, your current weight, specific relationships—whatever currently feels on target. Then proceed to the upper left corner and the category of "over stressed." On this list, record items which cause chaos, overextension, unmanageability, excessive behaviors, and crisis management. These items keep your life on the edge. To the right of each item list a specific step you can take now to change it. At the top right is an optimum list: if you fixed this problem, what would the optimum look like? Describe that optimum as you would have it in your life. To complete the sequence go to the middle left of the page where an arrow asks you, "What opens you up to such chaos that you need to let go of?" This question aims at your investment in negative behaviors that continue to hurt you. There is some reason in the form of a belief, or relationship, or secret to which you hold on. Listing and addressing this investment in your chaos makes an incredible improvement in your focus.

Similarly, turn your attention to the bottom right corner and give the category of needs a closer look. The target here is your lack of action in the form of procrastination, feeling paralyzed, resistant, rigid, frozen, and even self-destructive. On your decision table, these would be the items of great importance for which you have no energy or readiness to fix. Then list specific steps you know you can take that would start the process of changing each item. The bottom left category is for the optimums. If you fixed these issues, record what those situations would look like. The middle arrow on the right presents the investment question again: "What pulls you down that you are willing to let go of?" Usually this requires letting go of something that keeps you stuck.

When finished you have a channel laid in which you would grow and thrive. Also the beginning steps (usually the hardest) are laid out for you. Plus your investment arrows tell you where therapy and your program can really help you. The behaviors simply represent the deeper issues in which you are clinging to even though they are no longer useful to you. The zone tool becomes a lens that brings focus to where you need to be. Like any lens, as you move you will need to refocus. This worksheet is only a start. We highly recommend that you keep your original work as it will be helpful for you to see your progress down the road.

Some other things now may have occurred to you. You may now see your decision table somewhat differently. Combined, the two tools do work collaboratively together. The Recovery Zone is a very useful way to help your table work be more effective. You may also have noticed that some items actually fit in both the under and over stressed categories. When that happens it is frequently because both ends are affected by the same issue you are clinging to. Yet that phenomenon is often hard to see by yourself. Most of us need help to see the connection when that happens.

Complete the zone process and then move to the next chapter which presents the addiction interaction map, another way to examine what is on your table.

The Recovery Zone

The Recovery Zone

Optimum Would Look Like:
1.
2.
3.
4.
5.
6.
7.

What pulls you down that you are willing to let go of: (not good at, don't wish to do, not necessary)
1.
2.
3.
4.
5.
6.
7.

UNDER STRESSED: Rigid, Resistant, Restricted, Paralyzed, Procrastination, Self-Destructive, Inaction, Freeze, Fail to Respond

Current Behaviors:
1.
2.
3.
4.
5.
6.
7.

The Recovery Zone

Current Optimums:
1.
2.
3.
4.
5.
6.
7.

Steps to Take:
1.
2.
3.
4.
5.
6.
7.

OVER STRESSED: Chaos, Unmanageability, Excessive Behavior, Over Extension, Crisis Management

Current Behaviors:
1.
2.
3.
4.
5.
6.
7.

Steps to Take:
1.
2.
3.
4.
5.
6.
7.

What opens you up to chaos that you need to let go of: (relationships, beliefs, situations, actions)
1.
2.
3.
4.
5.
6.
7.

The Recovery Zone

Optimum Would Look Like:
1.
2.
3.
4.
5.
6.
7.

Exercise 2.2

Chapter 3 **The Addiction Interaction Map**

One of the scariest moments in human experience is when you have to admit there is something wrong with your brain. One of the worst of those moments is admitting that you are an addict. For the vast majority of addicts the very worst is admitting that you are addicted in many ways. Consider the power of this difficult moment. For years you have convinced yourself that you could handle your behavior. Your problems were really about other people, circumstances, history, and even God. It was seldom that you needed to change your behavior. Temper it a bit maybe. In most cases you had been trying to prove to others that you could handle it. In other words you were proving what was not true. Even your perceptions were that you were fine.

When you admit to having an addiction or co-addiction, you admit that others were right. You see that all the effort you put into proving true what was untrue was useless. In fact they were lies. A lie at a time one can ignore. Taken together, all the lies show you have a real problem. Because of your problem you have been deceptive and betrayed those you love. And this is most difficult when you have prided yourself on being trustworthy, honest, and loving. Worse, you have betrayed yourself. The very worst, however, is that you cannot trust your perceptions. You have lost contact with reality—which is what insanity really is. In your current state you cannot trust yourself to make the next right decision. When you truly accept that, it is very scary. To paraphrase a famous cartoon, you should be very afraid.

In my forty years of working with addiction, I have never known an addict or co-addict to argue that they need more time in treatment. Usually, the addicts argue over whether or not they have a problem. If they do recognize an addictive problem, they believe it is not as extensive as people think. And surely, it will not require as much time, effort, or money as people suggest. The world is crumbling around them, but they work to stay in the bubble of illusion. One of the most difficult moments for any therapist is when a patient who has been through inpatient treatment five times, admits that he or she will die if he or she uses again, then refuses the recommendations of the treatment team. Then the addict does it his or her way and does, in fact, die. In therapy we call this, "Talking to a dead man who is walking." It is a great stressor to all addiction therapists.

Compulsive attachment is not exempt. Consider the highly reactive codependent whose life is filled with drama and rage at other people's behavior. In her righteousness, she fails to notice the distance between herself and her children, her friends, and her colleagues. People can tolerate only so much intensity. As she ages she realizes she has not been successful at maintaining a long-term successful, significant relationship. She is right about a lot of what she saw, but she is also alone. She has insidiously burned through the brain chemicals that give her a sense of well being and protect her body from disease. Evidence shows that she is much more likely to have serious health problems. The stress takes a toll. So she is right, and alone, and probably sick.

The great irony is that if the patients did surrender to the truth around them, they would have so much happiness. Recovery exists because so many have proven that true.

In this scary moment, the biggest problem is in admitting how much is wrong. Consider Jonathan. His story involves both addiction and codependency, yet serves as a great example of the ways both can masquerade under many guises. Jonathan was a race car mechanic who loved the travel and romance of his career. He would later admit how much he was hooked on the stress and excitement of it. He was good at coaxing more power from the extraordinary machinery on which he worked. Eventually, travel, drug use, and compulsive infidelity created so much chaos he became a liability to his team. He went to treatment twice but both times relapsed within days of his return. The team owner sent him to treatment for one last time. Jonathan knew that he would probably die if he started using again. He told his group, "I don't have another run in me."

During treatment, he was having a hard time focusing: so many problems in so many places. Much of early therapy was about pointing out inconsistencies. At one point, Jonathan admitted to having constantly used various types of drugs, including heroin and cocaine, since he was about eleven. So given his recent forty-eighth birthday, he had thirty-seven years of constant drug use. A deeper problem was that he had convoluted relationships including a compulsive prostitution problem. He had been married for ten years and had three young children. His wife told him she had lost hope and would not come to another family week.

He denied that he had a sexual problem. He felt sure he could control his sexual acting out because he only acted out when he used drugs. When he was sober, he claimed, he did not have a problem. His therapist reminded him, "Jon, you have just documented for us that you have not been sober since you were eleven." Everyone laughed at the contradiction, including Jonathan. Then his therapist bored in. "The problem is you are hooked on your own excitement hormones, and you use drugs to help manage that. What would happen if you just stopped your life long enough to give your brain time to heal? And further, what will make this treatment different? You cannot stand being away from the circuit. You constantly keep your family in turmoil, so the open road feels like freedom. If you do not stop and do the work, there is no point to having a chair in this group. We are talking to a dead man." One by one, the group members added more examples of how out of control he was.

The real issue involved more than sex. If Jonathan admitted to a sex addiction it weakened his position to spend less time in treatment. This might mean another four to six weeks of residential work. He was fearful that he would lose his lead position on the team if he did not return quickly. He had responsibilities to his wife with three small children. Plus, he had some secret "relationship issues" to clean up with other women before talking about these issues further with anybody. He especially did not want to talk about these problems with a therapist.

His therapist suggested to the group that they make a list of what the group knew so far about Jon. They started listing facts on a large piece of paper:

- Using drugs constantly since the age of eleven
- Saw his first prostitute at the age of seventeen
- Prostitutes are one of his principal sources of drugs
- Jonathan has semi "rock star" status in the racing world with women approaching him wherever he goes
- He has very convoluted relationships with women he rescues, including some tortuous ones with prostitutes who have taken him for lots of money
- His wife was a race car fan who fell in love with him but also had a troubled life. (Jonathan was her shining knight although a little tarnished at the moment)
- He is codependent but hates the term (he does admit to the rescuing part and that much of his life's troubles stem from that)
- His national and international travel created even more instability and lack of accountability
- He loved the excitement of what he did—and the thought of not doing it was "like death"
- He grew up in an alcoholic family in which he would take care of his mother who was frequently battered by his father
- He learned very early how to take care of women by being the person who comforted his mom
- He was deeply resentful toward his father (which extended to anyone who tried to set limits on him)
- He was a master of the quick solutions, whether it be getting a car to run, pulling out of a scrape with a woman, or finding drugs in foreign cities (he also loved being the hero in all these situations)
- He now had hepatitis, which he could have contracted either sexually or with drugs (therapist adds note that, even among addicts there are few who do not know how they contracted this disease)
- Three near-death experiences, all of them involving drugs and sex, the last of which brought him to this treatment
- He is forty-eight years old and has had a problem for thirty-seven years (but he is arguing over how many weeks he needs to be in treatment)

When the list was done, Jon was amazed at how much the group had put together. Further, he literally saw the writing on the wall. Fixing one thing would not stop the process. They were all hooked together. Moreover, it would not be fixed in a few weeks. Finally, he knew that the list was still partial because there were secrets he had not shared, including a child no one knew about.

When he admitted that he saw it was all one problem and that it just came out in different ways, the group smiled. His therapist underlined the moment by pointing out that addictions are hooked together. He added, "To just focus on your chemical use, is why you relapse. You have to see how the addictions hook together, and then you need to understand what drives them. You have to go back to the source."

So how do addictions start and more importantly, how do they hook together? Like Jonathan, we have to go back to the source.

The Making of an Addict

Addiction starts with the genetics of your family. It is no accident that addiction runs in families. As we learn about our genomic structure, it is clear that addicts tend to have some differences from the general population. For example, the dopamine strands (technically the D1, D2, D3, and D4) tend to be shorter for people who have alcoholism, eating disorders, compulsive behaviors, attention deficit disorder, and Tourette's syndrome. Dopamine is a chemical in the brain which is core to the addiction process. A meal will raise your dopamine levels 50 percent. Sex and alcohol will raise it over 100 percent. Nicotine will raise it 150 percent. Methamphetamines will raise it 1,100 percent. All of these are ways to feel better. And if you start life with an insufficiency of dopamine, you are behind the curve in terms of having feelings of well being. Dopamine is just one chemical. We will give more examples as we go along.

Genomic evidence is starting to appear that addicts have a DNA sequence which comes from nomadic peoples. There seems to be in their genes more need for novelty. These early findings are intriguing, given the proven role of a part of the brain called the anterior cingulate. This groove at the top of your brain is the "gear shifter" of the brain, allowing us to multi-task. In all the addictions, there is a body of evidence which shows that novelty seeking is core to the addiction process. A principal culprit in the mind of the addict is "more is better." Addiction researchers are convinced that novelty and arousal are principal factors in developing tolerance, causing the addict to need more. The searching for new perspectives also is core to creativity, which echoes our conversation about how talent and creativity are entwined with the addictive process.

While we do not have the full genomic profile yet, we know some people are much more vulnerable than others to addiction. This brings us to the question: when do the factors that make an addiction start? The answer is immediately after birth. The first two years of life are critical because that is when the basics of attachment occur. During this time the parent will gaze at the child. This is not about feeding or entertaining or changing diapers. Optimally, the parent and child simply look at each other. The gaze of the parent is the beginning of intimacy. Busy parents who are hard pressed for time do not provide this core ability of establishing a bond. Since the brain always seeks something to do, as we have learned, the children busy themselves. Or, they can become an "observer" or do a myriad of other things to occupy their time.

One definition of addiction is that it is a failure to bond. The inability to establish secure attachment has been repeatedly demonstrated as a key factor in addictive disorders. If you do not trust people, you may find that alcohol, sex, food, and excitement do what they promise causing you to feel better—at least for the moment. Plus, if you grew up in a family in which adults had excessive behavior, the modeling confirms that this is how to "do" life. The bottom line is, addiction can start as an intimacy problem.

A child learns from a parent how to access, utilize, and learn from feelings. Essentially, the child borrows the frontal lobes of the parent. When something difficult happens, the parent sets limits, helps develop decision-making skills, and soothes upset feelings. Our feelings are critical to our ability to develop a sense of self, or what is sometimes called a self-concept. The definition of "self" is much more than an idea. How to deal with feelings is one of the most essential life skills. Families where feelings were discouraged or not tolerated create kids unable to access their feelings. The children then have difficulty being with themselves. They will always seek distraction.

The greatest escalator of all is the feeling of fear. Fear changes the brain. Through a complex process (we will describe in Chapter 4 to Chapter 8), fear alters the very structure of the brain. Chemicals that keep the brain in a high arousal are generated in excess, and the chemicals that soothe and help in decision making actually decline. Take the fear away, and the child will feel something is missing. And if prolonged enough, that child will grow up to be an adult who will be in constant crisis, live on the edge, place him- or herself at risk, and use addictive behavior to manage stress.

The evidence that trauma and anxiety is foundational to every addiction is overwhelming. Whatever the addiction, stress is a component. Whether it be:

- The alcoholic who is trying to make sense out of what happened last night
- The cocaine addict making a buy on the street
- The high roller executive who has bet everything on the next deal
- The battered spouse who tells herself this will be the last time
- The adult child of an alcoholic who kept secrets as a child and now as an adult is keeping them in the office
- The pastor whose affairs with congregants inevitably will surface
- The spouse who discovers her husband's secret life
- The emergency room physician who volunteers for the swat team to escape his affairs with staff and patients
- The wife whose drug use, spending, and binge/purge eating have to be kept secret

All of these situations involve stress. All addicts stay in such turmoil, because chemicals such as cortisol and norepinephrine keep their brain in a heightened level of alert and awareness. They are addicted to the flood of neurochemicals that depend on a life in crisis. The other brain problem that goes with this is that the ability to make decisions becomes compromised, especially decisions that involve inhibiting behavior.

How did this problem with the brain happen? Sexual, physical, and emotional abuse can impact the brain. Other circumstances include early losses such as death of a parent or catastrophic illness, living in a home with addicted parents or simply living in a dysfunctional family. One of the most insidious contributing factors is neglect. Children who do not get the care or help they need—or if they do get the help, they are made to feel that they were a failure or a problem when they needed help, also fit the profile. Or being in a minority in a culture in which there is high stress will do it. Being African American, Native American, or just realizing that you are gay in what you perceive is a straight world is enough. All a child needs is enough fear to get hooked on the stress of it.

Addiction is not always based in childhood problems. For example, we sent people to Vietnam who had no history of addiction or abuse in their families. But they came back heroin addicts, sex addicts, and risk junkies. War, natural disaster, or government collapse are examples of catastrophic stress that has been shown to precipitate addictive behavior in all forms.

The other problem is exposure. Early excessive behavior is a problem especially in the ages from twelve to sixteen. Adolescent drinking episodes dramatically raise the adult onset for alcoholism. Smoking as an adolescent is a critical precursor for nicotine addiction. The part that is deceptive for kids is that nicotine remains in the brain of an adolescent for thirty days. So what they see as occasional use, is the beginning of a problem. Kids who gamble on the internet are much more likely to have an adult money problem. Kids who are sexually abused or experience early sex are much more likely as adults to have problems with sexually compulsive behavior or sexually aversive behavior—or both.

From a Recovery Zone perspective it is extremely instructive to note that the kids least likely to become addicts are the ones who have an early passion or experience of excelling or learn early to focus on meaningful activities. Adolescents who struggle with addiction or the periphery of addiction have been shown to be much more likely to control their behavior if they discover ways in which they can excel or be passionately engaged. Remember, a difference exists between obsession and focus.

Again, the roots of addiction are not always based in childhood stress. The stimulation of cybersex or cocaine can be so pleasurable that people who have none of the typical profiles of an addict will become addicted. Often it is associated with some high stress, but it does happen without the stress component. Part of exposure is availability. For example, the more casinos that exist, the more compulsive gambling occurs. In that sense each culture presents its issues—alcoholism in Russia, obesity in the United States, and gambling and sex in certain Asian cultures.

Part Two of this book is designed to untangle the underlying factors that drive addiction. To start, however, requires acknowledging what addictions exist now. It is the hardest part, but without acknowledgement, there is no traction to untangle the underlying factors. And without that, there is no meaningful lasting recovery.

Multiple Addictions

Unfortunately, all these factors are complicated by the reality that addictions compound by nature. Like a debt that keeps growing, addictions have the ability to morph into something powerful and biologically tenacious. Once the initial neural pathway is laid down, other addictions become overlays using some of the same circuitry. All the problems become magnified:

- Decision making becomes more distorted, which adds to the stress
- Obsession grows to feed the biological changes occurring
- The craving for more distorts the brain's thinking, causing a person to lose contact with reality
- Loss of control on more than one addiction domain adds to stress and relationship problems
- Survival requires creating even more separate compartments or realities that require deception and risk
- The synapses of the brain grow and demand to be soothed or fed more stimulation

In short, the brain has become damaged. It feeds on itself and demands more. We can see the damage in brain scans. We can see pictures of dendrites which grow in size and dimension but in unusual and twisted ways. They look like trees which grow out awkwardly because of sun deprivation.

To the addict, it feels normal. So we are back to the scary moment of admitting a problem. Our story of Jonathan is a good example because he fits so many of the typical patterns. He had addiction in his family and spent much of his youth scared. He started using very early at his brain's most vulnerable moment. He exploits women like a drug and has little ability to be with them unless they need him in unhealthy ways. Consequently, he often feels used by them. Jonathan is an engineering genius and he loves the excitement of the race. He resents deeply, however, that the credit often goes to drivers and the owner even though without him they would not be winning. So he is driven by a deep resentment yet is thrilled by his own notoriety. He uses drugs and alcohol to cope with the stress and even—he tells himself—to improve his performance. How do we make sense of all these issues when they are so interwoven?

Here is a map that helps sort this out. **Figure 3.1.**, below, provides a map to constellations or "families" of addictions. We start with substances which are most widely accepted as being addictive. Alcohol, cocaine, methamphetamines, nicotine, heroin, and prescription drugs for many are a nightmare. Nicotine, for example, is pernicious. When smoking, addicts feel that their mental abilities are enhanced. They are accurate in that memory momentarily improves. However, nicotine attacks the brain's ability to remember. You are trading a moment of improvement by sacrificing your ability to remember. Similarly, you temporarily lose the ability to multi-task. Research shows that when executives who are smokers are contrasted with non-smokers of equal skill, the smoker's ability to handle complex, multiple tasks is impaired. This is the addiction double bind. For temporary relief, you sell your soul. As we have described earlier, this is the bargain with chaos.

Addiction Types

Substances	Process
• Alcohol	• Sex
• Cocaine	• Work
• Methamphetamine	• Exercise
• Nicotine	• Video games
• Heroin	• Food (anorexia, bulimia & binge)
• Prescription drugs	• Money (gambling, shopping, E-trading)
• Caffeine	• Internet and/or cybersex
• Marijuana	
Feelings	**Compulsive Attachments**
• Rage	• Seeking and staying with troubled people
• Fear	• Pathological giving, rescuing and becoming a hero
• Self-loathing	• Intensity, drama and crises
• Intensity	• Impression management
• Love	• Codependency
	• Co-addiction
	• Traumatic bonding

Figure 3.1   © Copyright P.J. Carnes, 2009

Then we have the process addictions such as food, sex, work, exercise, and money. These are vital processes that are central to our well being as humans. However, ask a person who has a process addiction and an addiction to a substance, which is more difficult to recover from. Usually, the recovering person will respond that the process addiction was the greater challenge. An alcoholic does not have to use alcohol to live a normal life, so he can simply not use it. For a compulsive overeater, every meal is a challenge. For the sex addict, every day presents challenges. For instance, exercise is vital to our health. Yet, consider the sex addict who obsesses about staying at less than 8 percent body fat and exercises six to eight hours a day. He does this so he can have more sexual conquests. For those who use work and money to escape, they live in a culture which constantly invites them to do more. Money and work are normal components of leading a responsible life, but they have become two of our greatest spiritual struggles in this day and time. As we have learned, anything can become addictive when focus becomes obsession and the obsession starts to order how you live your life.

With compulsive attachments, relationships become addictive. This includes the classic "that man is your drug" phenomenon. We include codependency, which is becoming obsessed with the addict and the addict's behavior. The parent searches the adolescent drug user's room to find evidence. The spouse marks every bottle to monitor the partner's drinking. The co-sex addict hires the private detective to catch her partner or pores through years of bills and bank withdrawals to pinpoint unexplained expenditures. Codependents are case builders who exhaust themselves proving their worst fears.

Danger, fear, and risk are allies to codependent obsession. Some actually seek out dangerous or hurtful people. We call this traumatic bonding, where the essential ingredient is fear: staying with a battering partner, remaining loyal to an exploitive boss, or covering your partner's illegal behavior. Another form is hooking up with someone who needs you and is unreliable. We step in with money, time, and solutions, enabling round after round of crises. Or the addictive risk might be in romance. A romance junkie will aggressively court someone but abruptly drop that person when it is time to commit. Their lives are about constantly "falling in love" but never succeeding in attachment.

We call this quadrant Compulsive Attachments because it is where intimacy and addiction become most obvious. All these relationships have commonalities:

- Usually they involve seeking and staying with troubled people
- They involve pathological giving, rescuing, and being a hero
- Inevitably there is intensity, drama, and crisis
- Boundaries collapse so what is obvious to everyone else is overlooked
- Impression management causes secrecy as well as believing in improbable events
- Conflict avoidance asks for peace at any price including living as one who has to walk on eggshells

Notice that the hallmarks of secure attachment and successful intimacy are absent: safety, reliability, trust, vulnerability, creativity, and intentionality.

On that morning of surrender when Jonathan saw his life issues written on the wall, he started to get the extent of his compulsive attachment issues. His life was filled with high stress work and "high maintenance" women. He had a long relationship with a woman, which started in a strip bar. They had a child and she demanded a great deal of money or she threatened to tell his wife about the child. So he kept the peace by paying her, and her volatility made for sexual excitement as well. This, plus his travel and prostitution, made his life a financial house of cards with credit cards, bank accounts, and bonus money that no one could track. Jonathan winced when his therapist told him he could be a poster child for Debtors Anonymous. Another addiction to add to his list.

Addicts do not want to add codependency to their list just as codependents are beyond slow to acknowledge their own addictions. The spouse who is righteous and angry about an addict's behavior constructs a formidable wall around personal issues. Similarly, the addict who does not see the codependent part of himself leaves the door open to the righteousness of entitlement. When it boils down to the essences of the problem, addicts and codependents are mirror images of each other. Nothing makes this clearer than our fourth quadrant, which is about feelings or affect that the addict uses to keep the addictive circus going.

Alice Miller, the famous pioneer on trauma therapy, described early in her career the "addictive dependence on feelings of pain." As in so many things, she described the phenomenon long before modern therapy and neuroscience could document it. She was referring to the fact that people could be, as the song says, "hooked on a feeling." We have all seen "rageaholics" who consistently act out their rage and have difficulty stopping. There is also growing evidence about people who obsess about their unworthiness to the point of being crippled by their self-loathing. There are those who cultivate their feelings of misery and despair. Unresolved feelings of loss perpetuate their need for soothing. Fear and risk become essential to relationships. Think of addictive feelings like weighted wheels in a steam engine: they keep the momentum going between puffs of steam. Jonathan had a mix of feelings of rage, fear, self-loathing, and intensity that kept his life driven.

In the brain, these forms of "affect" become part of the neural pathways of addiction. This happens at a molecular level in the very synapses that convey the energy of addiction. Thus, what we know about recovery parallels the classic peeling of the onion. Most people start with substances or processes, or both. Then, underneath the addiction, they have to unravel the compulsive attachment issues. As those are exposed, another layer of dysfunctional feelings are revealed. Almost always these feelings are rooted in what we call the "grievance story." Dismantling the grievance story is a core process to recovery. By doing it, feelings are transformed into guides to well-being and success. Without emotional consciousness we can never reclaim the knowledge of who we are. In therapy we describe this as differentiation. This process of dismantling and reclaiming is the focus of Part Two, Chapters 4 to 9.

Jonathan was no different than most addicts. They start with the issues most obvious in their lives. But as they see the patterns, they are confronted with a more complex reality. If they do not look deeper, they relapse. If their caregivers do not push them or provide ways for them to do that work, they become part of the problem. That is why the Addiction Interaction Map is so important to use to clarify these issues. It has proved to be an important tool to make sense of addiction and its complexity.

Use the following worksheets to orient yourself to the map. In **Exercise 3.1**, Addiction Types, think of the four quadrants as a way to describe addictive behaviors and feelings you know you have. List all of your substance addictions, processes, attachments, and feelings that are problematic to you. For *each* item on your list, complete an "Addiction Impact Summary." These summaries will ask you to list:

- Your "worst moments" because of that problem
  (Select the most difficult, embarrassing, shameful, or painful examples)
- Your "effort to stop"
  (Give examples of ways you tried to limit, cut down, or eliminate the problem)
- Your "impact on relationships"
  (How has this behavior, relationship, or feeling affected your family or friends?)
- Your "signs of obsession"
  (Give examples of how this problem took up space in your mind)
- Your "other addictions present" (List what other substances, processes, attachments, or feelings were involved)

By completing the summaries in detail, you will then look at how those interact—which is usually at the core of relapse.

* **Note**: You have been provided with thirteen "Addiction Impact Summary" worksheets in this book.

Addiction Types

Using the four quadrants below, describe addictive behaviors and feelings you know that you have.

Substances

- _____
- _____
- _____
- _____
- _____
- _____

Process

- _____
- _____
- _____
- _____
- _____
- _____

Feelings

- _____
- _____
- _____
- _____
- _____
- _____

Compulsive Attachments

- _____
- _____
- _____
- _____
- _____
- _____

Exercise 3.1

Addiction Impact Summary

Addiction type (circle one):   Substance   Process   Attachment   Feeling

Addiction description (use your words): _____

Worst Moments:

_____
_____
_____

Efforts to Stop:

_____
_____
_____

Impact on Relationships:

_____
_____
_____

Signs of Obsession:

_____
_____

Other Addictions Present:

_____
_____

Exercise 3.2

Addiction Impact Summary

Addiction type (circle one):   Substance   Process   Attachment   Feeling

Addiction description (use your words): _____

Worst Moments:

_____
_____
_____

Efforts to Stop:

_____
_____
_____

Impact on Relationships:

_____
_____

Signs of Obsession:

_____
_____

Other Addictions Present:

_____
_____
_____

Exercise 3.2

© Copyright P.J. Carnes, 2009

Addiction Impact Summary

Addiction type (circle one): Substance Process Attachment Feeling

Addiction description (use your words): _____

Worst Moments:

_____
_____
_____
_____

Efforts to Stop:

_____
_____
_____

Impact on Relationships:

_____
_____
_____

Signs of Obsession:

_____
_____
_____

Other Addictions Present:

_____
_____
_____

Exercise 3.2

Addiction Impact Summary

Addiction type (circle one):   Substance   Process   Attachment   Feeling

Addiction description (use your words): _____

Worst Moments:

_____

_____

Efforts to Stop:

_____

_____

Impact on Relationships:

_____

_____

Signs of Obsession:

_____

_____

Other Addictions Present:

_____

_____

Exercise 3.2

Addiction Impact Summary

Addiction type (circle one): Substance   Process   Attachment   Feeling

Addiction description (use your words): _____

Worst Moments:

_____

_____

_____

Efforts to Stop:

_____

_____

Impact on Relationships:

_____

_____

Signs of Obsession:

_____

_____

Other Addictions Present:

_____

_____

Exercise 3.2

© Copyright P.J. Carnes, 2009

Addiction Impact Summary

Addiction type (circle one):   Substance   Process   Attachment   Feeling

Addiction description (use your words): _____

_____

Worst Moments:

_____

_____

_____

Efforts to Stop:

_____

_____

_____

Impact on Relationships:

_____

_____

_____

Signs of Obsession:

_____

_____

_____

Other Addictions Present:

_____

_____

_____

Exercise 3.2

Addiction Impact Summary

Addiction type (circle one):   Substance   Process   Attachment   Feeling

Addiction description (use your words): _____

Worst Moments:

_____

_____

_____

Efforts to Stop:

_____

_____

_____

Impact on Relationships:

_____

_____

_____

Signs of Obsession:

_____

_____

Other Addictions Present:

_____

_____

_____

Exercise 3.2

Addiction Impact Summary

Addiction type (circle one): Substance Process Attachment Feeling

Addiction description (use your words): _____

Worst Moments:

_____
_____
_____

Efforts to Stop:

_____
_____
_____

Impact on Relationships:

_____
_____

Signs of Obsession:

_____
_____

Other Addictions Present:

_____
_____
_____

Exercise 3.2

Addiction Impact Summary

Addiction type (circle one):   Substance   Process   Attachment   Feeling

Addiction description (use your words): _____

Worst Moments:

_____
_____
_____

Efforts to Stop:

_____
_____
_____

Impact on Relationships:

_____
_____
_____

Signs of Obsession:

_____
_____

Other Addictions Present:

_____
_____

Exercise 3.2

Addiction Impact Summary

Addiction type (circle one):   Substance   Process   Attachment   Feeling

Addiction description (use your words): _____

Worst Moments:

_____

_____

Efforts to Stop:

_____

_____

Impact on Relationships:

_____

_____

Signs of Obsession:

_____

_____

Other Addictions Present:

_____

_____

Exercise 3.2

Addiction Impact Summary

Addiction type (circle one):   Substance   Process   Attachment   Feeling

Addiction description (use your words): _____

Worst Moments:

_____
_____
_____

Efforts to Stop:

_____
_____
_____

Impact on Relationships:

_____
_____
_____

Signs of Obsession:

_____
_____
_____

Other Addictions Present:

_____
_____
_____

Exercise 3.2

Addiction Impact Summary

Addiction type (circle one):   Substance   Process   Attachment   Feeling

Addiction description (use your words): _____

Worst Moments:
_____
_____
_____

Efforts to Stop:
_____
_____
_____

Impact on Relationships:
_____
_____
_____

Signs of Obsession:
_____
_____
_____

Other Addictions Present:
_____
_____
_____

Exercise 3.2

Addiction Impact Summary

Addiction type (circle one):   Substance   Process   Attachment   Feeling

Addiction description (use your words): _____

Worst Moments:

_____

_____

_____

Efforts to Stop:

_____

_____

_____

Impact on Relationships:

_____

_____

_____

Signs of Obsession:

_____

_____

_____

Other Addictions Present:

_____

_____

_____

Exercise 3.2

Addiction Impact Summary – Part 1

In the space below, on the left side, list the worst specific problems each addiction has created in your life. Then in the area on the right, circle the level of impact that each problem has had on your life with 1 = not at all, 5 = somewhat and 10 = extreme consequences.

Ex. Lost a great job opportunity due to a positive drug screening for cocaine.	1	2	3	4	5	6	7	⑧	9	10
1.	1	2	3	4	5	6	7	8	9	10
2.	1	2	3	4	5	6	7	8	9	10
3.	1	2	3	4	5	6	7	8	9	10
4.	1	2	3	4	5	6	7	8	9	10
5.	1	2	3	4	5	6	7	8	9	10
6.	1	2	3	4	5	6	7	8	9	10
7.	1	2	3	4	5	6	7	8	9	10
8.	1	2	3	4	5	6	7	8	9	10
9.	1	2	3	4	5	6	7	8	9	10
10.	1	2	3	4	5	6	7	8	9	10
11.	1	2	3	4	5	6	7	8	9	10
12.	1	2	3	4	5	6	7	8	9	10

Exercise 3.3A

Addiction Impact Summary – Part 1 continued

13.	1	2	3	4	5	6	7	8	9	10
14.	1	2	3	4	5	6	7	8	9	10
15.	1	2	3	4	5	6	7	8	9	10
16.	1	2	3	4	5	6	7	8	9	10
17.	1	2	3	4	5	6	7	8	9	10
18.	1	2	3	4	5	6	7	8	9	10
19.	1	2	3	4	5	6	7	8	9	10
20.	1	2	3	4	5	6	7	8	9	10

Observations

_____

_____

_____

_____

_____

_____

Exercise 3.3A

Addiction Impact Scale – Part 2

List below the addictions present in your Impact List. Add up the ratings you gave for each problem which involved specific addictions. Thus, if the problem involved cocaine and you rated the problem as severe, you would add seven to the total for cocaine. If the problem involved both cocaine and sex, both would then get seven added to their respective totals. When the totals are complete, you will be able to make a new list by ranking the impact each addiction has had. The addiction with the highest total, is number one in impact. After you have ranked the addictions, compute an interaction impact score. Go back to your problem list, and then total all the ratings for each problem that involved more than one addiction. Also determine the number of problems listed that involved multiple addictions out of the total twenty listed. Compute the percentage of problems then that are about multiple addictions.

List of all addictions on impact list	Total of impact rating	Rank order of all addictions on impact list	Total of impact rating
1.		1.	
2.		2.	
3.		3.	
4.		4.	
5.		5.	
6.		6.	
7.		7.	
8.		8.	

Interaction Impact Total Ratings Score

Number of problems involving multiple addictions

Percentage of problem list (multiply times 5)

Exercise 3.3B

Family Addiction History

In the space below, on the left side, list all family members who have addiction(s). Then in the area on the right, circle which addictions the individual has. If their addiction is not listed, please write it below or beside their title (ex: Dad/video games). Please include parents, grandparents, siblings, aunts, uncles, and cousins, if appropriate.

Ex. Maternal Grandmother	(Alcohol)	Drugs	Food	Sex	Money	Work	Codependency	(Feelings)	Nicotine	Caffeine
	Alcohol	Drugs	Food	Sex	Money	Work	Codependency	Feelings	Nicotine	Caffeine
	Alcohol	Drugs	Food	Sex	Money	Work	Codependency	Feelings	Nicotine	Caffeine
	Alcohol	Drugs	Food	Sex	Money	Work	Codependency	Feelings	Nicotine	Caffeine
	Alcohol	Drugs	Food	Sex	Money	Work	Codependency	Feelings	Nicotine	Caffeine
	Alcohol	Drugs	Food	Sex	Money	Work	Codependency	Feelings	Nicotine	Caffeine
	Alcohol	Drugs	Food	Sex	Money	Work	Codependency	Feelings	Nicotine	Caffeine
	Alcohol	Drugs	Food	Sex	Money	Work	Codependency	Feelings	Nicotine	Caffeine
	Alcohol	Drugs	Food	Sex	Money	Work	Codependency	Feelings	Nicotine	Caffeine
	Alcohol	Drugs	Food	Sex	Money	Work	Codependency	Feelings	Nicotine	Caffeine
	Alcohol	Drugs	Food	Sex	Money	Work	Codependency	Feelings	Nicotine	Caffeine
	Alcohol	Drugs	Food	Sex	Money	Work	Codependency	Feelings	Nicotine	Caffeine
	Alcohol	Drugs	Food	Sex	Money	Work	Codependency	Feelings	Nicotine	Caffeine
	Alcohol	Drugs	Food	Sex	Money	Work	Codependency	Feelings	Nicotine	Caffeine
	Alcohol	Drugs	Food	Sex	Money	Work	Codependency	Feelings	Nicotine	Caffeine
	Alcohol	Drugs	Food	Sex	Money	Work	Codependency	Feelings	Nicotine	Caffeine
	Alcohol	Drugs	Food	Sex	Money	Work	Codependency	Feelings	Nicotine	

Exercise 3.4

brain parallel other domains of nature in which energy flows. Like ...d then join together, the neural pathways of addiction will form a larger ...al energy. These connections will be deeper, wider, and swifter. There ...que high is created, the roots of which exist down to a molecular ...entists have shown that combined alcohol use and tobacco use form ...tion. This is why relapse is higher for people who are addicted to ...the addict gives up alcohol but not nicotine, the tendency to relapse is higher. That is because a major portion of the river still flows. Both addictions work together to provide the most relief for the addict's pain. Damming one river does not help. (Plus, you have the problem of where all that water goes. This pressure must find a medium of excellence which is why living in the zone is so important.)

In the early years of addiction treatment, there were those who said treat one addiction at a time. Too much change at once was considered bad. Now we understand that poor success rates are rooted in part by the complexity of how addictions interact. Now we address the way addiction begins and the way they work together. Here are the patterns that clinicians look for:

Cross Tolerance: Cross tolerance happens when two or more addictions increase the addict's ability to engage in more addictive behavior. Thus, the alcohol use and sexual behavior increase at the same time. Cocaine creates more arousal drive when masturbating to porn on the Internet. Working a hundred hours a week, making high risk investments, and using amphetamines amplify the joining of rivers taking things deeper, wider, faster. Eating disorder studies have provided an abundance of research on how compulsive eating and compulsive drinking accentuate each other. Another way to see cross tolerance is when an addict switches from one addiction to another, with the new addiction starting at a level of someone who had developed high tolerance over a long time. An example would be someone with a long history of high risk sex, who upon discovering cocaine begins immediately using cocaine in amounts that would typically take a long time for the body to handle.

Withdrawal Mediation: This occurs when one addiction is used to help stop another. A great example is smoking at an AA meeting. Nicotine is a hard drug and smoking is a certified health disaster. But it numbs feelings, elevates mood, and helps a person feel more on top of things—while it erodes your brain from the inside. It has been used by addicts for years as a "cushion." When one addiction is used to assist stopping another, interaction occurs. Withdrawal mediation is like diverting one river into another.

Replacement: When one addiction replaces another with all the behavioral features, an interaction problem exists. Usually in these situations the addict has stopped for some time. The time element makes it a different category than withdrawal mediation. So consider a broker who works in the high stress of trading stocks in a stock exchange. He uses marijuana to relax and get through the day. The marijuana becomes a problem, and he goes to treatment. Sober, he returns to work. After a year, the stress gets to him but he does not want to use marijuana. He discovers massage parlors. Soon sexual behavior assumes the former role of his marijuana use. It becomes his coping mechanism with all the secrecy and lies of his former marijuana behavior. He still considers himself in recovery and fails to notice how he has slipped into the same patterns. Of course, he maintained his high risk, adrenaline soaked work pace.

Alternating Cycles: Addictions have rhythms and become cyclic. Consider the woman who is out of control with sex but anorexic with food. Then she gets married and reverses the processes. She becomes sexually anorexic and eats compulsively. She gains one hundred pounds. She gets divorced and becomes anorexic and promiscuous again. Over four marriages she repeats the same process. Most addicts recognize cyclic repetitive patterns in their lives by looking at a timeline. An example would be sexual acting out for a period of years and then bingeing for a period of drug and alcohol use. This would be followed by another era of sexual acting out. Definite patterns repeat themselves, weaving in and out of an addict's life.

Masking: "I did it because I was drinking" is a refrain used by sex addicts for years to mask their other behavior. Blaming out-of-control sexual behavior on alcohol use puts the blame on drinking, which is a more socially acceptable addiction. Often, addicts who do both would rather give up drinking than the sexual activities. A typical scenario is to go through alcoholism treatment and convince the spouse that the sexual issues were due to alcohol. However, when the sexual behavior continues even though the drinking stops, the truth appears—much to everyone's pain. Or consider when alcohol is an excuse for rage, or work stress is blamed for compulsive eating or gambling. Of course, angry outbreaks can be justified as being a "tough" manager, and high risk investments and deal chasing can be justified as part of being an entrepreneur. Whenever one behavior is used to cover another, you have masking.

Rituals: When the rituals of one addiction are the same for another addiction, the joining occurs at a synaptic level too. The movie, *Looking for Mr. Goodbar*, tells the story of a teacher, Theresa Dunn, going out to seduce men and get high. Her rituals in dressing and preparing for the bar scene are examples of how more than one addiction can be accessed by the same ritualistic behaviors. Most addicts are able to see certain things that "rev things up" so that judgment is clouded. Driving in certain areas where there are casinos, drug dealers, or sex-oriented businesses is not accidental. Such cruising is part of the "I am going to binge" process. Addicts kid themselves about why they end up in those neighborhoods, but the brain knows what is going on. It is part of the preparation scenario that activates the pleasure centers of the brain.

Fusing: Clinicians note how one addiction will amplify the impact of another. About 50 percent to 70 percent of cocaine addicts also have problems with sexual compulsivity. Sex on cocaine is a different experience. When two addictions are used simultaneously they become one entity and the term we use to describe it is *fusion*—the addictions become fused. The addict then will not use cocaine without sex, nor be sexual without cocaine.

Numbing: Trauma therapists have long noticed a rhythm in people who have post traumatic stress disorder. They will seek out high risk and pleasurable experiences, and after the binge they will soothe themselves with some numbing behavior. A common pattern is to do high risk behaviors all evening, and then they drink, masturbate, overeat, or even cut on themselves as a way to soothe or calm down. So the pattern is high arousal followed by numbing, high arousal followed by numbing.

Disinhibiting: Disinhibiting occurs when one addiction helps you to relax so that you could do something that when in your "right mind" you would not ordinarily do. The behaviors can become an interactive pattern. "I would think of what I wanted to do sexually, but would have to get drunk to do it." One addiction paves the way for another.

Combining: When addicts combine behaviors to achieve the right "high" and maintain that edge, we call it combining. Classically, chemically dependent people will mix uppers and downers to stay in that zone. Like surfers catching a wave, they try to ride as long as they can. But there are so many things to add, such as danger, nicotine, a little alcohol, something illegal, spending, or even swinging. You will notice that many of the novels that fly out of airport bookstores have a character who is an expert at mixing obsessions. John Sandford's *Prey* novels, Robert Ludlom's *Bourne* series, or David Baldacci's *Camel Club* series are great examples. *The French Connection* is an excellent example if you are more of a cinema person. Once you understand combining, you start seeing how it is very much part of human experience to ride the wave.

Inclusive: Sometimes there is one addiction that is always present and it serves as a background to the others. So if you smoke when you eat, drink, work, or have sex in an addictive way, this addiction is fundamental to the addictive neurocircuitry of your brain. It becomes the neurochemical touchstone for all your other behavior. So check to see if there is an addiction that serves all the others.

An essential part of deep recovery is to identify interactive patterns in your life. The more complete the identification, the more profound the change. The addiction interaction map becomes a portal to the reclaiming of self and the releasing of talent. You cannot take your life into the zone without a complete inventory of how addiction has perverted your focus into obsession. So many people start recovery by getting sober in one or two addictions. Maybe they attend to their codependency, but they keep some of the old patterns and addictive ways around. The result is that they get so far and somehow the promises of recovery elude them. Life is better, but they end up asking themselves, "Is this all there is?" The audit for addictions has to be ruthless in its honesty and complete in its detail.

The following pages will help you start to identify addiction interaction in your life. Each page has a definition and examples. Record patterns you see from your own history. Some categories will not fit for you. In those that do, list as much as you can think of. At times you will find behavior that can fit in more than one category. For example, lighting up a cigarette can be listed as part of a "combining" pattern but also could be a ritual prior to other behaviors. Be complete and "rigorous" in your honesty.

Addiction Interaction Master List: Cross Tolerance

Cross tolerance is when two or more addictions increase the addict's ability to do more behavior. One example is how the use of alcohol and sexual behavior increase at the same time. List ways that you have used cross tolerance in your life with items from your Addiction Impact Summary (pages 57-69). Describe worst moments for each.

Cross Tolerance Interaction	Worst Moments
1.	
2.	
3.	
4.	
5.	
6.	
7.	
8.	
9.	
10.	

Exercise 3.5A

Addiction Interaction Master List: Withdrawal Mediation

Withdrawal mediation is when one addiction is used to help stop another, like a "cushion." A great example of this is smoking at an AA meeting. List ways that you have used withdrawal mediation in your life with items from your Addiction Impact Summary (pages 57-69). Describe worst moments for each.

	Withdrawal Mediation Interaction	Worst Moments
1.		
2.		
3.		
4.		
5.		
6.		
7.		
8.		
9.		
10.		

Exercise 3.5B

Addiction Interaction Master List: Replacement

Replacement is when one addiction replaces another with all the behavioral features. Usually the addict has stopped for some time. For example, the stressed out stockbroker who used to use marijuana to relax but after getting treatment for drug use, he used addictive sexual behaviors to "relax." List ways that you have used replacement in your life with items from your Addiction Impact Summary (pages 57-69). Describe worst moments for each.

	Replacement Interaction	Worst Moments
1.		
2.		
3.		
4.		
5.		
6.		
7.		
8.		
9.		
10.		

Exercise 3.5C

Addiction Interaction Master List: Alternating Cycles

Most addicts recognize cyclic repetitive patterns in their lives by looking at a timeline. Consider the woman who is out of control with sex but anorexic with food. Then she gets married and reverses the process by becoming sexually anorexic but eating compulsively. She gains one hundred pounds, gets divorced, and becomes anorexic and promiscuous again. List ways that you have used alternating cycles in your life with items from your Addiction Impact Summary (pages 57-69). Describe worst moments for each.

Alternating Cycles Interaction	Worst Moments
1.	
2.	
3.	
4.	
5.	
6.	
7.	
8.	
9.	
10.	

Exercise 3.5D

Addiction Interaction Master List: Masking

Masking is when one behavior is used to cover another. Consider the person who blames out of control sexual behavior on alcohol use. List ways that you have used masking in your life with items from your Addiction Impact Summary (pages 57-69). Describe worst moments for each.

Masking Interaction	Worst Moments
1.	
2.	
3.	
4.	
5.	
6.	
7.	
8.	
9.	
10.	

Exercise 3.5E

Addiction Interaction Master List: Rituals

Rituals involve the preparation, "getting ready," or "revving up" to act out. Driving in certain areas where there are drug dealers or casinos is more than accidental. List ways that you have used rituals in your life with items from your Addiction Impact Summary (pages 57-69). Describe worst moments for each.

Rituals Interaction	Worst Moments
1.	
2.	
3.	
4.	
5.	
6.	
7.	
8.	
9.	
10.	

Exercise 3.5F

Addiction Interaction Master List: Fusing

Fusing is when two addictions are used so simultaneously that they become one entity. An example of this would be the addict who will not use cocaine without sex and will not be sexual without cocaine. List ways that you have used fusing in your life with items from your Addiction Impact Summary (pages 57-69). Describe worst moments for each.

Fusing Interaction	Worst Moments
1.	
2.	
3.	
4.	
5.	
6.	
7.	
8.	
9.	
10.	

Exercise 3.5G

Addiction Interaction Master List: Numbing

Numbering involves seeking out high-risk and pleasurable experiences, and after the binge, the addict soothes him- or herself with some numbing behavior such as drinking, masturbating, or overeating. List ways that you have used numbing in your life with items from your Addiction Impact Summary (pages 57-69). Describe worst moments for each.

Numbing Interaction	Worst Moments
1.	
2.	
3.	
4.	
5.	
6.	
7.	
8.	
9.	
10.	

Exercise 3.5H

Addiction Interaction Master List: Disinhibiting

Disinhibiting is when one addiction helps you relax or gives you courage to do something you would not ordinarily do in your right mind. Basically, one addiction paves the way for another. An example of this might be wanting to act out sexually with a stranger but getting drunk first so you could then act out sexually. List ways that you have used disinhibiting in your life with items from your Addiction Impact Summary (pages 57-69). Describe worst moments for each.

Disinhibiting Interaction	Worst Moments	
1.		
2.		
3.		
4.		
5.		
6.		
7.		
8.		
9.		
10.		

Exercise 3.5l

Addiction Interaction Master List: Combining

Combining exists when addicts "combine" addictions (such as using uppers and downers) to achieve or maintain a specific balance or edge. Examples are food and wine, fear and sex, the dangerous partner and cocaine — combinations which reinforce one another. List ways that you have combined items from your Addiction Impact Summary (pages 57-69). Describe worst moments for each.

Combining Interaction	Worst Moments
1.	
2.	
3.	
4.	
5.	
6.	
7.	
8.	
9.	
10.	

© Copyright P.J. Carnes, 2009

Exercise 3.5J

Addiction Interaction Master List: Inclusive

Sometimes there is one addiction that is always present and it serves as a background to the others. So if you smoke when you eat, drink, work, or have sex in an addictive way, this addiction is fundamental to the addictive neurocircuitry of your brain. List ways that you have used inclusion in your life with items from your Addiction Impact Summary (pages 57-69). Describe worst moments for each.

Inclusive Interaction	Worst Moments
1.	
2.	
3.	
4.	
5.	
6.	
7.	
8.	
9.	
10.	

Exercise 3.5K

© Copyright P.J. Carnes, 2009

88 | Chapter 3 **The Addiction Interaction Map**

Recovery Zone The Internal Tasks

As you go through the rest of this chapter (and later ones) you will have new insights. Return to this master list and make it a living document of what addiction has done in your life. Before we finish, the master list of interactions will become very important.

Identifying the Patterns

Shortly after Jonathan had his moment of realization about his behaviors, he was flooded with insights about how it fit together. One of those insights came out during a psychodrama session. The therapist who did psychodrama had divided the room up into four squares which represented the four quadrants of the addiction interaction map. Each patient did a "dialogue" with their addictions in each quadrant. A dialogue is an imaginary conversation between parts of the self. The "inner observer" represents that part of the patient that was functional, fully accessing the executive processes of the brain (the frontal lobes). This inner observer then talks with the addiction in order to coax into consciousness aspects of the self. This dialogue is effective as an insight tool, assisting with the internal fragmentation of the addict. Most importantly, this dialogue promotes the integration of new circuitry in the brain by forcing the neuropathways to connect in new ways. Psychodrama is one of the many formats in which these dialogues occur in therapy.

When it was Jonathan's turn, he started with his sex addiction. Jonathan was prompted to ask his sex addiction what he was in denial about. As his sex addict, Jonathan responded, "Let's start with how many women there have been." When the inner observer was puzzled, the addict continued, "You only count the ones you have paid. There were others that you started with and discarded." The therapist then asked how Jonathan could figure that out and the sex addict said, "Go by city. Make a list by each city." The psychodrama therapist coached Jonathan to pick a city and make a list out loud. So he picked Charlotte, North Carolina, a frequent racing stop for his team, and came up with ten women. Only two were prostitutes. Jonathan was stunned and scared because his denial had broken.

The psychodrama coach then asked why he was so angry with women. Jonathan had not been aware of how his behavior was driven by so much anger. The therapist responded, "Such disregard for others has to come from somewhere." Jonathan turned toward the affect quadrant of the map and asked his anger why he treated women that way. The anger response was almost disdainful because there was so much that was obvious and had been ignored:

- There was anger because his mom did not protect him from his dad.
- He always had to help his mom and he knew she was in too bad of shape to nurture or help him. He recognized how terrible it was for her, so he felt he could not be angry with her. With no connection with his dad, she was his lifeline.
- He did not trust women, so the only ones he would stay connected to were the women who needed him financially or in some other way. Attractive, independent women really infuriated him.

- His resentment for his wife was like a cauldron because she was at him all the time to do things. He felt he could not get mad because he could see she was overwhelmed with their children and money problems. She was trying hard and he loved her for it, but he often wanted to flee from her.

- His wife never gave him credit for how hard he worked and how good he was at it. Nor did she acknowledge that he made a lot of money, even though they seemed to be financially desperate. Part of it was how she spent money, but a major part was also his spending—a good portion of which was hidden. His wife was not the only one who did not give him credit. The team owner overlooked the fact that the team drivers could only be as good as the tuning of their engines. At race parties when a woman told him how she admired his success he could not resist going to bed with her. He was a sucker for any compliment, but he hated himself for his sexual behavior. Drugs helped to make it seem like fun, more like a party.

- When he saw prostitutes he would fall for their compliments. He knew they were insincere and it was a game to them, but he was so desperate for acknowledgment that he would play anyway and often could not wait for the sex to be over. And from his courtesans he was able to buy drugs. He hated needing them for that, but it was the quickest, easiest way.

He had noticed the sex and the drugs, but he had missed the anger. His clothes were damp with perspiration and tears. In the debriefing with the group, he admitted how obvious the patterns were and how out of touch he had been. Various group members had been asked to pick out categories of addiction interactions. For example, one member was struck by how his drug use was frequently used to numb out his pain around sex. Another underlined how the background to everything was excitement and crisis. Several thought his sexual and drug behaviors were fused.

His therapist gave him the task of making a list by city of women who he had harmed and to continue his dialogues in written form. In the final dialogue that night, his anger responded, "You must come to terms with me or I'll take you down." Jonathan clearly heard the message. At that point he did not know how to do it. After the day's work his therapist had said to him, "All you have to do now is get clarity." Those words and his therapist's kindness were a comfort.

Your therapist will also ask you to work for clarity. One of the principal tasks you will be asked to do is an addiction timeline. Typically, you will be asked to look back over your life and specify when each addiction started and how it affected other addictions. A good practice is to note when major life events such as a death in the family or specific abuses occurred. The goal is to connect your addictions, their interactions, and the key stress points of your life. In the following pages you will find a timeline worksheet. More than likely you may want to create this on a large piece of paper, using the worksheet as a model. It is important to record the totality of it. For this exercise you will need several colored markers or pens. You will begin by filling out the legend on page 92. List each addiction you have or have had in the past. In the small boxes on the left side of the legend, use the colored pens or markers to assign each addiction you have listed a different color.

Legend for Timeline Addictions

Example Addiction: Smoking Cigarettes

☐ Addiction 1: _____

☐ Addiction 2: _____

☐ Addiction 3: _____

☐ Addiction 4: _____

☐ Addiction 5: _____

☐ Addiction 6: _____

☐ Addiction 7: _____

☐ Addiction 8: _____

☐ Addiction 9: _____

☐ Addiction 10: _____

Multiple Addictions Timeline

Using the legend that you created on the last page, map out a timeline for each addiction listed based on your age when use started until your current age (or when the addiction stopped) and the severity of the addiction. Example: Started smoking at age fifteen, a few cigarettes a day and now I am thirty-five years and smoke a pack a day, so severity has increased.

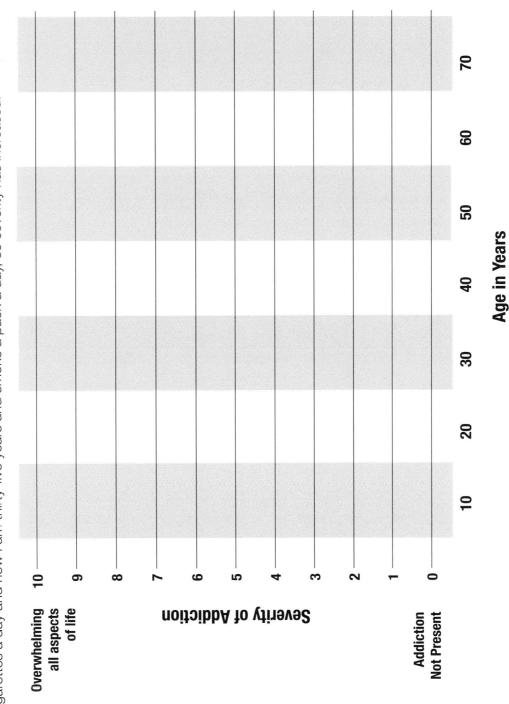

Severity of Addiction

Overwhelming
all aspects
of life — 10

9

8

7

6

5

4

3

2

1

Addiction
Not Present — 0

Age in Years

10 20 30 40 50 60 70

Exercise 3.6

A frequent assignment designed to foster internal dialogue is to write a letter to yourself from each addiction. An extension or variation of that theme is to identify addicts in your family history who are now deceased. Write a letter to yourself from the deceased person about your addictions. This "letter from the dead" exercise can be powerful and moving. They also serve the purpose of helping you access your own wisdom. It is hard to get clarity without these devices to assist you in making conscious what you know but is not in your awareness. At this stage clarity is everything.

The Interaction Sobriety Imperative

Sally was struggling with her husband who had recently returned from treatment for his alcoholism. He is a physician who now had his license conditionally until he completed the five-year state physician's health program. He had returned to his old work patterns of being on-call and working long hours in the emergency room. Lately, he had outbursts of irrational anger which he dismissed as a sign of working too hard. Sally knew the pattern. Long hours led to rage, which led to drinking, which led to violence. When she raised the issue he was dismissive. He was the doctor and knew best about these things. She hated that arrogance. Even more, she hated how he would just stop talking to her in silent rage.

The other problem was with Martha, who was Sally's mom. Her parents had been divorced for about twenty years. Martha clearly had developed an alcohol problem, and Sally had several fights with her about her drinking. Sally felt caught because she was the only sibling who saw the problem. Her siblings did not acknowledge or understand the addiction. She was overwhelmed and discouraged. She recognized that her efforts to control both her husband and her mom were becoming counterproductive—but it was so hard to let go.

One day Sally was riding in a car with her dad, George. She was sharing some of her struggles with recovery and wanted to talk about family issues. Her dad had been in recovery for decades for his drug dependence and his eating disorder. He had years of Twelve Step experience and would be candid about addiction in their family. Her dad smiled and said, "Yeah, it is like your mother and me and food." Sally was puzzled so he continued. "At the height of my compulsive eating I was obese. And I was secretly drinking. Your mom could not see all my drug use but she could see my weight. Whenever I took seconds of food or had what she thought too big a helping she would say something like 'do you really need that?' I would immediately feel a stab of hunger, say yes, and reach for more." Sally was really surprised and told her father that she had never seen that dynamic. In fact, she was somewhat skeptical.

Her father added more to the story, "When we divorced, and my weight was in a healthy range again, she told me that I did not even look like a husband anymore. That is when I got the piece about her being invested in me being overweight. For all of her nagging, she in one way needed me to have the problem."

A few weeks later a favorite uncle of Sally's died after surgery. The vigil in the hospital threw Sally's dad and mom together for lunch alone. And then that night all the family had dinner together. After placing their dinner orders, her mom leaned back over a drink and said, "You should have seen the lunch your dad ate today. It would have fed an army!" Sally looked at her dad who smiled in return. She was stunned that this pressure around food had been in the family for years and she was unaware of it. Sally later told her dad that she could not believe her mom's words, she was so surprised.

Sally also told her therapist who helped her put more of the pieces together. Her therapist started by comparing addiction to a complex tapestry of interactive threads that weaves addictive codependency with other addictive behavior. She gave two examples out of Sally's current circumstances. First, Sally's husband was very thin, verging on anorexia. He ate very sparingly often leaving up to two-thirds of the food on his plate. His comment would be that he would eat it later—which he seldom did. It served several purposes. One, as a doctor, he prided himself on his trim appearance. Second, he hated that Sally had put on so much weight. He was trying to teach her that she should eat like he did. Then she would be more attractive to him. At every meal he modeled a lesson to her, underlined by an air of medical arrogance.

Her therapist pointed out to Sally that the patterns of food and chemical dependency that had been in her parent's marriage had reemerged in her marriage. Further, her therapist wondered if Sally's weight was more than just about having children. Could the weight be a layer of safety to minimize sexual interest in her because she was so hurt still by her husband's behavior? The other possibility was she was using food to soothe herself.

The second example her therapist provided was about her husband's smoking, which Sally hated. She constantly nagged him about it. When he came inside after smoking she would roll her eyes and ask him to move away from her because she could not stand the smell. She would not let the kids ride in his car because it smelled so bad. She would righteously point out that as a doctor he should know what second-hand smoke does. It was a constant source of bickering in the marriage and had frequently been brought up in their therapy. Her therapist concluded, "Every time you nag you become part of the problem. When your mom nagged your dad, he would reach for more mashed potatoes. When you nag your mother about drinking she becomes more resentful and defiant about her drinking. And when you nag about his smoking, you are as arrogant as he is."

Her therapist added that the only way to change the nature of the tapestry was to change her own behavior. Sally's therapist told her, "You must state clearly what you see that concerns you. If you have boundaries, set them. Then you have to let go of it and let the natural consequences run their course. You must take care of those issues that truly are your own, such as your own eating and codependency. That will go further toward changing the family than anything else you can do. Nagging creates the dynamics of resentment. Doing your own work brings respect. Finally you absolutely must see how all these pieces fit together and work on them constantly. It requires deep focus for a long period of time, which is why meetings and therapy are so important. Recovery is not something to fit in. It must be the priority. The improvement in your life will let all else flow into your life."

The last observations really hit home for Sally. She had been aware of her spotty Twelve Step attendance and the difficulty she seemed to have in attending therapy appointments. Children, work, and financial challenges felt overwhelming. When she commented on that, her therapist persevered and said, "Much of your time and attention goes into these dynamics. The stress of it keeps you hooked and wears you out. But becoming clear on what you need to do and resolutely following the clarity is the only way out of the mire of addiction interaction. It is the only proven path. Difficult, yes. But it will create a seismic change in how good your life can be."

Sally's therapist helped her to get in an intensive outpatient program for food issues. She owned up to having done some purging in high school and realized that it was related to her bingeing as an adult. Now she did not purge, she simply used "comfort" food. It made her angry because food did not put the family's well-being at risk as her husband's alcohol use had, nor did it lead to violence. She surrendered to the fact that being overweight is a health issue. She hated there was truth in her husband's dinner time lessons. Righteousness blinded her to the damage she did to herself. She told her therapist, "Righteousness was my refuge. That and food."

One of the addiction interaction exercises Sally was asked to do was the interaction, sobriety imperative. An imperative is really a list of what a person in recovery must do. In Twelve Step programs it is used as a way of defining sobriety. She listed what sobriety meant for her from her codependency and from her eating disorder. Then she was asked to go back over the master list, and do her "worst moments" from an interaction point of view. Sally described one of those moments to her group. She had made a meal she liked, but her husband wanted to skip it and get to his hospital shift. She clearly saw that she provoked her husband into a rage and he hit her. He was on his usual express train schedule, but she just wanted him to stop and hear how desperate things were for her in the house. She was also righteous about his drinking before working in an emergency room. She said awful things and berated him terribly. He became irate at what she said. After the violence he smashed the side of the garage door in a dramatic exit. Sally had actually laid her body down on the driveway in order to stop him, and he drove over the lawn and through a garden to make his wheel-spinning exit.

"No drama in this," she wryly observed. Then, with a determined voice, Sally added, "No excuse either. For either one of us." She broke into tears as she described her shame because all of their kids and many neighbors witnessed the process. As people helped her on her feet, she never before had felt so embarrassed. For two very educated people, to create such a scene eviscerated her sense of pride. She had no doubt that everything was present: anger, alcohol, food, overwork, stress, and drama. The whole "enchilada," she observed.

From this, Sally formed an interaction imperative: She at all costs must not create, add to, or be part of unnecessary drama. By stating these obvious guidelines to recovery, the interaction imperative becomes central to building recovery. For Sally, it gave her a way of seeing "the trees, the forest, and the planet."

While in treatment and therapy, Sally completed her addiction interaction map. It took time to put all the pieces together, and she had to get help with the house and the kids. She was amazed at how many people would help, including her mother. Her hard work showed. She could ignore her husband's silent tirades and arrogant lectures. She no longer got caught in un-winnable debates with him. Sally's mother started to get the picture as well and went to an outpatient program. Sally was able to avoid getting trapped in her mother's tirades as well. She was verbalizing needs and boundaries, and she told her husband that if domestic violence ever occurred again, there would be zero tolerance. She no longer would be tyrannized by the fear of his loss of his medical license. Plus, she lost weight, exercised, went to meetings, and was now seeing food as an adventure. How and what she ate changed, as did the family dynamics. Her therapist joked with her about having a "black belt" in Al-Anon.

The following pages create a format for you to determine your interaction imperative. Start with the worst moments you have had in your addiction history. Out of the worst moments list what interaction dynamics are part of your powerlessness. Then describe your sobriety for each addiction that you have. Then carefully think through what interactions you have to avoid in order to remain in recovery.

Interaction Imperative

Review your Addiction Impact Summaries (pages 57-69) and your Addiction Interaction Master List (pages 78-88). Select ten of your very worst moments involving more than one addiction. List them below under Interaction Worst Moments. Make another list of guidelines for your recovery goals. List them under Interaction Imperatives.

Interaction Worst Moments	Interaction Imperatives
Example: Escalating drama and compulsive eating created neighborhood scene and acting out.	Example: Do not create, add to, or be part of unnecessary drama.
1.	
2.	
3.	
4.	
5.	
6.	
7.	
8.	
9.	
10.	

Exercise 3.7

Sobriety & Interaction Imperatives

List each addiction and list the behaviors you no longer do (sobriety or boundary). Then name the critical interactions and what is imperative for you to do for your recovery.

Interaction Imperatives

Interaction Worst Moments		Interaction Imperatives

1. Addiction Sobriety:

_____

_____

⬆

Critical Interactions Imperative:

_____

_____

_____

2. Addiction Sobriety:

_____

_____

⬆

Critical Interactions Imperative:

_____

_____

_____

3. Addiction Sobriety:

_____

_____

⬆

Critical Interactions Imperative:

_____

_____

_____

4. Addiction Sobriety:

_____

_____

⬆

Critical Interactions Imperative:

_____

_____

_____

5. Addiction Sobriety:

_____

_____

⬆

Critical Interactions Imperative:

_____

_____

_____

Exercise 3.8

You Are Here

At the end of each part of this book, we will take stock of what we have done up to this point. So far we have looked at some of the hard realities of addiction and its complexity. With the Decision Table, we have learned a way to help us prioritize challenges. Then we explored the concept of a zone of excellence which helps us to re-examine those challenges in light of where we are at our best. The final tool we have used is the Addiction Interaction Map which further helps to determine what is in the zone for us and what is not. **Figure 3.2** graphically shows us how far we have come.

Reclaiming Self

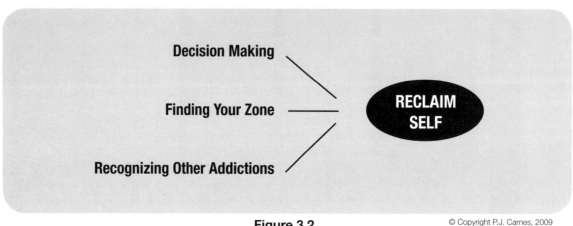

Figure 3.2

© Copyright P.J. Carnes, 2009

The next step is to reclaim our personal and moral compass. In our addictions we have lost our way. Now that we have some clarity, we need to reclaim what we have lost. Ironically, we can find that sense of direction by looking at how we lost ourselves. This requires us to go deeply into our pain and the underlying feelings from which we flee. By facing them we will make them allies in good decision making. We call this next part, "The Dark Night of the Soul."

Remember, as you use the book, recoveryzone.com is a great companion. You can get forms and further resources for each of the tools and tasks you encounter here. A book is limited in its formatting. Recoveryzone.com can make this much easier. Plus you have all the other support resources.

Recovery Zone **Part Two**

Chapter 4 **The Dark Night of the Soul**

The story of Buddha is
"the universal soul journey that begins asleep and ends awake."

—Deepak Chopra, *Buddha: A Story of Enlightenment*

So many great teachers begin by saying that life is a dream. Plato told a story of how our lives are like waking from a dream. His famous allegory of the cave describes a group of people raised from birth in a cave. They were prisoners who were chained so all they could see were shadows cast on the wall of the cave. When their captors walked in front of the fire, the prisoners named the shadows cast on the wall. They thought the shadows were reality. When they were allowed to turn around, they could see their captors whose shadows they thought were real. They were stunned when they grasped the new reality. When the prisoners were subsequently released from the cave, their understanding of the world again expanded dramatically. Plato's allegory is about developing a higher level of consciousness. As we assimilate to new levels of reality, we have to adjust to change.

Much of life is a series of progressive realizations. Sooner or later, most of us adults have the opportunity to hear the cry of a child and remember how a parent protected us from ourselves. A child in the "terrible twos" would not last long without a parent's protection. Every parent has told a toddler not to do something, but the child attempts to do it anyway. Or, when you think of the angst of an adolescent, you probably remember the lack of reality during your own painful adolescent strivings. Most of us can remember wanting to do something that was beyond our capabilities. We also can remember our feelings of outrage and injustice at unyielding parents. I have often thought, as I struggled with kids and grandkids, about how I pushed my own parents.

This developmental struggle is critical. The brain does not organically finish maturation until just short of thirty years of age. At two years old, a child is experiencing intense feelings but does not have sufficient frontal lobe development to manage them. Thus, when a two year old who is scared or angry grabs his mother's skirts, the mother soothes the child and supplies a story or explanation to help do that. In therapy we call this the "narrative." Adolescents need to witness parents who struggle and overcome difficulties. Observing their parents help the brain of the teenager develop the circuitry to inhibit behavior and make good decisions, and the parents must remain in good relationship with the teenager while the conflict continues. This produces adults who have secure attachment. Also, the teenager feels valued because they were "worth" fighting with. Again, there is a "borrowing of perspective" that the teenager does not yet have.

This struggle prepares the child for life's realities. Life is often unfair. Suffering, fear, and hurt will be there. We must know how to transform bad experiences into assets. We call this resilience. In the Twelve Step programs, the widely used phrase, "nothing is wasted" captures the truth that there are always critical lessons in the struggle. No matter what the disaster is, we must seek learning, meaning, and opportunity. Finding peace and joy in the struggle is humankind's most important task. Notice the following elements in the struggle:

- **A story evolves.** We all have a story starting with our parents' narrative. The story is at the heart of how we perceive ourselves. Our internal narrative is the brain's way of helping us make sense of the world. The telling and hearing of stories is the most complex activity the brain does and it is critical to engineering new neural pathways. The success of Twelve Step programs lies in part in the tradition of story telling. We truly do meet ourselves in the story we use to anchor our realities.

- **Feelings become regulated.** We must be able to access and manage our feelings. We have to be able to tolerate and even embrace their presence. In families where strong feelings were not tolerated or used well, kids become vulnerable to the addiction process. If the family is toxic or abusive, feelings may be overwhelming. Whatever our history, once sobriety is established, early recovery is accessing and learning from feelings. The term *emotional intelligence* is used to describe an important way we understand life. Recovery in many ways is reclaiming our knowledge and how feelings help us. They are an essential part of our moral compass.

- **Meaning and passion emerge out of the struggle.** Mistakes, setbacks, challenges, obstacles, and catastrophes contribute to a larger sense of purpose that we often describe as spiritual development. Feelings of serenity, value, and purpose co-reside in the midbrain along with our emotions and our deepest attachments. Writer Viktor Frankl described those who survived the concentration camps of Nazi Germany as able to "transform suffering into meaning." The very essence of recovery is turning bad life experiences into good.

- **A detached "inner observer" emerges.** Key to brain functioning is a part of the brain that creates a psychological distance and evaluates what happens in one's own internal world. This detachment is fundamental to mental health and can be cultivated in the neural pathways of the brain. What started as a "loan" of frontal lobes from the parent continues and reaches a peak in most humans during their mid-sixties. Researchers find that by that age, enough "bad experiences" have occurred to provide a perspective called "wisdom." In essence, wisdom is the ability to know what is worth being upset about. The recovery process is a proven recipe for creating an inner observer, a part of the self that has psychological distance sufficient to limit our overreactions.

Physician and writer Deepak Chopra's recent novel on the life of Buddha has the same message: "Take care to examine your own perceptions lest you lose the perspective that suffering simply is." Buddha's story is all about how he lives in a protected reality and progressively comes to the realization of how illusory his world is. Similar to Plato's cave dwellers, his new perceptions are jarring. As his awareness expands, he understands more about coming to terms with pain and suffering. Buddha describes this as waking up from a dream.

We lose serenity when we invest in the pain. Mostly, that means resisting change or believing we have more control than we do. As theologian and writer C. S. Lewis observed, the core of Christ's message was surrender. Lewis wrote in *The Problem of Pain* that Jesus accepted the will of the Father. He wryly observes further that we humans "are rebels who must lay down our arms." Growing up means abandoning what we once believed to be true, divesting ourselves of those impassioned arguments about fairness, and allowing the larger force of the universe to work through us.

In our addictions we were very invested in our unreality. Our recovery process painfully lays bare our pretenses. Our emotional nakedness teaches us about the legitimacy of our feelings, despite how long we nursed our illusions. We wrestle with our control and our grievances. We realize we justified and blamed others. Recovery, we learned, starts with acceptance of what is. We do all that we can to change our behavior. We give our best effort, and we no longer put energy into things that no longer matter. This is the essence of the Serenity Prayer, in which we give up battling that which we cannot change. We lay down our arms. The Serenity Prayer is really a mental tool to help our inner observer with the spiritual task of change.

The Serenity Prayer

God grant me the serenity
To accept the things I cannot change,
Courage to change the thing I can,
And the wisdom to know the difference.
—Reinhold Niebuhr

When we learn these lessons, those of us in recovery often say it is like waking up from a dream. In fact, most of us measure our recovery by contrasting how it is *now* with how it was *then*. We come to see that all of life is like that of the prisoners in Plato's cave, waking up to a new reality and surrendering to change and expanded awareness. This process makes our story more complete.

Toltec teacher Don Miguel Ruiz helps us with some basic rules for this process which he calls the "four agreements." Each agreement is a basic rule for examining the traffic in our mind. Taken together these agreements assist in managing our reactivity and self judgment.

- **Be impeccable with your word.** Speak to others and yourself with integrity. Avoid toxic talk about others and reject the toxic voices in your own internal dialogues.
- **Don't take anything personally.** We create needless suffering when we personalize the projections of others. We have no way of knowing their reality.
- **Don't make assumptions.** Have the courage to know the difference between what you can and cannot do. You can express your needs, ask for clarification, and communicate what you mean. Don't assume you know the realities of others.
- **Always do your best.** Change is constant. If always we do our best, we can set aside our self-judgment. Best efforts mean mistakes become learning opportunities, and we gain a greater sense of reality. Acting with excellence helps our brain stay in focus.

How does Ruiz start his introduction to these principles? He writes, "What you are seeing and hearing right now is nothing but a dream." The path out of the dream is to use these simple rules as boundaries in our thinking. The four agreements help us cultivate a "detachment" or an observer which notices when our thought patterns are toxic. That is what our daily meditations, internal dialogues, and therapies are designed to do. This inner observer becomes an internal guide out of the dream.

One of the more striking descriptions of this process comes from writer Paolo Coelho in his new introduction to *The Alchemist*. As an author I always search for writing that is elegant and persuasive. These few pages introducing this wonderful tale of a boy's growing up are exquisite.

Coelho suggests that there are obstacles to waking up from our current dream. The first is that we have to "disinter" the dream. This is the process of reclaiming our true voice from all the voices who told us we could not have our own dream. We know the toxic voices that echo in our minds. We struggle with them when we strive to keep our word (and mind) impeccable, despite our self-talk.

The second obstacle stems from our love for others. Our misplaced loyalty may keep us from realizing our dreams, because change can be threatening to our loved ones. We may try to keep the peace at too high a price. Remember, telling the truth about ourselves will benefit them too. We must realize that when we reach out and make changes, we help loved ones disinter their own dreams. And we become better partners.

The third obstacle is our fear of defeat. A famous Japanese proverb applies nicely here: "fall seven times, stand up eight."

Similarly, Ruiz suggests in the fourth agreement that we always do our best. Coelho describes the last obstacle this way:

> Oscar Wilde said: "each man kills the thing he loves." And it's true. The mere possibility of getting what we want fills the soul of the ordinary person with guilt. We look around at all those who have failed to get what they want and feel that we

do not deserve to get what we want either. We forget about all the obstacles we overcame, all the suffering we endured, all the things we had to give up in order to get this far. I have known a lot of people who, when their personal calling was within their grasp, went on to commit a series of stupid mistakes and never reached their goal—when it was only a step away.

Coelho comments that the last obstacle is the most dangerous. Not only does it appeal to our feelings of unworthiness, but to our sense of deprivation as well. Life's misplaced loyalties and disingenuous sacrifice can masquerade as nobility. Many a recovery is lost because of the sabotage of "stupid mistakes." Trusting our inner observer to help us disinter the truth about our dream is key to the recovery process.

Recovery parallels waking up from the dream.

Wake Up Calls

The problem with waking up is that it never stops. It was early December in Minnesota and I had settled into a contented night by the fire. The temperature had plummeted and brought with it the first real snow fall of the year. I was a single parent at the time with four children, all of whom happened to be gone for the evening. For me at that time, a moment alone was beyond precious.

One of my sources of stress was a daughter who at the age of fifteen had a drinking problem. She seemed to skip the experimentation stage, and when she drank, the goal was to get drunk. I had been alerted by other parents, she was losing friends, and school was becoming a problem. Police involvement occurred in various ways. I had discovered hidden bottles and drugs. The battle over what was real and not real, sorting out lies and truths, was wearing me out. I had told her that the next episode would most likely end up with her in treatment. This particular evening she was having dinner with her mom, so I felt I could relax. In light of all the turmoil, a night alone felt like a real blessing.

The phone rang. It was her mother, who inquired how she was doing. I answered, "I thought she was with you having supper." Her mom responded, "No, a few minutes after she got here we got into a fight and I sent her back to you. But she ran out the door and left her coat. That was hours ago." An instant clarity hit me. My daughter had run away. She knew this event would probably land her in treatment, so she ran. Without supper. Without money. And without her coat.

Later that night, I stood out in our driveway. The lights of Minneapolis were obscured by the haze of the snow. All I knew for sure was that my daughter was out there somewhere. I could imagine how cold and scared she was. I had heard too many stories about the dangers of street life. Desperate kids did desperate things. I wanted to find her, hold her, comfort her, and bring her home. The pain of the moment is indescribable. There was nothing I could do.

I also had shame. Here I had a doctorate in psychology and I had a daughter who ran away. I had taught parenting classes, helped other families, and had worked hard on my own therapy. In the blackness of the moment, none of that seemed to matter. I wondered what I had done to make it so unsafe that she could not at least come home. The hardest part was acknowledging how much I missed her and the sorrow I felt.

Then the wake-up call came: this is what it was like to be with me when I was active in my addictions. This is what it was like for those who loved and worried about me. The lies I told, the disappearances, the impulsiveness and self-destructiveness came rushing back to me. All I could do was whisper through my tears into the wind and snow how profoundly sorry I was for what I did. Old grievances melted and formed waves of compassion for those I had harmed. Parallel scenes from my past floated in front of me. The truth about myself emerged in such a deep way. That moment brought my recovery to a profound place of resolve. I had a whole new level of appreciation for how precious pain is. Nothing brings focus like pain.

I hope never to experience another night like that. Even so, this lesson is one that I carry close to my heart, and I would not trade it for anything. Along with other such moments, this lesson continues to empower that part of me that wants to make a difference, that part of me that recognizes my impact on others, and that part of me that accepts the humbling realization of the deep realities of my story.

Eventually my daughter was found and entered treatment. We talked a lot about what happened to each of us that night. I thanked her for the gift she gave me in all of this. I was also appreciative of myself. I did not resort to high drama or old behaviors. I did not blame all the people I could have. I stayed focused on what I could take away from this experience. My support community helped me maintain that focus and weave the realizations into the lessons about what integrity is.

Of course, the wake-up calls continue, and the process of disinterring the dream is constant. If you are reading this book, you more than likely have had some recent wake-up calls of your own. As you clear out the fog of active addiction, it is incredibly important to go through your history to sort out feelings and harvest the important lessons you missed. From a brain perspective, accessing anger, fear, shame, sorrow, and pain are central to fostering new growth. Not only will you acknowledge feelings that you have "walled off," you will cultivate that inner observer so that you can be more clear about who you are and acquire critical resilience skills.

Like my dark night of the soul, we will all walk through painful moments. The process is not easy, but at the end it is very rewarding. Our research shows that these internal tasks are essential to a successful recovery. In Twelve Step recovery, this is core to your Fourth and Fifth Step work.

We set the goal of accomplishing this in two hundred days, or roughly thirty weeks. Working with each task takes time so the brain can percolate, network, and integrate. Also, the internal tasks require concentration. The feelings you have will demand that you process and debrief with others. Your therapists, loved ones, and Twelve Step support people will be important resources. The tasks also may require action on your part. All of this takes time.

In earlier days a Fifth Step would be done in a matter of hours or days. We now know that this approach will not give you the full benefits you want. Also, people put off these painful processes and stretch them over years. They lose the benefits of concentration and momentum. Your therapist will want you to be in a directed, focused, and time-limited process to prepare you for the next stage. That is what we have found works best.

After all, you are waking up from a dream.

The Fourth and Fifth Step

Bill W. and Dr. Bob found that the self-examination process was core to recovery, followed by admitting powerlessness and accepting that one needed help. Stopping the behavior and having the perspective of others help lift the fog from the addictive nightmare. It starts with a deep, reflective process called the Fourth Step inventory, which basically asks you to sort through your story for what worked and what did not. The early pioneers of Alcoholics Anonymous knew that alcoholics had been lost in the chaos and needed to be "disinterred from the dream." The Fourth Step is meant to be a search through the darkest corners of one's soul. Of special interest to those early authors were the ugly feelings of anger, fear, shame, and loss, and how they played significant roles in addiction. Most significantly, this was not a journey to take by oneself.

Looking back, it is remarkable how many of their early insights have been validated by science—especially neuroscience. To summarize:

- The telling and hearing of stories are critical to the change process. Refining the stories involves facing reality and integrating new solutions.
- Greatest change occurs when a person feels safe and trusts their caregivers.
- Change occurs most effectively when deep bonding also occurs. Often that occurs most successfully when others have faced the same issue.
- Accessing and utilizing feelings is central to "emotional intelligence" which gives us a sense of conscience, life satisfaction, and commitment.
- Change occurs best when issues are shared with others.
- Structure that fosters internal dialogue and a language to understand oneself add to the paradigm shift.
- Sorting out inconsistencies, anomalies, and compartmentalization is key.

The Twelve Step process captures these profound principles of human change. The Alcoholics Anonymous program has been adapted to address many forms of addiction and codependency. The success of this self-help movement is a testimony to the insights of those early Twelve Step ground-breakers and their agonizing efforts to find sobriety.

With what we now know there are some practices that are different. The original Fourth

Step inventory was shared during the Fifth Step with one other person. There was tremendous relief in telling another soul the whole truth and finding unconditional acceptance. Also, the sharing helped the sorting process. Sometimes a Fifth Step went on for some time—a binge of sharing that could last many hours. Once the ice was broken, more could be shared with others. This, combined with a good sponsor, helped to get the person grounded in reality. In some ways it parallels early childhood development. People in recovery "borrow" the frontal lobes of others because their own judgment is still impaired.

We now recognize that a Fifth Step introduces us to the basics of building a human support system. Most recovering people have a range of people with whom they share deeply. Using a therapist was not part of the picture in 1935, but therapy has dramatically improved the quality of recovery. Also, group psychotherapy has changed how we do this work. With a sponsor or sponsors, Twelve Step groups, therapists, and therapy groups, there are a wide range of people who can hear the story and not flinch. Indeed, the process works out better. The evidence is quite clear: we are smarter together than we are separately.

We recommend that you see this process as like finding people to be on your own personal board of directors. Picture them as consultants who provide you with needed perspective as you go through the process. Select people who will support you as well as hold you accountable. **Exercise 4.1** will help you choose people with whom you wish to share your work. Even if you are in a Recovery Zone group or other type of group, you need a few people besides your therapist to listen to all of your reflections and insights. Likewise, all your "sharing" can't be done in groups. So take the rest to your board. As we progress, we will make suggestions on how to do this. Your therapist will also have suggestions for you on this process.

Fourth & Fifth Step Consultants
1.
2.
3.
4.
5.

Exercise 4.1

Traditionally, the instructions for a Fourth Step inventory were more descriptive and open ended. A fearless, searching moral inventory was intended to strip away denial and face the dark and secret side of the self. To return to Plato's allegory of the cave, this is the opportunity to meet the shadows on the wall. Facing the harm done and the secrets kept means taking full responsibility for yourself. Most significantly, it requires sorting through all your feelings. It is part of waking up from the dream of addiction and codependency.

Today we understand even more clearly the importance of the words *searching* and *fearless* to this critical activity. Your Fourth and Fifth Steps need time for focus and processing. There are essential skills of "emotional or affect recognition" that come out of the step work. For example, anger is an empowering feeling that is vital to standing up for oneself. Anger, when it is used to bully others or entitle destructive behavior, becomes corrosive. Being paralyzed by fear does not help. Recognizing when something or someone is dangerous to you is an essential life skill.

Figure 4.1 provides an overview of the Fourth and Fifth Step process in terms of learning about how to utilize feelings. This task requires more than a few days of thinking and a few hours of "confessional" experience. First, it requires deep focus. The learning of skills requires practice. Thorough inventories often reveal elements of the self that a person did not recognize. Often we are ruled by that which is unconscious to us. Finally, the brain requires the focus to rewire itself so that feelings can become empowering.

The format that we use should take just over six months. Going too quickly is like a pressure relief valve that reduces the pressure but does not address the problems. Some people would stretch the Fourth and Fifth Step process out forever. They just cannot seem to get it done. We have found that the target of two hundred days of concentrated effort is just about right. One of the great spiritual writers of the sixteenth century, St. John of the Cross, described this very human journey as the "dark night of the soul."

To go through your dark night will accelerate your waking up from the dream. Here is some advice about doing it:

- Do not put off the tasks. You will prolong the agony.
- Keep things focused and simple. This is a time of consolidation and learning. It is not a time for making change or starting new ventures.
- Be thorough. Some parts may not seem as relevant but in retrospect will be important to you.

The Fourth & Fifth Steps

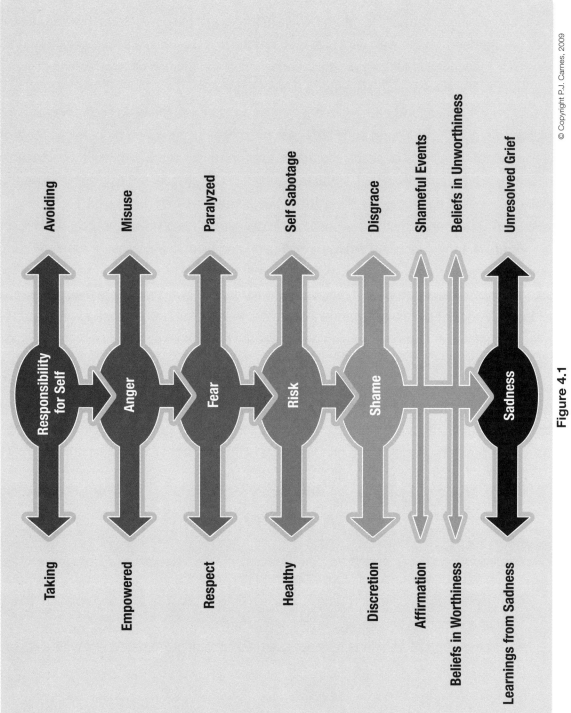

Figure 4.1

© Copyright P.J. Carnes, 2009

Chapter 5 **Naming the Demons**

In *How the Grinch Stole Christmas!*, Dr. Seuss pointed to how the Grinch's own childhood suffering drove him to be so mean spirited. He was singled out, shamed for his differences, abandoned and hurt by those he trusted and loved. He withdrew and became obsessed with those whose thoughtlessness hurt him so deeply. His lifestyle and all that he did was organized around this original pain. Vengeance was the logical conclusion of his obsession. This wonderful, holiday tale holds a deeper truth: our grievances feed obsession, especially addictive and coaddictive obsession.

Joseph Campbell's fundamental insight was that all the great stories held the same themes. We have already noted how in all the great stories, heroes and heroines were transformed by facing their worst fears. Villains, however, are almost always transformed into evil by their grievances. For example, the character of Dracula is based on the true story of a prince who courageously fought for the church in the crusades. When he returned and found his fiancée dead and the church he loved as central to her betrayal, he became the vicious monster of legend. Lord Voldemort, the evil wizard in the *Harry Potter* series, was betrayed at birth, lost his family, and placed in an abusive orphanage. Voldemort's cruelty and ruthlessness was rooted in a profound conviction never to be vulnerable or to rely on anyone else again.

Anakin Skywalker, the central character of the *Star Wars* saga, never met his father, was not readily accepted into the Jedi Order, and because of his devotion to duty, he felt his mother was tortured and killed. He became Darth Vader because of his perceptions of mistreatment by the order, many of which were really misperceptions. For Anakin some things were unfair. Other issues were simply an adolescent struggle with a world that was not the way he wanted it to be. The emperor was able to play on Anakin's feelings of being misunderstood. He appealed to Anakin's adolescent feelings about acceptance by insinuating, "The Jedi really do not understand you, do they?" At another point, he suggested that the Jedi were afraid of Anakin's power and were holding him back. His whisperings mobilized Anakin's resentful perceptions. In a later movie, as Yoda was instructing young Luke Skywalker and cautioning him that the "dark side will turn you," he was clearly mindful of Luke's father, Darth Vader.

These stories illustrate how unexamined grievances can lead to trouble and the dark side. Psychologist Carl Jung described clearly how the dark side of the self works. We all have parts of ourselves that we wish to keep hidden. These are our mean spirited thoughts, our lusts and desires, our hurt feelings and personal wounds. The dark side is also the haven of our willfulness best described by the recovery refrain: "I want what I want when I want it." Jung taught that dark desires and feelings were distorted by self-absorption and maintained their power because they were kept secret. By sharing these internal struggles, you can begin to heal from hurts, see your own self-indulgence, and gain perspective from others about what is "real." By explaining these hidden thoughts, you gain important knowledge about yourself.

Our mental health depends on sharing our internal struggles. So does recovery. At the heart of the Twelve Step program are the Fourth and Fifth Steps, which involve the "fearless" inventory of oneself to be shared with others. Every Twelve Step program talks about the role of resentment as critical to this process, starting with Bill Wilson's fabled "grudge list." Note how the columns below are divided into, "Who" the grudge is held against, "What" the person did to him or her, and "How" the individual making the list felt.

Grudge List from Big Book, pg. 65

I'm resentful at:	The cause:	Affects my:
My employer	Unreasonable—Unjust—Overbearing—Threatens to fire me for drinking and padding my expense account.	Self-esteem (fear), Security.

Figure 5.1

Facing yourself does require courage. Both Harry Potter and Luke Skywalker grew up without their parents. Both ended up in difficult circumstances such as facing Lord Voldemort and Darth Vader. Yet, their stories are about transformation. They had to be fearless about their realities and stare down their internal resentments. As Aristotle pointed out, without this fundamental courage, no virtue can exist. Life did not deal with them fairly. Their stories didn't hinge on justice; rather, their stories were about challenge and how challenges transformed them. The essence of the heroic journey is resilience. The core of recovery is resilience. In recovery, we take the bad and transform it into something good.

There is a story told about God from the ancient Jewish tradition of the Kabbalah. As the story goes, God was lonely so He created humans. But God had suffered as He became more conscious. In order to keep himself company, He knew that humans would have to struggle as well. So God introduced chaos into the world so that humans would struggle. Chaos is a refining process that calls men and women to be better people. The interesting irony for many of us is that the original word that the Kabbalah used for chaos is *Satan*. The "bargain with chaos" is essentially to skip over reality. Or to use a phrase from the Big Book, seeking "an easier, softer way."

The ancient Greeks knew this lesson well. They used the word *virtu* to mean excellence. No matter what the challenge, Greeks saw it as an invitation calling for them to be their best, whether that challenge was intellectual, athletic, or emotional. The Greek games were a metaphor for this outlook. An athletic contest was a scheduled stress. Training for it meant to build endurance, to develop strategies, to acquire skills, and to plan. The word *agony* comes from the Greek *agonists*, which refers to the pain one goes through when facing the inevitable struggle.

Each of us will face challenges that we can not foresee. It may be so difficult, it will take your breath away. Recovery is actually a training program in which you prepare for inevitable stress. You will need strategies, skills, endurance, and a plan. As we learned in Chapter 2, meeting challenges in which we are at our best will bring us contentment and joy. When we made bargains with chaos, we took short cuts in an attempt to skip the agony.

Recovery is a heroic journey. Every month I watch a new group of people enter treatment, stop their lives, and face what they have been running from. The process has moments of agony tempered by moments of resilience. Resilient people do not get caught up in arguments about fairness. Resilient people learn from their betrayals, disappointments, and hurts. They acknowledge their flaws, mistakes, and harm to others to keep perspective. They commit to reality at all costs. This means they have to be honest about themselves, no longer hiding behind false images. Resilient people remember what they have learned from others, and let go of past grievances.

Resilient people know that suffering gives them no special rights, but it does offer the opportunity of integrity and creativity. They have proven that a good future is exempt of indulgent feelings like defensiveness and denial. Feelings, however, become guides to knowing the next right thing to do. Avoiding feelings always means trouble.

Recovering people understand the adage, "It is not the cards you are dealt, but how you play them." For recovering people, the agony starts with acknowledging the ways they have blamed others and not taken responsibility for what their part was. In the harsh light of that reality, the righteousness of resentment crumbles.

The Grievance Story

We all have grievance stories. For example, we all will experience some form of betrayal. Even those who love us will still let us down sometimes. The grievance story is a tale we tell to comfort ourselves and to explain why something so painful happened. It provides focus for our anger, reasons for our grief, and answers to our feelings of unworthiness. Most importantly, grievances feed our fears, allowing them to become disproportionate. We may disown our responsibility for causing or adding to our pain. The grievance story, therefore, masks realities we do not wish to see in ourselves.

Bad stuff happens. The sexual or physical abuse of a child is clearly the fault of the adult. The early death of a parent creates havoc for a child. Alcoholism in the family leaves children with scars, invisible and visible. Even catastrophes such as Hurricane Katrina are beyond our control.

How we respond to these challenges is the measure of our resilience. If we respond poorly, it keeps us in our own darkness.

Sometimes, however, we bargain with chaos and make *an alliance with self-deception*. A portion or maybe all our problems were caused by ourselves. Consider the jealous lover who is so controlling that he drives his partner away. He blames the partner for all the problems in the relationship and misses an important lesson. Such one-sided blame will cause him to repeat the pain. Each time we fail to learn a lesson, we are destined to learn it again, and probably more painfully each time.

Likewise, if your workplace performance is poor and you vehemently challenge every management decision, you should not be surprised if you are fired. Similarly, a driving-while-under-the-influence charge is not the arresting officer's need to meet a quota. The stress of being a single parent, divorced, elderly, or lonely, are not legitimate excuses for drinking and putting others at risk. The "inconvenient truth" is that you have created a problem for yourself and others. The convenience of the grievance story places the blame on others.

One of the sure signs of grievance distortion is *entitlement*. If you justify your affairs as a sex addict because your spouse is not sexually responsive, you obscure the reality that you are not making yourself sexually interesting to that partner. Further, to blame it on the partner's weight or drinking does not excuse your hurtful behavior. Or as a codependent, discovering your partner's infidelity, drug use, or secret money dealings does not entitle you to break boundaries of privacy. Invading the personal journals, letters, and phone calls of kids, parents, and partners, is evidence of you being out of control. The legacy you need to face is your deep distrust of others and your willingness to violate the privacy of others.

Grievance scenarios are at their worst when *the narratives are hidden* in the recesses of the self. Often we are unaware of how powerful these grievances are since we have never let them see the light of day. In therapy, I have always been struck by events that are horrifying, destructive, or sorrowful, and the patient starts telling the story with "I have never talked about this before." They may even wonder whether it has any bearing on their addictive behavior. All who hear it immediately see that it was a watershed event which determined that person's whole life. If the family had "no talk" rules, and there was no safe person to coach the child through the tragedy, the event becomes a secret code which affects all decisions. The adult will later miss the significance of the grievance.

The grievance story can be a sign of *negative intimacy and unacknowledged grief*. Consider two people whose relationship ended in divorce. Ten years later, one partner has grieved the losses, worked hard in therapy, and learned about him- or herself. That partner is now remarried and has a rich, rewarding relationship. The other partner has done no significant therapy and tells "war stories" about how awful the other partner was. The passion and feelings of these embittered narratives are as if they happened yesterday. This partner is alone and has children who stay distant because they cannot bear the tales. Negative intimacy occurs when grief is blocked. This partner does not want to admit the significance of his or her own mistakes and failures. Nor can he or she accept how deep the loss was. Every time the partner tells the story, the old partner is, in effect, still very present.

Further, every time the partner shares the stories, the old feelings of anger, stress, risk, and sadness are recycled and kept fresh. *Addictive affect and intensity* reign—as they always have. Letting go of destructive feelings is perhaps the hardest of all to reconcile. Notice that *grief* and *grievance* share a common root. The original source of the word is about "holding emotions close." With brain scans, we can see that people who have "complex" grief, tap into the pleasure centers of the brain.

All the above *undermines resilience*. The capacity to learn from mistakes, failures, and loss is blocked. The agony of creating the emotional depth for the next challenge never takes place. So the grievance story leaves a legacy of brittleness, rigidity, and addictive obsession.

Dismantling the grievance stories is arduous and necessary, but the work does not have to be grim. I always liked what Mark Twain said about his life. He observed that throughout his life there had been many serious crises, some of which actually happened.

We start with the Grievance List. In the following pages list your grievances. Next to each grievance describe what happened in detail. Then record what feelings were present as a result of what happened.

Grievance List

"WHO" I have a grievance with …	"WHAT" That person did … …	"HOW" I felt …
1.		
2.		
3.		
4.		
5.		
6.		
7.		
8.		
9.		
10.		

Exercise 5.1

Dismantling The Grievance Story

One of the great Greek stories is about the House of Atreus. It starts with Atreus trying to become a god and challenging the gods, always a mistake in Greek mythology. A curse was put on the family in which bad things happened. Atreus was punished but so were all of his descendents. His daughter Clytemnestra was the prototypical battered woman. In order to protect herself and her children, she killed her husband. Her son Orestes was left with a terrible decision. One of the highest values for a Greek soldier if your father was murdered was to avenge the murder. For Orestes this would mean killing his own mother. In the Greek ethos of the time, one of the worst things you could do was to harm your mother. Yet that is what Orestes did. He took his mother's life and as a result, he was pursued by demons called the Furies. These demons tortured him night and day.

Some of the gods thought this unfair. Apollo in particular took offense. There was a court-like scene in which Apollo advocated on behalf of Orestes. Like a good defense attorney he pointed out that the curse on the family was intended for Atreus, the grandfather of the family. The murder of Orestes' father was by his mother. No matter what Orestes did at that point, he would be cursed by the gods. The unfairness of the curse was made patently clear.

Orestes, however, did not make a good witness. When it was time for his testimony, he stated clearly and regretfully that his grandfather and his mother should not be blamed for what he did. He still killed his mother. No rationale could take away the significance of his action. The gods were moved by his sorrow and his integrity. He was given "tasks" to do. When he completed the tasks, the Furies were transformed into the three Eumenides, the sources of wisdom.

I love this story as a metaphor for recovering people. Like Orestes there are reasons behind our behavior. But as addicts and codependents, we have to own the behavior and to express our remorse for it. Understanding how we got there does not excuse what we did. I also appreciate the fact that peace with the demons that pursue us is made by performing tasks that teach us. Like Orestes, we have these difficult tasks to face. When the tasks are completed, that which tormented us can actually become the source of wisdom. The irony is not lost on me, that in the Serenity Prayer we ask for this wisdom.

One of those tasks is to get our "inner observer" on board and revisit our grievances. The first step in dismantling the grievance story is the search for commonalities. Review the various grievances in your life to see if patterns occur in the story. Are there themes such as trusting too much, or ignoring reality, or being self-destructive? Record these commonalities. Then sift through these events and commonalities to see if common stories exist. In other words, most of us find certain scripts and scenarios that we repeat. For example, the woman who marries the same type of abusive alcoholic three times is repeating a pattern. One of the most helpful things you will ever do in your recovery is to identify these core patterns. Do this by writing down what the narratives have in common on page 122. Usually there are two or three main narratives.

The clarity of these stories will change your life. First, you can now identify the scripting that has kept you stuck. Second, you cannot escape the obvious in that the common denominator is you. The structures of your various defense mechanisms are laid bare. You can no longer defuse, confuse, or refuse the truth about your part in this. Once you have these basic stories or patterns in your life down, they help you identify your core life issues. They become a window to your soul, and the dark side can no longer hide. Make a list of these core life issues, for these are the primary goals on which you need to focus in your therapy. This list will help you and your therapist get the most out of your time together.

To further help you we have included a Grievance Analysis worksheet. Start by doing what Orestes did when he clearly owned his misdeeds. List what your part in all these grievance stories was. How did you behave to precipitate, complicate, or facilitate all the harm done? Usually our denial is rooted in some truth that we feared. For example, people who are often jealous are very unreliable in relationships, so they fear their partner will be like them. Or the addict who responds abusively to nagging and complaining about his or her behavior, fears that the criticisms are true. A very valuable activity then is to make the connection between grievances and how they triggered your addictive behavior. If you were jealous, and you feared the truth of your own unreliability, did you use your jealousy as a way to justify sexually acting out? List all the ways you can think of how grievances triggered your addiction scenarios.

The Grievance Story Worksheet (p. 122)

Dismantling the Grievance Story starts with a search for patterns. Start by listing grievances you have accumulated over your life. You may find there are many more than the space provided here. If so, start with another sheet of paper and record your list. In this exercise, record each of the ten grievances in which you felt harmed. Then after each grievance describe the process by summarizing what happened to you. Follow the process description by listing the feelings that you experienced in each situation in the column labeled Affect Description.

After completing all three columns, you may see patterns. For example, you may notice a pattern in which you trusted people even though warning signs existed that they were not trustworthy. Or maybe you see a pattern where you sabotaged your own efforts. Situations which are familiar to you from your childhood transcend the grievances. Often patterns appear in how you felt about the situations such as rage or despair. These common patterns are like gold for recovery progress. While a pattern may not appear in every grievance situation, you can see how certain situations have shaped your life perceptions. Share the list with others and your therapist.

In the fourth column, list what commonalities you find. The commonalities can make a story that we call a narrative. Every human has a story about themselves. This narrative is how we make sense of our world. They are core to the paradigm from which we direct our efforts. The energy for addictive behavior, compulsive attachment, and dysfunctional feelings stems from these narratives.

Dismantling the Grievance Story Worksheet (p.123)

A clarifying narrative is really a story line derived from the commonalities. An example might read, "Authority figures show that they are not trustworthy, but I end up trusting them again. Then they use me as the scapegoat for their own hidden agendas." People often come up with two to five dysfunctional scenarios that they repeat. If you made a larger list of grievances, return to it now and see if these narratives have weaved in and out of your life. Record each narrative in the column labeled, Clarifying Narratives.

Certain life issues are now on the table. For example, these life issues might be "trusting authority figures," "trusting people who are untrustworthy," "being a scapegoat for others," and "hidden agendas or secrets." Identifying the narratives and the specific issues embedded in these scenarios is the key to dismantling the grievance stories and regaining your sense of power. List the specific issues which are now clear to you in the appropriate column.

Grievance Analysis Worksheet (p.124)

To complete the dismantling of grievances create an analysis of how you involve yourself over and over in the same process. Start with what your "part" might be. An example would be trusting someone who you know is dishonest. Or perhaps you take on the hero role. When dysfunctional behavior is repeated there is some truth that is feared. For example, you might fear the accusation that you did not trust others, that you were uncooperative, or that you were lazy. By acknowledging these things, you reduce the power of such situations in the future. It helps to identify the trigger that causes you to repeat the behavior. The trigger might be people who ask for trust which they have not earned. Consequently, when you meet people in the future who are flattering or seductive, you will recognize that the pattern is familiar.

The Grievance Story

	Grievance	Describe Process	Affect Description	The Commonalities
1.				
2.				
3.				
4.				
5.				
6.				
7.				
8.				
9.				
10.				

Exercise 5.2A

Dismantling the Grievance Story

Clarifying Narratives

Life Issues

The Commonalities (from *The Grievance Story*)

Clarifying Narratives

1. _____

2. _____

3. _____

4. _____

5. _____

Life Issues

1. _____

2. _____

3. _____

4. _____

5. _____

Exercise 5.2B

Grievance Analysis

	Grievance Trigger	Truth I Feared	My Part
1.			
2.			
3.			
4.			
5.			
6.			
7.			
8.			
9.			
10.			

Exercise 5.3

After completing your grievance analysis, share with your support community. Use their help in defining how your grievances have shaped your behaviors. Once you have completed your grievance analysis with their help, you are ready to maximize the lessons of all your "madness." With the help of your community and your inner observer, you now can clearly examine the nature of your anger.

Anger: Dysfunction, Empowerment, and Mission

Juan had been in recovery for many years. He was insightful and a powerful force within his Twelve Step communities, but every now and then he would lose his temper. He would use anger to bully employees and force his way in organizations. He was at his best in "helping people," always speaking up for the underdog. He was outraged by injustice although unaware of how he perpetrated his anger onto others. He was overly generous with time, money, and advice. He desperately needed to have people indebted to him because he could feel close to them in their need or injustice. Once they were in his shadow, he could be a devastating critic.

Juan was physically small so he compensated by being "scrappy." As a kid he had a reputation as a street fighter. As an adult he was very successful in business. The fact that he could claim years of recovery added dimension to his presence in Twelve Step meetings. His psychological presence was enhanced by the force of his personality. He was so perceptive and "zeroed" in on the flaws of others. He was quick to give feedback to others, which at times was devastating to the receiver. He would get impatient with those who refused to listen, which was perhaps the greatest truth about him. He rushed into situations where more compassionate or observant persons would have been wary. Troubled by authority figures, he always assumed they were covering up some dark purpose. Observers would note that as a CEO of many businesses, he could be ruthless. He always described these episodes as "past" behaviors.

All this came to a head because of an episode of road rage. He was driving home with his wife Shelly. A young driver cut him off, pulling up to a stop sign. Juan angrily pulled next to the other driver and started shouting. The other driver lost his temper and got out of the car. This driver was younger by forty years, much larger, and clearly not sober. Yet Juan got out of the car and exchanged blows. The drivers were quickly separated by passengers and family members. After the drama subsided, Juan and Shelly headed home. Shelly said, "I cannot stand it anymore. We are taking this to therapy." She refused to discuss it further until they saw their couples' therapist.

They had just returned to therapy because she was so unhappy. Recovery was supposed to bring more peace than this. Plus, Juan wanted to be sexual and she was so miserable she did not want to, and she had had enough recovery to know that sex would be a mistake for her. Further, his outbursts and impatience were having consequences. For example, he had retired early but invested in some companies that had not done well. Juan brought such turbulence to the companies that Shelly knew having Juan as an investor was actually becoming a liability for the companies. He promised more help than he gave, then things went awry because of his lack of attention, his failure to follow through, or his unwillingness to listen. He blamed problems on the executives of the company. He would switch from passive investor to devastating critic. He would then get locked up emotionally with board room politics and be miserable to live with. Shelley knew the companies were losing money because of him, and he was killing the spirit of the people he needed to be successful.

The clinic that Juan and Shelly went to was a large but established practice. They had originally attended sessions there after Juan got out of treatment for his alcoholism and sex addiction. Like many, they had drifted away from therapy because of travel and time commitments, and it seemed that things were better. Therapy went from sporadic to nonexistent. Shelly and Juan agreed to see Charlie, who headed the clinic. They started in couples therapy but then committed to group psychotherapy as well.

Even in therapy things became problematic. Juan, of course, presented himself as an "old hand" who was just in need of a tune-up—not because he had serious issues. Shortly after starting, Juan heard rumblings that the women were upset because their favorite therapist, Karen, was suddenly not in the women's group. Other therapists took over without much explanation. A number of the couples were having dinner after their late afternoon groups. Juan brought up the issue of Karen. Juan shared that he thought that Karen's absence was because Charlie was not willing to pay for an experienced therapist and had lost her to another clinic. He further assumed that the transition was not handled well, so he wrote a letter of protest and had everyone sign it. He also promised to "bring it up to Charlie."

In the session following the road rage incident, Shelly listed all the ways Juan's anger was a problem to her. She felt as though she had to "walk on eggshells" which was an old feeling that she hated. She loathed how he judged people, their children, the people in the businesses, and people in their various communities. She talked about how scared she could get when he would lose control. When he dismissed this with a hand gesture, she responded, "Juan, if people had not been around when you got into the fight at the stoplight, you could have been hurt or killed." She then sobbed and the tears were so heartfelt he realized how hurt she was. As the sobs subsided, she said, "You need to be such a hero, that you are even trying to run this clinic!" Referring to the protest letter about Karen, she added, "I just want you to pay attention to what is happening to us."

Juan started to explain, "I just wanted to help." Shelly interrupted, "Juan, it is not our fight. You seem just hooked on finding things to fight about!" Realizing no explanation would help, Juan remained silent. After a couple of minutes of sitting together without words, Charlie broke the silence, "Juan, we were in a terrible bind around Karen. She had just learned that she has stage four cancer and is dying. All the groups she was in are being told this week. You would have learned that later today in group." He added, "Fortunately, years ago we took the advice of our accounting firm and created a fund so all of Karen's expenses and needs will be well attended. We all are very sad but wanted to respect Karen's process in telling you." Stunned by the news Juan realized how presumptuous and uncaring he had been.

Charlie continued, "It appears that you assumed we had mismanaged things and were uncaring in something which really was not your business. It also strikes me that you were disrespectful of the women's group by taking away the opportunity for them to work it through for themselves. You are in the men's group and need to look after yourself. This seems to verify all that Shelly is fed up with. Your need to be a hero, foster dependency, and seek crises, are all strategies not to be responsible for yourself. The result is an intimacy deficit for you and Shelly." More silence.

"The biggest problem," Charlie added, "is you get lost in the process. It is incredibly important for you to figure out the anger that drives this struggle seeking. I am quite convinced it is also at the core of all your addictive processes." Charlie went on to explain how initial wounding can be carried in one's affect (the collection of our feelings) without being conscious of it. He felt, from what he knew of Juan, his need to be heroic, in charge, and perceived as a savior, was very connected to his feeling of being sacrificed by his parents. Charlie also suggested that it fit Juan's history of sexual abuse by a Catholic priest. His distrust of authority and his "instant" rage was symptomatic of unresolved resentment. Charlie also helped both Juan and Shelly to see that understanding the source of one's anger is an important way to figure out life priorities. Knowing what is worth fighting for is one of life's great lessons and worthy of deep reflection. Charlie also affirmed Shelly for bringing up how angry she was because having a relationship with Juan "was worth fighting for."

At the end of the session Shelly said she was relieved and appreciative of Charlie's support. Juan apologized to Charlie and promised to apologize to the other patients for his meddling. They both knew they had work in front of them. As they walked out Juan stopped, looked at Shelly, and simply said "I am sorry." They were back in therapy.

From Grievance to Anger

Dismantling the grievance story allows access to anger which is often the easiest feeling to acknowledge. One way to explore your anger is to make a list of moments of anger in your life. Pick the ones that were most upsetting, that you were able to say how angry you were, and that most affected you. Be aware that you need to distinguish between moments of truth and moments of denial. Moments of truth are moments of anger which emerged as expressions of your core sense of self. Examples would be:

- Speaking up when something really mattered to you
- Protecting yourself or others in your care (when it was your job or role as a parent)
- Pushing yourself to do whatever was necessary
- Finding the determination to see something through to completion
- Empowering yourself to do things beyond your comfort range

- Insisting on boundaries you knew you needed
- Reacting to harm done to you by others so it would be stopped or repaired
- Willing to fight for what matters to you

Many of us were trained by our families to be "nice" and our important feelings like anger were muffled. However, our recovery depends on our ability to create moments of truth and honesty. Moments of denial occur when anger is a mask to cover willful, addictive, or destructive behavior. Examples would include:

- Losing control to get "what you want, when you want it"
- Using anger to get what you want
- Using anger to bully or intimidate others
- Creating a distraction so others will not notice your bad behavior
- Getting even by vengeful or humiliating behavior
- Using anger to excuse addictive behavior whether chemicals, processes, or compulsive attachment
- Mobilizing anger in order to be self-destructive
- Justifying behavior that is invasive, hurtful, or illegal
- Taking action that violates your own values
- Involving yourself in issues and problems that are not your business
- Telling bad news, gossip, and even lies to discredit someone who knows the truth about you
- Being self-righteous so you do not have to be responsible for your part
- Creating righteous drama for legitimate causes while covering up your own not-so-legitimate purposes

When anger shields denial, anger truly becomes "madness." Think about when you have heard the word *madness*. Note that at its root, such madness is almost always about losing touch with reality, living in illusion, or deliberately distorting reality. Most high drama is built on madness of some sort. So discerning the difference between moments of truth and moments of denial becomes an important self-observation.

In **Exercise 5.4**, "Angry Moments," you will categorize whether the moment was "one of truth" or "one of denial." Then record why it fits in that category. For example, if you go through your partner's emails or private journals because you are angry with him or her, but it violates your value system, record that in the "moment of denial" column. If you attack someone by talking about him to others, but you do not have to address him directly, this is a "moment of denial." In contrast, if you talked openly with family members about ways you were hurt, record that in the "moment of truth" category. Some moments will fit both categories. For example, if when angry with another family member you speak up about the problem, but do it in a shaming, judgmental way to hurt him or her, you fit both categories. When they fit in both categories is where some of the greatest learnings reside, so be patient and thorough in reflecting on your moments of anger.

Another way to parse out "functional" versus "dysfunctional" anger is by constructing a resentment list. In **Exercise 5.5**, list the people for whom you have specific resentments. Then list the resentments you hold toward them. Then, using the spirit of "fearless" inquiry, ask yourself what the truth is. For example, if someone said something critical of you and it was done unkindly, is it possible that it was still an accurate observation. Maybe the statement was a truth you did not want people to see, but it was easier to dismiss it because of how it was said, rather than what was said.

The other question that is important to ask is, "What would happen if you abandoned the resentment (as in, not let it rent space in your mind anymore)? Does it really make sense to preserve the resentment? After examining the truth that might be obscured in the resentment, think about what your life would be like without the resentment.

I remember starting family week for my daughter. My ex-wife was there as well. The divorce was recent and I seethed with resentment. I stopped by the chaplain's office just to talk about how I was feeling. He pulled out the Big Book of *Alcoholics Anonymous* and read me the part about praying for those I resent. I thought at that moment such advice was useless, but I tried it. As I did it, my seething resolved and I saw how hurt and sad my ex-wife was. I clearly recognized how two wounded people tried to make a marriage and ended up hurting each other. I resolved that the cycle and my resentments needed to stop. I was able to focus on what was going on for us as a family. I believe it is one of the most succinct and helpful prescriptions I have ever received.

After all this work, you need to harvest what your experience with anger can teach you. Often times, the people who frustrate, betray, and disappoint us are our greatest teachers. I sometimes wonder if they are not picked to help us get the lessons we need. You would not be angry were it not important in some way. The task is to figure out what is legitimate anger and then why it is important. One of the most clarifying questions in life is, What are you willing to fight for? Similarly, even our dysfunctional anger reveals our core spirit. If we know what is important it can be shaped into a statement of purpose or calling. Sometimes we refer to this as a "mission" statement.

Read over your work in this chapter and use the concluding exercise on Anger and Mission to distill what you have learned about yourself. Words and phrases can be knit together into a statement of purpose. As we examine and reflect on the dark night of the soul, we will keep returning and refining this statement. It will be critical to how we formulate our recovery path and determine our best zone.

When Juan faced this exercise, three phrases kept coming to his mind: being fair, being kind, and being honest. His group and therapist pressed him on how he had implemented these practices in his life. He would be so angry when others would be neglectful, unkind, or dishonest.

Yet, in his own conduct he had harmed so many in the ways he detested. It rolled through his mind like a set of dominoes. All the righteousness, bad behavior, and justification became exercises in hiding. He had created stress and chaos, which he now accepted was part of the problem. He had stopped the obvious addictions but had failed to see the deeper need to keep the struggle going. To think it started with a street brawl. He told his group he wished he could find that kid who he had fought with, for he now realized that the young man he was so angry with had given him a gift. The bravado was a cover for his pain. With the help of his wife and people around him, Juan was starting to realize what was worth fighting for.

Angry Moments

Start with reflecting on angry moments in your life. List as many as you can in the column labeled "Angry Moments" and indicate whether it was a moment of truth or a moment of denial by describing how it fits in either category. If it fits in both categories, remember to note the difference between how it was useful and how it was not. The goal is to learn the patterns so your anger can be effective and not destructive to yourself or others.

Angry Moments	A Moment of Truth Because …	A Moment of Denial Because …
1.		
2.		
3.		
4.		
5.		
6.		
7.		
8.		
9.		
10.		

Exercise 5.4

Resentment List

Make a list of people with whom you have a resentment, and record what the resentments are. Behind each resentment, reflect on whether there is a truth you do not wish to face. Finally, ask yourself what would happen if you "abandoned" the resentment.

Persons for whom I have resentment towards	Specific resentments	Truths I wish to ignore	Life without the resentment
1.			
2.			
3.			
4.			
5.			
6.			
7.			
8.			
9.			
10.			

Exercise 5.5

Anger & Mission

After reviewing your work in this chapter, ask yourself what is truly worth fighting for, and summarize those things in a list of what is truly important to you. Distill those "important" values into words and phrases that describe yourself when you honor these values. Finally, put the words and phrases together in one or two sentences which describe your purpose in life. This will, in effect, be a "mission statement"—or what you are called to do. Another way of thinking about your anger is to consider as "evidence" who you are when you have legitimate anger and are true to yourself. How would you describe yourself when called to defend or act on your own behalf? Remember, this does not have to be perfect and you will have more opportunities to refine your mission statement.

Based on my legitimate moments of anger and truth, **the following values are important to me.**	Across these values, certain phrases and words seem to be in common (Examples: *being fair, kind, or honest*). **Record those words and phrases here.**
1.	
2.	
3.	
4.	
5.	Now work them into a sentence or two **which describes what you are called to do.**
6.	
7.	
8.	
9.	
10.	

Exercise 5.6

Chapter 6 **Becoming Friends with Fear**

Human security does not exist. Almost all of human misery stems from resisting that fact of life. No matter what we do to control outcomes, the unexpected awaits. The only solution is to learn to live with life's anxieties. It is possible to become friends with fear.

What does becoming friends with fear mean? First, stop and think about how much of your daily life has been given over in some way to fear. Perhaps you spend a lot of time reacting to what others say or do. Perhaps you spend a lot of time being fearful of something that may happen in the future or did happen in the past. Spending time "catastrophizing" about the latest drama obscures our clarity and postpones our decisions. Most people in recovery recognize that their lives have been ruled by fear.

The worst part is that many of our fears have been unfounded. Fear has existed despite no real threats. Fear without threat is related to being separated from our core. The truth is, we are perfect in the true consciousness of who we are. In that rhythm and connection, there is no fear. Pain can exist, but fear doesn't define our daily lives any longer.

Ah. But how do we get there?

Most of us in recovery become aware that our capacity for legitimate fear abandoned us when we needed it the most during our active addictions. Untrustworthy people, dangerous situations, and warning signs were brushed away with a callousness akin to dismissing an intrusive insect. An intuitive voice said, "Do not do this," but we did it anyway. Many catastrophes later, we wondered why we did not listen to that true voice. Again we are divorced from the core self.

Throughout this book we have referred to the "heroic journey," which is the story of everyone. In all the heroic journeys, the ordeal engenders courage in the hero or heroine. Courage is that God-given quality that allows us to do what we did not know we could do. Courage is the cornerstone of self-definition. Aristotle observed that no virtue could exist without courage. The early Twelve Step pioneers discovered this essential truth, which is why they termed the fourth step as a "fearless" inventory. Aristotle also observes that a lack of courage is about cowardice. However, he continues, fearlessness to an extreme creates recklessness, which can be worse. So how do we become friends with fear?

All of therapy and recovery is about coming to terms with fear. Becoming friends with fear means we reframe our fears into opportunities for learning. Concretely this means:

- Accepting our human limits and making mistakes
- Seeking challenges for self-improvement and excellence
- Being true to ourselves
- Cultivating an inner observer that gives us the psychological distance to know when we are over or under reacting
- Having rules of thought which help our mind discern what really needs our attention
- Accepting at our core that we can change some things and we cannot other things (and to spend time at the latter is high risk and a potential bargain with chaos)
- Having another set of rules of thought (and coping skills) to cultivate resilience (resilience being the ability to take the worst of life and make it a way to grow)
- Accepting at our core that nothing really matters except that which matters
- Committing to whatever it takes to make our lives better (our shoulds becoming musts)
- Knowing the skills for quieting the mind

Most of all, coming to terms with fear means we see how past problems and suffering can be integrated in a perspective that involves a higher "sense of purpose." Some people term this ability, a spiritual life. This is the "transformation of suffering into meaning," which is one of the basic premises of the Recovery Zone process.

The additional task for recovering people (Task Eight if you are keeping track), is to acknowledge the impact of fear. Alternating between cowardice and recklessness is common when we lose touch with the core self. When that happens, we no longer trust others or ourselves. Further, fear can bully its way into becoming the head "chemist" of the brain. One of the ways to define addiction is as "a maladaptive response to stress." At the most basic level this means that broken people can find solace and escape in addictive behavior. The sweet voice of escape helps us to cope with overwhelming pain. At another level, fear becomes a catalyst. For example, in sex addiction we find addicts for whom sex only works when it is dangerous. Part of the thrill of cocaine was based on using it in illicit circumstances. At the most integrated level, fear itself becomes the drug of choice. Debtors Anonymous talks about debt as a way to keep fear around. Codependents Anonymous (CoDA) addresses relationships that become compulsive because they are dangerous. In short, we become hooked on fear.

Stress and Fear: Core to the Addictive Process

Actually, fear may start before we are born. For example, researchers have documented how some second and third generation survivors of the Holocaust appear to have all the symptoms of post traumatic stress disorder (PTSD) despite having no major trauma in their lives. They did, however, have a parent or near relative in the concentration camps. Although they did not go through the camps, as children they heard the stories. Similarly, other researchers have suggested that sexual anorexia exists more strongly in African American women because they heard the stories of the sexual atrocities of slavery. In other words, these women have been profoundly affected by what they have heard about their ancestors. The fact that these atrocities are mostly unacknowledged by the larger community adds to the irrational terrors. No one is assaulting these women now, but the fear or sexual trauma persists.

Families with multiple generations of addiction often tell "war stories" about the previous generation. Frequently, stories are told as jokes because they are so improbable. If grandpa was so drunk he missed the garage and drove into the living room, the family laughs as a defense against the tragedy and chaos of the event. For a child listening, such pandemonium can be concerning, but the child's reality is everyone is laughing. The incongruity may make it hard for the child to ask questions. After all, if the situation is scary to you, but funny to everyone else, then there must be something wrong with your perceptions.

My father had only one eye. No one ever learned exactly how this happened. He had a glass eye that was noticeably different from his natural eye. I heard many different stories about how it happened, none of which were ever confirmed or denied by him. I knew that he got into fights all the time, and even with one eye he competed in Golden Gloves boxing competitions. The joke in the family was that he would often get into fights in bars and he would lose his hat. The humor was in losing the hat. As a child, I was a firsthand witness to his violence, and, at times, I was the object of my father's volatility, especially when he was drunk. I found the stories very believable since he was drunk most of the time. Thus began my lifelong issue of keeping the peace whatever the cost. When the family does not acknowledge the terror and tells the stories in ways that the kid cannot ask about, they leave a legacy of inherited fear.

The antidote to fear is attachment. Early attachment to caregivers provides an essential ability to be yourself. The parent gazes at the child without talking or doing anything. This profound intimacy starts with just being present. This gaze assures the child they have a place in the universe, that the child does matter. The child does not have to do anything to be acceptable. As the child grows, the parent soothes the child and starts to teach the child how to soothe him- or herself. The parent models judgment and perspective that contributes to the child's ability to have judgment and perspective. Fear does not overrule other emotions because the child trusts him- or herself and others. The following description of early attachment and the development of a sense of self is so helpful it is worth quoting at length:

> The Good [Mother] teaches the striving one. It helps him. But only in the way that
> the loving mother teaches a child to walk alone. The mother is far enough away
> from the child so that she cannot actually support the child, but she holds out her
> arms. She imitates the child's movements. If it totters she swiftly bends as if she
> would seize it—so the child believes that it is not walking alone. The most loving
> mother can do no more, if it be truly intended that the child shall walk alone. And

yet she does more; for her face, her face it is beckoning like the reward of the Good and like the encouragement of Eternal Blessedness. So the child walks alone, with eyes fixed upon the mother's face, not on the difficulties of the way; supporting himself by the arms that do not hold onto him, striving after refuge in the mother's embrace, hardly suspecting that in the same moment he is proving that he can do without her, for now the child is walking alone.

A reader might think this description comes out of current, professional descriptions of parenting and bonding. The great irony is that, it was written by Soren Kierkegaard, the renowned Danish theologian, in 1845. Kierkegaard was best known for his describing the spirituality of coping with "angst" or fear. He concluded that all of us must make a leap of faith that we are acceptable as we are. Even then it was obvious that it starts with a profound confidence and trust in the self.[6]

If that confidence does not appear, it is easy to be separated from your core identity. Fear gains leverage with a diminished self and a distrust of others. That is why attachment is so important. As mentioned in Chapter 3 of this book, a way to describe addiction is a "failure to bond." Without the self-certainty that comes with deep attachment within the family, addiction becomes a refuge for the anxiety one feels about being unacceptable to others. If you do not trust others, one thing that alcohol, sex, food, and excitement all do, is deliver on what they promise. The addict starts to have a relationship with the alcohol. The food addict becomes enamored of food and always needs to know when the next meal is served. Even sex addicts can reach the point where their partners cease to be real. What is real is the hunt, the risk, or the "behavior." Consider the child who grows up in the chaos of an addictive family. Nothing is certain. Survival means developing abilities to read the intentions of others so as to stay safe.

To find out about early intimacy and attachment in a patient's life, therapists ask how help and nurturing were given in the family. Like Kierkegaard's mother, was the nurturing supportive but not controlling? Without the ability to stand on one's own, the natural developmental process fails. Even here, the insight to know what you can influence and what you cannot control starts at our most precarious moments, for both children and parents. Reflect on what happened when you needed help. Was help given? Were there "prices" for getting help, such as having to endure lectures? Was help given in a way that stifled learning for yourself? Were you criticized for such things as laziness, lack of preparation, lack of effort, lack of talent, or an interest in something outside of the family's interest? Were you an inconvenient child? Was the family so absorbed in other matters: addiction, cultural crisis, economic survival, or other siblings that there was little time for you? Or was your experience parallel to Kierkegaard's mother image with parents who were always there, being supportive, but allowing you to grow into your own abilities?

How help was given to you is important to the attachment issue. The essence of resilience is the ability to come to your own assistance. Early nurturing sets up within a child the basic expectations of well-being. Developmentally, we then incorporate these basic expectations into our own efforts of self-care. An essential self-conclusion has been made: "I am worthy of saving."

Exercises 6.1A, **B**, and **C**, "Learning about Self-Assistance," walk you through this basic issue. Courage and resilience in the face of adversity rely on you clearly deciding that you are worth the struggle—you are not "just acceptable," you are worthy of facing your worst fears. Start by listing ways you were nurtured and ways you were not nurtured. Draw an image of how you accept help from others now. Then reflect on how that affects your ability to help yourself. Pick an age when lack of help and nurturing was most obvious and write a letter to that child from where you are now.

Learning About Self-Assistance – Part A

In the areas below, begin by listing ways that you were nurtured and helped by others and ways that others were **NOT** nurturing to you. Then, in the bottom quadrants, list ways that you have been nurturing to yourself and ways that you have **NOT** been nurturing to yourself.

Ways others nurtured you	Ways others were NOT nurturing

Ways I was nurturing to myself	Ways I was NOT nurturing to myself

Exercise 6.1A

Learning About Self-Assistance – Part B

Draw an image of how you accept help and nurturing from others now. Then reflect on how that affects your ability to care for yourself.

Exercise 6.1B

Learning About Self-Assistance – Part C

Pick an age when lack of nurturing and help was most obvious and write a letter to that child from where you are now.

_____

_____

_____

_____

_____

_____

_____

_____

_____

_____

_____

_____

_____

_____

_____

_____

_____

_____

Exercise 6.1C

Trauma and the Brain

I went to have my brain scanned. I did it, in part, because I wanted to experience a technology that I referred people to. I was also curious about myself. Part of the agreement with the physician working with me, was to see what he could find without knowing any of my personal history. My skepticism was that the imagery might be some kind of projection of already known history. He looked at the pictures and then asked, "Were you a battered child?" I was astonished. I asked how he knew and he indicated where he saw residual brain damage. Then he asked me if I ask people to repeat things, which is something I do all the time. My family, colleagues, and friends wrote it off to my deteriorating hearing. Not true, I learned. It was a problem of attention and categorizing that is characteristic of abused children.

Over the course of recovery, I have learned that things I merely accepted about myself had roots in growing up in fear. My dad started drinking after more than thirty years of abstinence. Facing this reality precipitated disturbing dreams that would distress me for days. My therapist encouraged me to go to treatment for help, so I went to an inpatient program that specialized in addiction and trauma work.

In treatment, I met my case manager, a tall lanky cowboy named Curtis. He did not look "professional" in his cowboy boots and worn jeans. I further learned that he had not graduated from high school. He had gone into counselor training out of his own recovery experience but had no college degree. I had just completed ten years of graduate work in counseling psychology and was quite ready to write this all off as a bad idea.

Curtis started by asking how my family would describe me as a child. I responded that the consensus in my family was that I was bright but always getting into trouble. He asked for examples. I listed some of the events:

- When I was two and a half, I found some turpentine under the sink and drank it. I had to have my stomach pumped.
- When I was three, an employee of my parents found me in my snow suit in a lake three blocks from our home, having waded up to my neck.
- When I was four I got into my father's station wagon and pulled it out of park. The car rolled a hundred yards down a large hill and crashed into our milk house. (The joke, of course, in the family was that I totaled my first car at the age of four.)
- My father was drinking one morning, I fell out of the car, and he drove over me thinking he was avoiding hitting me.

The list grew but Curtis stopped me. He said, "Pat, you were not a difficult child. The truth is, no one was watching you." He went on to question how a child is left alone long enough to drink turpentine, walk for blocks into a lake, get into a car and pull it out of gear, and fall out of a car and get run over.

Have you ever witnessed a glass or bottle that was shattered and then watched the film reversed? It looks like all the shards and slivers come together into a whole. That moment with Curtis was like that. For years my family had characterized me as always being a problem. The truth was my early attachment years were spent in the presence of an alcoholic who was out of control and dangerous. Out of those circumstances flowed a series of events that would affect me profoundly. Curtis became what Alice Miller, the great trauma therapist, called "an enlightened witness," and Robert Heinlein referred to as a "fair witness"[7] in his book, *Stranger in a Strange Land*. The fair witness is a person who has no stake in a situation but can attest to the presence or absence of truth about an event. I still seek fair witnesses. A short time ago, I asked an aunt who is the last living person of that generation if she knew what was happening in our house. Her lovely, aged face became clouded as she talked about it. She looked at me and said, "Every time you were in the hospital I would come to be with you. But I could never get your mother to tell me how you would get injured." Another fair witness.

In therapy, we use the term *transformational insight* which means achieving a new understanding that fundamentally alters how you perceive your life. The realization that I was not the problem brought me extraordinary relief, but I also realized how much fear I lived in. Any transformational insight creates what we term a *transformational cascade* where one insight leads to others, sending ripples throughout all your perceptions. When this happens, we experience a *paradigm shift*, a term discussed earlier. Like shards of glass returning to their proper place, what used to look separate and unconnected becomes whole.

My paradigm shift included a deep gratitude that Curtis came into my life. My own arrogance almost got in the way of Curtis' wisdom. I have often laughed at the scene where Luke Skywalker meets Yoda, whom he regards as a pest. Certainly, he was not the Jedi teacher Luke sought. Help often does not look like assistance when you first encounter it. That is embedded in all of our great stories. It certainly was true for Curtis and me. His humility, insight, common sense, and droll humor bypassed my defenses. I began to learn about fear and the importance of safety. There are certain therapists who intuitively and innately know how to slip in and teach without being obtrusive. Similar to Kierkegaard's mother, you feel their support, but, in fact, you are standing on your own as you do your work. No graduate program creates that.

Curtis was in that tier of helpers. He made me sit there until I accepted the fear. He looked across the group of people and asked, "Why are we here if stuff did not happen?" To tell the truth did not mean that I did not love my family. Nor did telling the truth diminish their challenges and accomplishments. If I admitted to the fear, of course, I would have to admit to the shame, the anger, and, at that point, what seemed to be an unutterable sadness. Curtis recently died. Every day I am grateful for his wisdom, because he gave me entirely new insights into my life.

When fear becomes the head chemist of the brain, trauma actually affects the biological structure of the brain itself. Violence can leave residual marks on how the brain grows. The flooding of neurochemicals alters the brain into a state of being heightened, empowered, and aroused. Fear produces chemicals that in themselves are addictive (norepinephrine, cortisol, adrenaline) and stunts the ability of chemicals that provide balance and good judgment (oxytocin). The brain overreacts and has trouble managing impulses that would give relief. The frontal lobes do not work as well to inhibit behavior. Hippocampal volume, gray matter, the myelination of the brain (like the insulation on electric wires) and the size of the corpus callosum (which produces oxytocin which helps calm and focus the brain), are diminished by inordinate fear.[8] There is an overwhelming body of science that shows the impact of early "adverse consequences" of which addiction leads the list.[9]

Once we have the fear, we hold onto it. Bessel van der Kolk, M.D., at Harvard describes this as "addiction to the trauma" in which we compulsively repeat the scenarios of trauma and fear.[10] Why? We seem to be driven to recreate the neurochemistry of fear and the sensation of being most alive. The result is a myriad of issues including:

- Post traumatic stress disorder in which the simple stressors of living activate high stress responses to events that are quite ordinary
- Personality disorders such as borderline or antisocial personalities
- Mood disorders such as depression and bipolar disorder
- Deprivation disorders such as food anorexia, sexual anorexia, or hoarding, which are all about the cultivation of terror
- Compulsive attachment, in which a person becomes the addiction because of the danger or uncertainty they bring
- Addictions because they give relief and perpetuate danger and crises

Figure 6.1 provides an overview of the impact of fear on our mental health.

Figure 6.1

Note that every addiction at its core has a stress component. The list includes the gambler's tolerance for risk taking, the sex addict's deceptions, the cocaine addict's drug buy, the alcoholic's DWI, the codependent's skill at holding things together, the domestic violence victim's cycle of abuse, the debtor's chaos, the co-sex addict's detective work, the cybersex addict's ability to hide. Stress and fear are the dreaded twins that are core to the addictive process. Addictions are very deceptive because they provide relief and mask the fear.

To summarize, sources of fear may have been present before you were even born. The key antidote to fear is successful attachment. If healthy bonding does not occur or there is sufficient fear in childhood in the form of physical, emotional, and sexual abuse, the potential for addictive patterns rise dramatically. As noted in earlier chapters, early excessive use or early exposure to sex, alcohol, drugs, and nicotine further ramps up the probability of addiction. Abundance of access is the other key variable in our recipe of making an addict. Throughout this book we have been building a model of addiction which takes into account genetics, brain changes, stress, challenge, trauma, and availability. **Figure 6.2** graphically presents how these factors converge into the many faces of addiction. **Exercise 6.2** is a modified timeline entitled "Stress as a Core Element of Addictive Process," which is designed to help you sort out how your history of these issues fits the pattern.

Stress as a Core Element of the Addictive Process

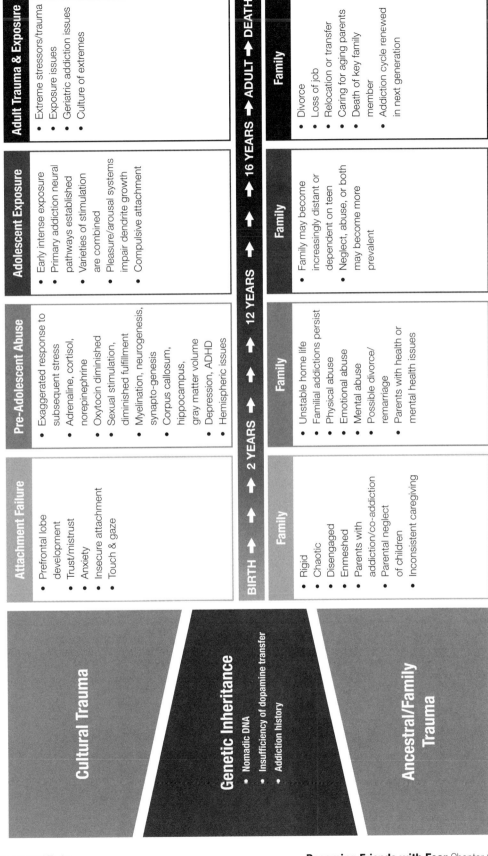

Attachment Failure
- Prefrontal lobe development
- Trust/mistrust
- Anxiety
- Insecure attachment
- Touch & gaze

Pre-Adolescent Abuse
- Exaggerated response to subsequent stress
- Adrenaline, cortisol, norepinephrine
- Oxytocin diminished
- Sexual stimulation, diminished fulfillment
- Myelination, neurogenesis, synapto-genesis
- Corpus callosum, hippocampus, gray matter volume
- Depression, ADHD
- Hemispheric issues

Adolescent Exposure
- Early intense exposure
- Primary addiction neural pathways established
- Varieties of stimulation are combined
- Pleasure/arousal systems impair dendrite growth
- Compulsive attachment

Adult Trauma & Exposure
- Extreme stressors/trauma
- Exposure issues
- Geriatric addiction issues
- Culture of extremes

BIRTH → 2 YEARS → 12 YEARS → 16 YEARS → ADULT → DEATH

Family
- Rigid
- Chaotic
- Disengaged
- Enmeshed
- Parents with addiction/co-addiction
- Parental neglect of children
- Inconsistent caregiving

Family
- Unstable home life
- Familial addictions persist
- Physical abuse
- Emotional abuse
- Mental abuse
- Possible divorce/remarriage
- Parents with health or mental health issues

Family
- Family may become increasingly distant or dependent on teen
- Neglect, abuse, or both may become more prevalent

Family
- Divorce
- Loss of job
- Relocation or transfer
- Caring for aging parents
- Death of key family member
- Addiction cycle renewed in next generation

Cultural Trauma

Genetic Inheritance
- Nomadic DNA
- Insufficiency of dopamine transfer
- Addiction history

Ancestral/Family Trauma

Figure 6.2

Stress as a Core Element of Addictive Process

In the spaces provided below, you will be reflecting on your own life experiences as they relate to this timeline. In the top group of boxes, reflect upon and list your own life experience during that time period. In the bottom group of boxes, reflect upon and list what was happening in your family during that time or age period. In the far left-hand column, list any significant cultural, genetic or ancestral family history that would be significant to your addictive process.

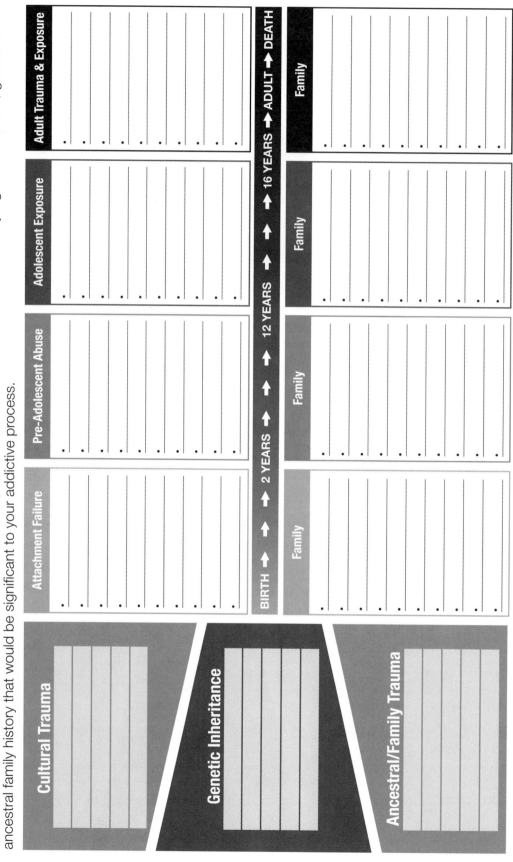

Exercise 6.2

Recovery Zone The Internal Tasks

Of all these factors, the core catalyst is fear. The grievance story and the anger is what we used to justify our behavior, but what drove us is the fear. All of this brings us to the trauma egg. My first encounter with the trauma egg occurred after treatment. I was referred to a trauma therapist named Marilyn Murray. One of the first things she asked of me was to take a large piece of paper and starting with my earliest memories, draw small pictures of moments of fear. More shards of glass from my childhood came into focus. She continued what Curtis and my therapist at home had started. It was an arduous process but extremely useful. Marilyn Murray's trauma egg today is widely used to help people understand the scope of fear in their lives. Once that perspective is established, it helps create the reservoir of commitment the deep therapy of change requires. To use the language of the heroic journey, the trauma egg is part of the ordeal and the call.

How To Do The Trauma Egg

1. Find a large piece of paper. A standard size is 24" × 36" and can be found in tablet form at any office supply store. You will also need felt tip colored markers that you can write legibly with.
2. On the paper, draw a large oval that takes up most of the page. About three-quarters of the way up, draw a dotted line across the oval as in the figure that follows:

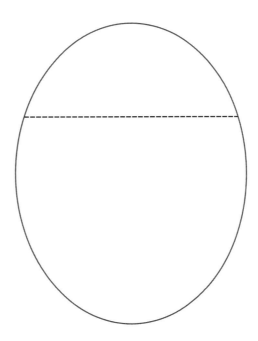

3. Outside of the oval and at the bottom of the page, write words to describe your parents or original caregiver. Put the words you associate with Mom on the right and words you associate with Dad on the left. You only need five to ten words.
4. Now think of events in your life that were painful or difficult. Usually these are events in which there was profound disappointment, betrayal, or abuse. Think of times when you were

embarrassed or let down, or when there was some upset or crisis that involved you. Starting with the earliest events that you can remember from early childhood, draw a small symbol for each event and separate it by a small curve. Do not use words; only use symbols.

5. With all these events recorded, the bottom of your oval will start to look like a honeycomb. Keep adding events through the various phases of your life: preschool, elementary school, early teenage years, young adulthood to the present. Fill the oval up to the dotted line. The most recent events should be near the top and the earliest at the bottom. Done well, this should take many hours to complete.

6. Before going on to the next instructions, show your work to your therapist or your sponsor. Ask this person to look for themes that are common to the events. Examples would be: "Many of the events represent some type of abandonment" or "The event seems to indicate extreme neglect." When you have these repeating themes clear, proceed to the next step.

7. Outside of the oval, in the upper-right corner, list what roles you played in the family (such as hero, scapegoat). Outside of the oval, in the upper-left corner, list family rules that affected you (such as "don't show feelings").

8. On the basis of all this work, write what you believe your family's expectations of you were. Write it in the form of a mission statement. This mission statement should accurately state what you perceived your family wanted you to do with your life. If you were the loyal kid or the hero, what were you supposed to do in life? Record this mission statement in the top quarter of the oval, above the dotted line.

9. If you had the power to clone yourself—meaning the same you with no programming—what mission would you give yourself? Write that mission down. In your journal, respond to the following questions:

    ■ How does the mission given to you by your family relate to the trauma bonds you experienced?
    ■ How did the original mission create repeated events throughout your life?
    ■ What are you willing to do in order to change the mission?
    ■ What steps would that take?
    ■ Who can help with it?
    ■ How will you start?

Suggestion: In this task of changing the mission, there are two books that can help you with the process. *The Artist's Way*, by Julia Cameron, and *First Things First*, by Stephen Covey.

Patterns of Jeopardy

By now it should be clear to you how fear shaped your history. It is time to look at the legacy of that fear in the present. Your therapist might ask you to complete an instrument that assesses the impact of fear and trauma on your life. Such assessments help us to see how fear has shaped our lives by contrasting us with others who learned to manage their fear better. The good news is, we can learn skills to manage fear better. We can rewire our brain so that we are not so vulnerable to this "Chief Chemist" of the brain. We start as we started this chapter, by accepting that there is no human security. Part of the driving force behind our compulsive use of addictions, relationships, and feelings is the feeling of fear itself. Fear has power because it is biologically wired to our survival. Learning how to manage it, use it, and let go of it is essential to mental health.

The place to start is with our own "patterns of jeopardy." The Trauma Egg helps us to see how the early patterns started. The hard part is to see how these patterns manifest in our lives today. The following worksheets will help you to locate how the early experiences echo in your life now. The first creates a matrix between risk and drama. Four scenarios are possible:

- **Low Risk, Low Drama:** In your fantasies and daily lives, you frequently upset yourself when there is really nothing to fear. You may agonize, procrastinate, and catastrophize, all for naught. You realize you put yourself through lots of anxiety when there is nothing to fear.

- **Low Risk, High Drama:** Sometimes to keep fear around you will create an unnecessary tirade and upset people. Rumors can do this. Family arguments, which have nothing to do with what is at stake fall into this category. Often, these scenes are much ado about nothing. They are just high drama.

- **High Risk, Low Drama:** These situations usually involve secret behaviors, which no one knows about but the behaviors are highly risky. There are no upset witnesses, challenges, or ultimatums. Only you know how over the edge you are.

- **High Risk, High Drama:** These situations involve dangerous behavior with a stage full of players who are not only witness but also add to the drama.

The first set of worksheets asks you to list behaviors that fit in each of the "windows" of the matrix. When complete you will have an expanded awareness of ways you use fear as part of your addictive patterns. Most of us have to learn that life provides an abundance of things to be fearful about. We do not need to create unnecessary and unwarranted anxiety.

To make this awareness complete, we ask that you draw your "Stressmaker." How do you keep dysfunctional and unnecessary stress in your life? Visualizing your Stressmaker puts a face on the Chief Chemist of the brain. That Stressmaker can become your greatest ally. It is the difference between being driven by fear or driven by courage.

Patterns of Jeopardy

The following worksheet can help you categorize how risk and drama have manifested in your life. List your behaviors in the areas below each label. You should be able to see the ways that you use fear as part of your addictive patterns.

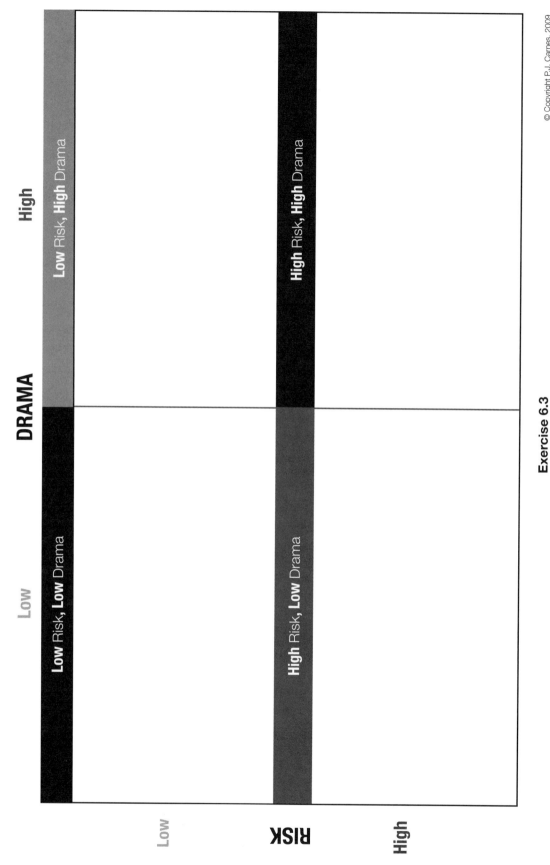

DRAMA

Low | High

Low Risk, **Low** Drama

Low Risk, **High** Drama

High Risk, **Low** Drama

High Risk, **High** Drama

RISK — Low | High

Exercise 6.3

Recovery Zone The Internal Tasks

Stressmaker

Draw your Stressmaker. How do you keep dysfunctional and unnecessary stress in your life? Visualizing your Stressmaker puts a face on the Chief Chemist of the brain.

Exercise 6.4

Making Your Alliance With Fear

Pam was a young mother and an educated lawyer. She had a problem with cocaine and seducing men. Everyone noticed her beauty. Naturally blonde, she had a willowy figure that was almost breathtaking. Two children had not changed her impact as she walked in the room. Her investment in her body led to bulimic behavior. She could not bear the idea of putting on weight but sought comfort in food. Her convoluted relationships included a double bind of her own making. She would seduce men to get her way and affirm her beauty, yet she was enraged to learn of her husband's use of escorts. The bind was being mad at him for infidelity when she had the same behavior and more shame about it.

Her therapist, Steve, was a bald, Jewish man whose upscale offices were in a fashionable part of New York. Steve talked very directly but made points with beautiful stories and analogies. It was like having a rabbi lead group. Pam had been to treatment and was attending an ongoing recovery group. The group had just completed the Stressmaker exercise. Her drawing showed her convoluted relationships because of work, children, and being the wife of an unfaithful CEO. Her Stressmaker was central to her addictions and the group laughed heartily with her about some of the outrageous risks she took to add fear to her life.

Steve noted that in the midst of her Stressmaker was a drawing of a vase with a dozen yellow roses that were a striking counterpoint to all the frenzy of her Stressmaker. When he asked what the roses were about, Pam responded that they symbolized her maintaining appearances and dignity. Steve wondered aloud if there were not more to that. He asked Pam to pretend that she was the bouquet and he would interview her. His questions started innocuously. She was asked to describe herself as a bouquet of roses, and talk about where she came from and how she sustained herself once she was picked. The last query made her uncomfortable. Her response was to say that she now depended on outsiders in order to survive. She no longer had roots. More discomfort occurred when Steve asked what she was used for and she admitted that she was a decoration to make everyone feel good. Finally, Steve asked what happens when you lose your beauty. Pam, seeing where this was headed, blurted out that once the beauty was gone, she would be thrown away.

Pam sobbed as the implications of the role-play seeped into her consciousness. Steve's voice, which was deep and comforting, summarized the significance for her. Pam only trusted her looks, not her immense talent. Underneath the Stressmaker and the attendant addictions was a deep fear. She believed from very young that the only way she would be cared for was to be sexy and alluring. It is how she got through childhood, law school, and even marriage. All that she had depended on was her sexual impact. Steve pointed out to the group that the Stressmaker distracts from the deeper fears by creating new jeopardies. Recovering people have to notice the distractions for what they are—new ways to perpetuate the neurochemistry of addiction. This is especially true of recovery that asks the individual to look at addiction to fear itself. A person must first find what the deeper fears are and where they come from.

He turned to Pam and simply said, "The deeper fear is ..." Pam concluded the sentence, "that I am dispensable, a throwaway." Others in the group started to speak about their deeper fears.

- A highly educated man from a wealthy family spoke of being a trust fund kid who did not believe he would ever be able to exceed his successful father and grandfather. He was not even sure he could hold a job. Cybersex was a way to disappear into another universe in which he counted.

- An artist who loved making art told how she made projects that her art teachers did not believe she could do by herself. Her parents would not support her by calling the teacher so she received "C's" for good work. Her family thought her art interests would never make an income, so why bother? She was passionate about art, but the voices in her head said her interests were useless. While drinking she could silence the voices, but could not finish her art projects.

- An obese man observed that he had the "opposite problem of Pam." By staying overweight, he kept people away and he could be intimidating in business. Wheeling and dealing in his Stressmaker added to "his bigger than life" image. If he lost weight, he would lose control.

- When the last of the responses were made, Steve broke the silence to point out the obvious connections they all shared. When fear becomes the chief chemist of the brain, the true fears are lost and with them the voice of the true self. The paradox here is that making an alliance with fear helps transform the Stressmaker into focus. With focus, you can reclaim your power.

This conversation occurs in recovery therapy groups every day all over the country. The Fourth and Fifth Steps examine the shadowy corners in which our worst fears lurk hiding from our awareness. Remember, our worst fears are tied to our dreams, challenges, and our best selves. If we ignore our dreams, we're not trusting ourselves to be true to ourselves. After all, would you trust a person:

- whose family did not nurture, or worse, disabled others with messages of defeatism?
- who ignored gut feelings about the truth?
- who allowed people to take advantage and be exploitive?
- who discounted deep, personal desires and needs to avoid rocking the boat?

Most of us could add to the list of ways we have discounted our fear. The Stressmaker is a "bargain with chaos" providing an easy way out. Remember the bargain with chaos was a term modeled on the notion of selling your soul (like Faust and the Devil), a short cut to temporary peace with ourselves. When anxiety and fear are created and mixed into our addictive behavior they become part of the bargain. They become core to the neurochemistry of the moment of escape, a neurochemical cocktail that distracts us from our deeper legitimate fears. Ironically, failure to acknowledge those deeper fears drives addicts to seek the sweet voice of escape, but inevitably the devil will be paid. Part of the cost is ignoring the legitimate fears, which call into focus the best part of ourselves. Our fears are a direct line to that which is important.

The bargain starts when the family talks the child out of being afraid, despite obvious circumstances to fear (Dad really did just hit Mom). The family may have rules about speaking up (If you cannot say something nice, say nothing at all). If the family has its own bargains with chaos, the child has no choice but to participate. For many of us, our Stressmaker (the part of us that likes the chemicals we experience when in jeopardy) started when we would recreate with our behavior that original neurochemistry of feeling threatened in our families. For all of us, at some time, we were asked to deny our own experience. We were talked out of our fears and even our dreams. When children participate in these ways, clinicians use the phrase that the kids then become part of the "affect regulation of the family." We as recovering adults must always remember that truth can be very threatening at first, especially in families. Swedish Nobel Peace Prize winner Dag Hammarskjörd put it another way, "Never, never, for the sake of peace, deny your own experience."

Let us summarize what we have learned. We start with the core reality that there is no human security. Fear is legitimate. All of life is about facing challenges and discovering our excellence. No matter what cards we are dealt, the true test is finding meaning in the struggle, and getting up one more time than we fall. If families did not handle fear well and failed to appropriately nuture and help us with challenges (akin to Kierkegaard's mother), we will seek short cuts (addictions) and fear itself (our Stressmakers). The path to recovery starts with debriefing in therapy about trauma and fear in our life. We acknowledge how we misused fear by continuing to create chaos and jeopardy in our lives, and how that drives the addiction process. We are not just dredging up the past. Rather, we are beginning the process of reparenting ourselves.

The problem is how to come to your own assistance as a good parent would. You have to start trusting yourself, listen to your fears, and examine them in the light of day. Making an alliance with our fear leads us to our power and our success. Great courage comes out of this relationship with fear. Without this alliance, all abundance, success, integrity, and intimacy will elude us. So how do we start? We start by noticing how fear has tried to help us. This is the beginning of a trust relationship between our fear and ourselves.

All of us have heard an inner voice that has told us, "Don't do this." We use phrases like "trust your gut" to help us follow our intuitions. There were many moments when we set aside uneasiness, but we would have been much better following our gut intuitions. The truth is scary and sometimes messy. Yet compared to what actually happened, the temporary mess would have been so much better. For example:

- Marrying someone who you knew was not the best match
- Supporting someone who did not deserve it
- Agreeing to cover or overlook bad behavior
- Staying in an abusive work environment
- Trusting a business partner with a history of known deceit
- Allowing a disrespectful joke because it was funny
- Believing someone who had lied many times before
- Helping people who really despise you
- Keeping employees who do not do their work
- Allowing kids to argue with and manipulate you
- Being used by friends or family members who only show up when they need something from you

In big and small ways, we added to the bargain with chaos. All the time our fear has warned us. It is we, who did not attend to the problem. Our fear is a friend. Back to Kierkegaard's mother. When a child is learning to walk, it is a great challenge and there is a fear of falling. The loving parent encourages the fear. "Be careful," she says, pretending she is still holding the child. With caution, the child takes the successful first step. The mother has empowered the child's courage by utilizing fear to make a success of walking. Courage always respects the reality before it.

Exercise 6.5 will help you think about the times when you ignored your intuition. Start a list of those times you had misgivings but went ahead anyway. These are the moments when you should have trusted your gut. You may find certain patterns in your life. For example, suppose family members unmercifully teased you. When you protested, you were told "it was just teasing," or it was only a joke, or that you were being too sensitive. You accepted disrespect because you doubted your instinctive reaction. That would not be an event but a pattern. List the patterns too.

As you develop the list, ask yourself what kind of mess would have been created if you had been true to yourself and your fear. Would you have lost money, friends, or even family members? Would you have caused problems? Describe what would have happened. For each item, also describe the actual result. What did turn out to be true? How was your intuition accurate? Then detail how that has impacted your life.

Intuition Insight Exercise

In the column on the left, list ways or times that you have ignored your gut instinct. List life patterns, too. After each example, note whether your intuition was accurate and how it impacted your life.

Way I have **ignored** my gut instinct	What would have happened if you had **listened** to fear

Exercise 6.5

Intuition Insight Exercise continued

What did actually happen?	What was true or accurate?	Impact on life

Exercise 6.5

All the great stories are about facing and utilizing fear. The hero or heroine has to face great danger, failure, or suffering, but they are transformed by it. They have to do something without knowing for sure how or if they will make it. The struggle matters so much that the challenge is worth it. Without fear there would be no challenge. Like any partner in a risky venture, your feelings of fear must align with your belief that the struggle is worth it. With caution, you can realize your dreams and achieve your passion. The good struggle is worth it, but beware, fear is not to be "overcome" or ignored. Rather, you reconcile yourself to listening to intuitive cues to be cautious and you heed your needs for self-care. Moreover, understand that fear is always about some truth. Sometimes it is cautionary, but often it is the call to be extraordinary. Sometimes it is fear that helps us to do what we do not want to do whether that is pursuing a dream or living our own truth.

Now we will plot this out. **Exercise 6.6** is called the Hero Map. It is composed of three categories:

- Cowardice: when you avoid the truth and back away from what you need to do
- Courage: when you accept the challenge of what really matters and, most importantly, when you are in the zone of personal excellence
- Recklessness: when you live in the land of jeopardy, throwing caution to the wind

Now think of these three categories from the point of view of your past. Record when you really backed away from the challenge of being true to yourself. Acknowledge when you acted in a courageous way, even if you were in the fifth grade and you stood up to the playground bully. Acknowledge when you acted on your own behalf and how that helped you grow. If you look carefully through your history, you will see the examples of your courage and abilities. You will see glimpses of how you struggled to claim your dreams. Your history of courage starts to reveal your calling and your zone of excellence. Be sure to include all the courageous steps it took for you to get into recovery. Finally, list all the ways you ignored your fear, especially when the Stressmaker was driving your addictions.

Next, consider the present. What are you avoiding now that needs to be faced? Pay close attention to recovery matters that you want to resist. Remember the therapy adage, "What you resist persists." Also, give yourself credit for what you have taken on. Even if you are uncertain about the outcome, there is bravery in just doing all of this work. In the reckless category, ask yourself how you are playing in the land of jeopardy with your Stressmaker.

You will also need to consider the future. List the ways that you could sabotage yourself. If you addressed these issues, where would your courage lead you? Detail what those courageous acts would be. Do not forget the Stressmaker. How could you return to old patterns? How would you and your recovery friends know that was taking place? Be very specific about what such self-sabotage would look like.

Directions for Your Hero Map: In the blank areas in the following worksheets note times in the past when you have shown cowardice, courage, and recklessness in your life. Below each column reflect on ways that these behaviors, if used in the future, could affect your life.

Cowardice – Your Hero Map

When you avoid the truth and back away from what you need to do.

Past Behaviors

Present Examples

Future Implications

Exercise 6.6A

Courage – Your Hero Map

When you accept the challenge of what really matters.

Past Behaviors

ZONE

Present Examples

ZONE

Future Implications

ZONE

Exercise 6.6B

Recklessness – Your Hero Map

When you live in the land of jeopardy, throwing caution to the wind.

Past Behaviors

Present Examples

Future Implications

Exercise 6.6C

© Copyright P.J. Carnes, 2009

On The Making of Heroes

In Kierkegaard's writing about the child and the mother, the child had to take the first step just as we in recovery had to take the first step. Kierkegaard's reference to spiritual literature was his discussion of the "leap of faith." Core to the Twelve Step program is the belief that life and suffering have meaning. Every Twelve Step program has a version of its own Big Book. All of them speak to trusting the process. In the original Big Book, Bill W. writes of the transformation that occurs when an alcoholic comes to this acceptance of a Higher Power at work:

> We are then in much less danger of excitement, fear, anger, worry, self-pity, or foolish decisions. We become more efficient. We do not tire easily, for we are not burning up energy foolishly as we did when we were trying to arrange life to suit ourselves.

Even then, I believe Bill and his friends understood the Stressmaker. Bill put it succinctly when he wrote, "we reviewed our fears thoroughly."

All fellowships come to this point of honoring what fear can do. Debtors Anonymous talks of "fear of the mailbox." In the end, all fellowships come to the issue of courage which Al-Anon simply describes as "fear which has said its prayers." The bottom line is that when you focus on what matters, a transformation occurs. The stories included in all those publications across the Twelve Step community are really heroic. The stories addressed the way it was and how it is now. It took a leap of faith to dig their way out of the black hole we call addictions.

But there are some important parts of your relationship with fear we must acknowledge. One hero you may remember is Indiana Jones, who in hot pursuit of the Holy Grail, has to step on a bridge across a perilously deep gorge. The bridge was disguised so he could not see it. He was confident that he had solved the puzzle and simply had to step out—a leap of faith. But caution prompted him to roll some pebbles on the bridge which revealed that it indeed was there. Sometimes we have to roll pebbles out.

Inevitably, we have to take action. Author Tom Morris describes in his book, *If Harry Potter Ran General Electric*, a moment when Harry had to take a significant leap:

> Sometimes, when great values are at stake, you just have to take action, regardless of how things look and no matter how you feel. That is the way of courage. It's also a version of the famous "leap of faith," first vividly described by the great nineteenth-century Danish philosopher and father of existentialism, Soren Kierkegaard. It was Kierkegaard's insight that when momentous values are at stake, thinking and reasoning about what we should do can take us only so far. The evidence available will never be fully sufficient for any truly important personal decision. Confronted with uncertainty, we are tempted to engage in endless reflection for the sake

of getting a bit more clarity as to what should be done, but endlessly thinking it through can actually keep us from doing anything at all. As Kierkegaard states in his famous and seminal book *Concluding Unscientific Postscript*, "Reflection can be halted only by a leap." It is this inner leap—in the present case resulting in only a small but decisive step—which Harry, in the company of every real hero, is willing to take (pg. 55).

The Harry Potter series teaches basic lessons about working with fear. Morris summarizes Harry's basic strategies that include preparing for the challenge, surrounding himself with the support of others, engaging in positive self-talk within his mind, focusing on what was at stake, and taking appropriate action. How parallel those principles are to those of the Twelve Step communities!

Throughout the chapter, we have talked about a contract with fear, which is a contract with yourself about fear. Here are five basic abilities you need to have in order to make an alliance with your fear:

The ability to create safety. There is overwhelming evidence that part of healing the brain is to feel safe. In therapy and in your Twelve Step community you should feel safe. Further, the skills of meditation and mindfulness will allow you to create your own "safe place" in your mind. You can sift through challenges and distress using the rules and formulas you have learned to examine fear. The Serenity Prayer, for example, is a formula for looking at threatening situations and determining action. You can recognize patterns of jeopardy and know if your Stressmaker is at work. You can cultivate an attitude of resilience that prepares you to face challenges. While challenges seldom come in the form we expect, we can see them for what they are: another challenge that simply has to be met. Creating safety for yourself is part of creating the psychological distance you need in avoiding needless worry or suffering. We call this an Inner Observer. This Inner Observer moves your perspective from fear of failure to a sense of opportunity and learning.

The ability to focus on purpose. Fear will surface when, like Harry Potter, you see what is at stake. Like Indiana Jones, you may need to throw out some pebbles, but you will need to be steadfast to prevent greater losses, including the loss of your dreams or your integrity. Earlier we noted that to move from obsession to focus we had to have clarity about your purpose. In the Trauma Egg, you were asked to transform your family expectations into a mission statement that will be true for you. This mission statement is a critical method for your Inner Observer to fulfill Paulo Coelho's call to "disinter the dream" and reclaim your true voice. The goal is to put energy only into that which matters.

The ability to risk. Challenge makes us nervous, but when we understand how to properly channel fear, it is possible to mobilize all our abilities to be at our best. The only option is to take action. Being a great surgeon, writing a best-selling book, or giving a terrific speech all start with being nervous. As we learned with Alan Alda, his stage performances also brought his greatest joy and spiritual experiences. Fear motivates us to put in the time to be our best. Great achievement can also be found in starting new businesses, being vulnerable with our partners, being an involved parent, doing our Twelve Step work, allowing our therapists to help us, and coping with overwhelming odds and chaos. In this, we are all the same. Our recoveries give us another chance and a different way to risk. The Inner Observer, by disinterring the dream, is asking you to take action and heed the call. Your fear is there to help. Remember, walking became effortless. And to think we do it with just two legs.

The ability to trust oneself. We all have made promises to ourselves that we did not keep. Start keeping them. Build trust in the little things. See the dentist when you should. Do not put off self-care. Protect yourself from doing things that stretch you into ill health. Take care of the places in which you work and live. Keep your promises to others and to yourself so there is no unnecessary drama. Do great speakers, actors, or surgeons worry about mistakes? Yes. But they trust themselves to meet the challenge. They put in the hours of practice and study. For recovery to become an "unconscious competence," discipline and study is required. You may start by focusing on healing the inner child by being a good parent to yourself. Remember, the loving parent stays with the child to help the child become his or her own person. As you learn to appreciate all that you are and are not, you can discard the narcissisms of the past. You can relax and know you will make the next right decisions. You will begin to have successful relationships with others when you are right with yourself. Your Inner Observer already knows this. Creating safety, retaining focus, and taking action will build trust in your ability to take care of yourself. Trusting yourself is the core ability in coming to your own assistance.

The ability to have witnesses. All the above works best with witnesses. In families of abuse, the children who are the most resilient are the ones who somehow developed deep attachments outside the family. Other humans help us to share, and they supply perspective on our fears. Attachment is the antidote to the chief chemist hiring the Stressmaker as the head laboratory assistant. In fact, attachment makes for a new neurochemistry. Chemicals are released that help empower anxiety into endurance and direction. We have described addiction as a failure to bond. The Twelve Step program is essentially a re-attachment process in which we learn to live in consultation with others. Living in consultation, we become our most effective. Moreover, few other factors generate synaptic growth more than deep attachment. Our friends in the fellowships, our group mates in therapy, our therapists, our friends and family members are witnesses to our process. Similar to Miller's "fair" witnesses, they confirm our realities and affirm our progress.

Obviously, these abilities go beyond handling fear. Taken together they help us to trust the process, which is essentially the spiritual task that runs through all of them. If you trust yourself, you can trust others and you can trust that a Higher Power is calling you to your life's purpose.

By completing this chapter, you will have done an important part in completing a Fourth Step inventory and understanding how fear has played an important role in your addictive and co-addictive process. By sharing it with others in the program and in therapy, you will empower yourself to make an ally of your fears. We strongly urge a dialogue between you and your fear to make an explicit contract that is unique to you. Record a conversation between your Inner Observer and your fear. Make an agreement to recognize your fears and channel them toward achieving excellence in your life. **Exercise 6.7** provides a format and suggestions for that dialogue to take place.

Dialogue with Fear

Write an imaginary dialogue with your fear about all the work you have done in this chapter. Below is space and a list of questions to help you walk through the dialogue process. At the conclusion, create a contract that specifies how you will work together in the future. Use your journal or other resources if you need more space.

1. Where does the core fear stem from in your life? How does it affect you today?

2. In what ways has your fear helped or protected you? Hurt you? Have your fear tell you of ways it has attempted to help.

Exercise 6.7

Dialogue with Fear continued

_____

3. Discuss with your fear how to work together for a positive outcome. What would your life look like if you recognized fear as a friend instead of an enemy? Talk about that in your dialogue with fear.

_____

Chapter 7 **Out of Many One**

Despite the fleeting nature of human security, we do have the gift of knowing that we matter. The way that we know is through the depth of our relationships. The gaze of Kierkegaard's mother assures the child that he has a right to a place on the planet. He does not have to "earn" his place, because his value has already been established by his mother. The risk of that first step will be like all the subsequent risks in life. That risk will be taken because people will witness it, support it, and more than likely be helped by it. The antidote to insecurity is our mutual attachment.

In the movie *Shall We Dance?*, Richard Gere plays John Clark, a husband who seems to have everything but finds his life somewhat joyless. He stumbles on a ballroom dance class, and he starts lessons without telling his wife and family. John is unsure of what wanting to dance is all about, but he recognizes that he has passion for it. In preparing for a major dance competition he spends more time away from home. His spouse, Beverly (played by Susan Sarandon), eventually notices that he is behaving suspiciously and hires a private detective. He discovers that John is learning to dance. He is not having affairs, but he is on a divergent path about which she had not known. The detective is attracted to Beverly Clark and senses a sexual opportunity. He asks if she is going to stay in the marriage. She responds with a clear yes. He asks why, to which she responds:

> Because we need a witness to our lives. There's a billion people on the planet. What does any one life really mean? But in a marriage, you're promising to care about everything. The good things, the bad things, the terrible things, the mundane things. All of it—all the time, every day. You are saying "your life will not go unnoticed because I will notice it. Your life will not go unwitnessed—because I will be your witness."

When Beverly shows up at John's dance competition, she sees that he is good at it and has passion for it. As a result, they have to have what we shall term in this chapter a "difficult conversation." Every relationship has these moments of truth telling. In this case John has to admit his deception and unhappiness. Also, he has clearly discovered that he loves to dance. She in turn has to acknowledge his discontent and his reasons. At the end he invites her to dance with him. Although hesitant, she joins in the process. So like the beckoning of Kierkegaard's mother, the open hand of the husband to join the dance allows a critical new step for the wife. Out of this flows a revitalized relationship for both of them.

The great pioneers of psychotherapy have long noted this connection between accomplishment and human connection. One of the classic formulations was that of psychoanalyst Erik Erikson, who described one of the first stages of human development as "shame versus autonomy." The toddler who feels affirmed has the confidence to be more independent. In this sense of oneself, the child is taking important steps to a healthy self-concept. Within that positive sense of self, healthy shame becomes an important guide to what is appropriate. In that way the child starts to develop an awareness of honorable behavior.

Yet shame, when toxic, starts to dominate the self. Gershen Kaufman, one of the pioneers in shame research, described such shame as essentially a "break in the interpersonal bridge."[11] Failures of attachment precipitate deep feelings of unworthiness. Unworthiness becomes codified into a set of core beliefs that undermine the dreams and talents of all of us. Rather than being true to oneself, a person hides true desires and projects an unreal image to others. The distrust rests in the certain belief that if personal needs, fears, and dreams were really understood and seen, he or she would be unlovable or unacceptable to others. This person feels that there is no secure spot reserved for him or her on the planet. Bargains with chaos are made because of this belief that personal needs will never be met.

When such breaches of attachment occur, it is essential to surround yourself with a community of open hands who believe in you more than you do yourself. They then serve as witnesses to the true person within who has been obscured by beliefs in unworthiness. Twelve Step communities who see their members in their most broken moments help dispel toxic beliefs and beckon for people to be true to themselves. The break in the interpersonal bridge is repaired. With the intimacy deficits met, the true self can reach for the original dream. To use Paulo Coelho's words, to "disinter the dream," we have to put aside the voices who told us we could not be ourselves. We must allow our loved ones the anxiety of experiencing us being ourselves. Talent and passion are reclaimed. True love exists when you can be fully who you are in the other's presence, even if it means that you want to dance.

One of my most unique experiences in that kind of freedom started in the Bluebird Café in Nashville, Tennessee. I had been invited by Max Haskett, a therapist who is known for his compassion and his sometimes unorthodox ways of making a point. Many of his patients are in the music industry and are now in recovery. A small group had bonded and were composing and performing songs about recovery. They were going to perform at the café and specifically asked that I come. Invited to sit with them on stage, they would sing these lovely inspiring songs and ask for my reactions. I felt presumptuous to improve on what they had done, so I simply would reflect and tell stories which I hoped added to their work. As the evening went on, a rhythm and energy evolved. What started haltingly became a magical evening.

When we finished, we sat over late night coffee as well wishers passed by and expressed how helpful and enjoyable our "conversation and music" was. Several commented, "We should take it on the road" which caused our friend Max Haskett to smile. That was what he hoped we would do. So we did. It took us about a year to make the rhythm work because what we did was so different. It was more than a concert and more than a workshop. Over a three-year period, I did some of the best teaching and creativity of my professional life. A typical comment from colleagues and friends was, "I have seen you do that many times, but I never got it like I got it today." I am confident that part of that reaction was the power of the music. I am now a believer in music as a way to effect change in psychoeducation. I am also sure that the group called the Voices from AFAR brought out the best in me.

At each performance, we worked on really being in our best zones. It was fun and meaningful to feel that support from one another. It also was a challenge. People would think we were entertainment but we were far more than that. People would come prepared to work on themselves and appreciate how helpful music was in accessing parts of themselves that were beyond their awareness. We all worked a Twelve Step program and, in time, knew each other's stories. We could be witnesses for each other when we reached for an extraordinary moment. Bands are like families and there were issues. Imagine singing a song you wrote about your abuse as a child with the abusive father in the audience. A spouse of a band member needed treatment, so we all pulled together to help. One member had a series of hits that interfered with being able to be with us. I learned that my wife had a serious illness as we were walking on stage. We had difficult conversations facing uncomfortable realities. Yet I count those times on the road as some of my very best moments in which I was most truly myself and most in my professional zone.

When you are sixty years old and tell your wife you wish to go tour with a band, you can probably expect a reaction. Frankly, there was one, so I invited the group to spend a week with us up at our cabin in northern Minnesota. Music and laughter filled our home. My wife became a witness to our connection as a group. Some wonderful moments occurred. One night of music on the beach brought boats from all over to listen. People in our lives recognized some of the group members. These musicians could have made a lot more money doing their regular gigs, but were working for recovery at virtually no pay because it mattered. My wife is an astute woman. She quickly put together the dynamics and appreciated the place the group had in my heart. As they loaded up to go, we both got teary. It was like watching our kids go. She turned to me and said, "I can see why you love them so."

Ultimately I contracted a disease called Valley Fever and literally had to focus on the bare necessities for a few years. Our touring days stopped and my focus has been to crystallize my experience in my writing. Part of my vision for the future is another tour, hopefully around these Recovery Zone books, with the band members who were so much a part of this book's making. No matter what happens I know that my abilities grew dramatically because of the challenge they presented me and the love they gave me. It has sustained me in persisting with the Recovery Zone process.

Certainly, the lesson learned is the deep relationship between connection with others and being in the zone. Most of us have to go back, as Coelho says, to the very beginning in order to disinter the dream. That means returning to when we heard the voices of those who said we were not good enough, too lazy, or unrealistic in our childhood dreams. This means the family in which we grew up. A way to start the disinterment is to revisit family holidays. Holidays have a way of highlighting the best and worst of families. We call this process *therapeutic holidays*.

Therapeutic Holidays

Social and family researchers have long tracked what holidays do to families. In our culture these days reserved for celebration and contemplation often turn into extraordinarily stressful events. Gift giving, cooking, travel, getting everybody in the same place at the same time make holidays one big Stressmaker. For many families, the holidays mark extraordinary losses that add to the intensity of getting together. With stress and intensity, family dysfunctions are magnified. Addictions in spending, eating, and drinking thrive during the holidays. Research shows that suicides are most often committed after a family holiday or birthday, especially when addictions are present.

Researchers call this the "broken promise effect." Family members look forward to the holiday as a time of connection or even "this year it will be different." When the same sad scenarios occur, however, the disappointment is so profound that those vulnerable to suicide fulfill their suicidal obsessions. The purposes vary. The suicide can be a way out, or a statement, or the result of deep depression, or part of a grievance story or grief obsession.

A family is a system that repeats its rituals and rules. To expect a family to behave differently given the history, does not make sense. But one's hopes become expectations, and we can invest deeply in them. A good metaphor would be how cartoonist Charles M. Schultz presented various versions of Charlie Brown playing football with Lucy. Every fall Lucy promises to hold the football for Charlie. Despite his experiences, Charlie still trusts her to hold it for him, and every year she pulls it out from under him. A promise is broken.

Healthy family members can recall holiday memories that enhance their lives. Consider this wonderful story from Lucille Clifton:

> I remember standing there on stage in my new Christmas dress, trying not to cry
> as the church members smiled, nodded and murmured encouragement from
> the front row. "Go 'head, baby." "Say it now, Luc." "Come on now, baby." But I
> couldn't remember, and to hide my deep humiliation, my embarrassment, I became
> sullen, angry. "I don' wanna." And I stood there with my mouth poked out. It was
> a scandal! This fresh young nobody baby standing in front of the Lord in His own

house talking about what she don't want! I could feel the disapproval pouring over my new dress. Then, like a great tidal wave from the ocean of God, my sanctified mother poured down the Baptist aisle, huge as love, her hand outstretched toward mine. "Come on, baby," she smiled, then turned to address the church: "She don't have to do nothing she don't want to do." And I was at the same time empowered and made free ....

For most of us in recovery, growing up diminished our sense of self. We were told, don't "wear your heart on your sleeve," and "If you can't say anything nice, don't say anything at all." If we needed guidance it was because we did something wrong. If we received extra attention or help, we were criticized for needing it. We became experts at reading what others wanted. We became what they wanted us to be. As adults we use the words "image management," but basically we were taught to be dishonest about ourselves.

See if any of the following is true for you in regard to family gatherings:

- If you were not related to your family members you would probably not spend time with them.
- Extraordinary tension or unresolved issues exist between you and specific family members.
- It is a relief to leave family gatherings.
- You feel compromised when you leave family gatherings.
- You do not feel free to be yourself around family members.
- Your family members have no clue who you are, what you have done, or how your life is.
- You laugh at things to get along but have dread inside.
- You agree or do not contest things about which you have strong feelings.
- Holidays are the only times you talk, so that family members are not part of your regular life.
- There are certain family rituals that are unbearable but you go along anyway.
- There are one or more family members who are angry or opinionated and push agendas you really detest.
- You tolerate some members of your family so you can see others.
- When you leave you feel somehow diminished or "less than" others in the family.

These feelings of unworthiness are called "toxic shame" and they erode the very essence of our sense of self. The "interpersonal bridge" is broken because there is no acceptance of others as they are. Examine this issue for yourself by walking through your own family holidays. This process helps to disinter the parts of yourself that have been lost.

Holidays and Therapy

The holidays are an opportunity for those in therapy or recovery. Thinking systematically about them can illuminate the issues of therapy as well as refine your own sense of purpose. The following exercises are intended to assist you in being more conscious about what the holidays reveal about your family and your experience. Start by listing four holidays that are important in your family. Then think of nurturing memories you have about each holiday (warm, joyful, peaceful, or meaningful). Then list painful memories of loss, exploitation, betrayal, abuse, or other suffering.

Holiday 1	Holiday 2	Holiday 3	Holiday 4
_____	_____	_____	_____
Nurturing:	Nurturing:	Nurturing:	Nurturing:
Painful:	Painful:	Painful:	Painful:

Exercise 7.1A

Your Place in the Family

Are there any particular ways that you are treated by family members that come out during the holidays? Do you ever feel like you are a "different person" with your family, than when you are with other people? Do you feel that, at times, like you act "differently when you are around certain family members"?

Describe below how you become a "different person" around family members. Then describe what it is like when you are most yourself. Record who is most likely to be upset if you were yourself in the family? What do you think that would change?

How I act when I am a "different person" around family members	How I act when I'm relaxed and being my usual self.

Exercise 7.1B

Your Place in the Family continued

What changes are necessary for you to be yourself in the presence of these conflicts and norms? Now record the different ways these issues were part of your "bargains with chaos." Start by listing the ways you tried to make it easier on yourself. (What "shortcuts" did you use?) How do your addictions fit in with these family norms?

1. _____

2. _____

3. _____

4. _____

5. _____

6. _____

7. _____

8. _____

9. _____

10. _____

11. _____

12. _____

13. _____

14. _____

15. _____

16. _____

17. _____

18. _____

19. _____

20. _____

Exercise 7.1B

Your Place in the Family continued

What do these issues tell you about your family? What conclusions can you make about your family values, based on their struggles?

Sample conclusions might be:

1. It is more important to be right than accurate.
2. Family reputation is more important than individual happiness.
3. It is not important that the family stays connected.
4. Money equals success in our family.
5. Secrets are the norm in our family.

Conclusion:

1. _____

   _____

2. _____

   _____

3. _____

   _____

4. _____

   _____

5. _____

   _____

How have these issues affected you?

Exercise 7.1B

Your Place in the Family continued

Families have an ideal for how you are supposed to be. If you were the perfect family member, what would that mission or expectation be? Record what that mandate is below.

Mission given to you by your family:

What happens during the holidays to confirm your family's expectations or mission for you?

Is that the mission you want? When you are most yourself, what is your mission? Record your mission as you wish it to be: (You can borrow from earlier chapters and at the end of this chapter we will provide you with a new way to think about your mission. Know that each time you make an effort to define yourself like this, it brings you closer to what you need to figure out. At the same time it stimulates vital synaptic activity in the brain. Hence, give your best effort and add it to the mix.)

Exercise 7.1B

Losses

Holidays are very affected by losses the family has experienced. Frequently, holidays underline the suffering of the family. Example losses would be deaths, accidents, financial reversals, divorces and significant geographic moves. List below losses your family has experienced. Record the date of the loss. Note how the loss changed or affected your holidays. Ask yourself what the impact on you has been.

	Family Loss	Date of Loss	Change in Holidays	Impact on You
1.				
2.				
3.				
4.				
5.				
6.				
7.				
8.				
9.				
10.				

Exercise 7.1C

Issues and Conflict

Every family has issues. These are long-standing areas of conflict that reveal so much of the family story. Please take time to list these issues, their history, and how they affect the holidays.

	Issue	How issue started	How it affects the holidays
1.			
2.			
3.			
4.			
5.			
6.			
7.			
8.			
9.			
10.			

Exercise 7.1D

Family Expectations

Based on the good memories, what expectations do you have of family holidays? What has the reality been in the past?

Based on the bad memories, what expectations do you have of family holidays? What has the reality been in the past?

What rituals were important to you? Why were they so important?

Family Expectations continued

How was nurturing expressed in your family?

What norms exist in your family about:

- Money
- Gift giving
- Resolving conflict
- Making decisions
- Remembering deceased family members
- Children
- Prayer and spirituality

How have these norms affected you?

Identifying the Shame Core

I had purchased a brand new car. In the process of backing it out of the garage, I had misgauged the distance and had scratched the car all along its bright new shiny side. I said to myself out loud, "Well, it did not take you long to do that!" I was unaware that my wife had heard the comment. She said in a matter of fact tone, "I hear your father's voice." It was true. The statement had the same intonation, exasperation, and cynicism that he frequently used when talking about me. I immediately recognized the attack on myself. I had made a mistake. Given the narrowness of the garage, we struggled for years getting cars in and out without damage. But the voice I spoke with was the tone I had heard for so many years. It was toxic and unforgiving.

I dreaded going to family events as a younger man. I was in a second marriage (in a Catholic family in which this was such a deep disappointment) and I had four children. My two sisters were married to their first husbands with only two children each. Plus, they were financially successful. My dad had wanted me to go into business with him, but I chose not to do that because of all our unresolved issues. He did take my brother-in-law into business and helped forge successful businesses with him. Indeed, he did that with others who to this day talk of my father with gratitude.

I remember a family event when I had driven up with an old Plymouth station wagon, which was the vehicle we could afford at the moment. It had a rusty rear panel that exposed a bit of the spare tire in the rear fender. My father noticed the hole in the fender and he quipped that I had the only car he had seen that had the potential to change its own tire. The male members of the family laughed. On the surface, it was simply teasing. Underneath, I felt angry about the jokes at my expense, despair about my financial situation, and defeated by all the criticisms over the years. At the time I was in recovery, in therapy, and in school to become a psychologist. All those activities were seen by my family as wastes of time and "flaky."

My Inner Observer can stop and be objective about what was true. The fact is, I was raising threatening issues that would turn out to be very painful for the family. My dad's teasing was an effort to connect, but his humor was very hurtful to everyone. The comments were sarcastic and barely concealed his anger. Yet, I know he was using humor as a way to relate. What I really wanted was the kindness that he extended to other men my age. (I eventually did receive that in the last months of his life.) I was being a very diligent person putting together what has become a successful career. A further fact was that my children and wife shared the same dread I did. To this day they speak of it. Finally, I loved that old car. It was reliable, served us well, was actually quite fast with a big Hemi V8, and was affordable. If I could find another one, I would buy it in a heart beat.

We internalize those negative messages into what is called our shame core. In therapy we create our "internal observer" who is able to filter out what therapists term the "attacks" on the self. The internal observer sifts through the comments which are really unnecessary and self-critical but are part of our internal circuitry of the self. With psychological detachment, one can see the truth.

People in recovery will find that their families will be critical of them. My dad was profoundly caught up in his own alcoholism, shame, and anger. He was a rager who never really got the help he needed; and the car was a good car.

When I damaged my new car, my wife's thoughtful nudge brought my inner observer online and I could see that I was being hard on myself. Actually I was calling on deep feelings of rejection fueled by some of the most painful processes of my family. Without the capacity to identify the processes at work, despair, entitlement, and old patterns of behavior are ready to be recycled. Let us return to Ruiz's *The Four Agreements* as a way for the inner observer to think about my scratched up car. The four agreements you will remember were:

- **"Keep your word impeccable."** Do not say toxic things to others or yourself. Be gentle and kind. We make mistakes but are not inherently bad because of it.

- **"Do not take things personally."** We need to have "boundaries" about people's comments and opinions. Learn to separate what is merely about them and what might be useful for you to take to heart.

- **"Do not make assumptions."** To infer that I knew what my family members were thinking was to some degree mind reading. I was to learn later that everybody was unhappy.

- **"Always do your best."** It took courage for me to start my life over and go back to school. There was no need to apologize for getting into recovery, or being a psychologist, or living within my means. Instead of beating myself up about scratching the new car, I just needed to reorganize the garage.

Thus, through an internal dialogue my perspective lifts, my sense of humor returns, and I appreciate my smart wife.

In the *Lord of the Rings* there is a character called Wormtongue who is an advisor to an old king. He whispers half truths, distortions, and negative thoughts into the old leader's ear. Wormtongue serves the dark wizard Saruman. He manipulates the old king by playing to his vulnerabilities and is quite destructive until he is unmasked. Author Jeff Lindsay creates a similar dynamic in his novels about Dexter, a serial killer whose goal is to rid the world of other serial killers. While filled with dark humor and irony, Lindsay's character introduced the concept of a "dark passenger," who is smart and creates a feeling of great power, and who also does awful things. He goes to a Twelve Step meeting and says that he has a dark passenger and every addict knows what he means. In therapy we refer to this as a shame core, sort of our own personal dark passenger or Wormtongue.

In treatment we often use a story by C.S. Lewis in which he is transported to another world filled with all kinds of unusual beings. He sees a man who is walking around with a lizard on his shoulder. The lizard is constantly whispering into his ear and the man does things that are clearly not in his own interest. A very bright, powerful being approaches the man and points out that the lizard must be a problem for him. He asks if he could kill it for him. The man says no, the lizard actually means no harm. The being grows brighter and says that does not appear to be so because the man still does not act in his own interest. He asks again if he can kill it. The lizard chatters madly into the man's ear. The man smiles and says to the being, I will keep him for awhile. This conversation is repeated in a number of ways until finally the angel-like being seizes the lizard and kills it. Immediately, the lizard is transformed into a powerful, beautiful horse, and the man morphs into a strong purposeful warrior. They ride off together.

The story is useful because oftentimes a therapist ends up asking if the patient will let him "kill it," and the patient refuses to give up this old friend (the shame core). The patient provides all kinds of reasons to empower the toxic voice. Yet when the patient does give up the shame core there is this transformation that occurs in both the shame and the patient. Patients become what they were destined to be. The shame becomes an extraordinary sense of honor and purpose which carries and sustains the patient's recovery.

You have to be willing to give up the sweet voice of the dark passenger. Remember that in a bargain with chaos, be aware of who you are bargaining with. Remember the answer Faust received. Mephistopheles said, "I am the spirit who denies." Old Wormtongue is crafty at inserting the old voices. Like a chorus in ancient Greek tragedy, the voices of past abandonment and rejection combine together to keep us stuck. Part of the work of a Fourth Step is to find the shame core. The next exercises will help you think about the nature of your dark passenger.

Identify Your Shame Core: Child and Adolescence History

Use the following format to identify your shame core. Start with your childhood and adolescent years. Think of ten incidents, big or small, when you felt deeply embarrassed, ashamed, degraded, or diminished. These incidents can be about overheard conversations or unkind environments. They also can be events in which specific behavior, talents, or efforts were criticized. List these incidents in column one. In column two, record your best memory of what was said and by whom. In the third column, focus on what you told yourself. In the final column, from the detached perspective of your inner observer as an adult, what was the truth? In other words, did the critical comments hold any truth that can be useful to you?

Shame Incidents	What was said about you?	What did you say to yourself?	What was the truth?
1.			
2.			
3.			
4.			
5.			
6.			
7.			
8.			
9.			
10.			

Exercise 7.2A

Identify Your Shame Core: Adult History

Now work up the most shame-filled experiences of your adult life. Again, write the experiences in the first column and the condemning comments in the second column. In the third column write what you told yourself. Finally, what is the truth that can be useful? As you complete the process, you may start to notice parallels between both sheets.

Shame Incidents	What was said about you?	What did you say to yourself?	What was the truth?
1.			
2.			
3.			
4.			
5.			
6.			
7.			
8.			
9.			
10.			

Exercise 7.2B

© Copyright P.J. Carnes, 2009

Shame Core Revealed

The following worksheet will help you make sense of the histories you have created. Start in the upper left hand corner and summarize commonalities that were said about you as a child and as an adult. Use the list as a way to consolidate negative messages you heard. In the middle left, record your physical reactions when you hear such messages. Examples could be nausea, tears, weakness, or shortness of breath. These physical signs become the essentials of the attack on the self. Then make a list of those persons who appeared repeatedly in your history. Imagine they are like a chorus in a Greek play emphasizing those messages. Then, in the very center of the worksheet write five core messages which are at the core of all messages you have received. Usually these are statements about your values, talent, lovability, or character.

On the right side of the sheet, you start the work of detoxification. In the upper right hand corner, identify strategies to keep your word impeccable. What rules could your inner observer use to avoid the attack on the self? In the middle, review the truths and lessons learned that will allow you to see the shame core messages for what they are. Finally, a great strategy is to reflect on why people said what they did. Were they just being mean-spirited, repeating voices they had in their heads, afraid you would succeed or be right? The best way to uncover their influences is to write out what would happen if you were successful, healthy, and integrated. Would it be upsetting, threatening, or a reason to celebrate? Record your best queries in that corner. As always, it is important to share your reflections in your groups and with your therapist.

Exercise 7.2C

List ways to keep your word impeccable toward yourself.
Key identifiers of toxic talk you struggle with:

_____
_____
_____
_____
_____

Common truths and lessons learned:

_____
_____
_____
_____

What happens to the chorus if you are successful, peaceful, not in crisis, and accurate in your perceptions:

_____
_____
_____
_____

Commonalities in what was said about you:

_____
_____
_____
_____
_____

Shame Core Messages:

1. _____
2. _____
3. _____
4. _____
5. _____

Describe your body's reactions when:

_____
_____
_____
_____

Whose voices (like a chorus) add power to these messages:

1. _____
2. _____
3. _____
4. _____
5. _____

6. _____
7. _____
8. _____
9. _____
10. _____

Exercise 7.2C

The Many Faces of Shame

In Chapter 2 we quoted Bill W., who referred to how he felt he "was acting" all the time. Toxic shame works that way. Because the interpersonal bridge has been damaged somehow, fear of abandonment can be the result. No matter what we do or say, we may fear we will not be accepted, so we strive to meet the expectations of others. Our real self can be lost. Starting with the original family, we become experts at reading and matching the expectations of others. In secret or out of sight, different parts of our personality will show up, especially when we have what we perceive as needs that are unacceptable. Carl Jung described these aspects of self as the "shadow" side of ourselves. He helped us to understand that until these darker aspects of self are both examined and shared with others, the full power of the self will not blossom. Given Jung's role in the beginning of Alcoholics Anonymous, we see how strategic the Fourth and Fifth Steps were in Bill's thinking.

Author Robert Louis Stevenson described how this split in the personality could occur in the story, *Dr. Jekyll and Mr. Hyde*. The good doctor had a secret side that came out with the very destructive Mr. Hyde. This story was often thought to be a metaphor about alcoholism and how drinking brought out a different self. Recent research indicates it probably was more about sexual behavior. If you read Dr. Jekyll's last letter within that context, little doubt remains. Dr. Jekyll had a very shameful part of himself that he could not integrate, which ultimately destroyed him. All forms of addiction, including compulsive attachment, share this splitting of the self. Any codependent, for example, lives with feelings of unworthiness in his or her attempt to be all things to all people. It was Lois W., Bill's wife and cofounder of Al-Anon, who first put her finger on that erosion of the self that results from trying to keep up appearances.

Therapists have long recognized the disintegration of self. Terms like *subpersonalities* or *compartmentalization* or *neuronal subsets* are used. The bottom line is that in a shame-based life, multiple selves exist. The trick is to integrate these various parts of self. Family therapist Robert Schwartz makes the helpful observation that we carry around within us an "internal constellation" of parts, most often based on our family experience. Each part usually crystallizes around specific shame or trauma events in the family. The part that evolves was "frozen" at the time the shame or trauma occurred. Whatever behaviors you adopted around the traumatic or shameful moment become "distinct" pieces of personality. For example, if you "freeze" when there is conflict, you probably learned to do that for safety during some early conflict experience.

To have all parts of you show up at once is called *authenticity*. When people know the full truth about you and love you anyway, trust develops. With such trust you can risk being all you can be. The basic challenge is to live between two truths: You must be faithful to yourself, and you must be faithful to others. Embracing this paradox is essential. All of therapy is about those two facts of life. Jung called living between those two realities the most spiritual work that humans do.

The next worksheets will help you highlight how the faces of shame work. The first, "The Many Faces of Shame," is to help you identify your inner constellation of parts. The process helps identify those public selves that everyone sees and private selves no one sees. The second, called "The Congruency Check," asks you to list your most hidden and shameful secrets. Notice how the hidden selves (your versions of Mr. Hyde) relate to specific secrets. Then think of you and your five most trusted people. The exercise asks you to notice how much these people know about your darkest secrets and the dark passengers that accompany them.

The Many Faces of Shame

This sheet is divided into what everybody knows about you and what you hide from others. Consider the parts or compartments as "selfs" that you use in your life. Use the existing circles and if you need more, make more. Consider first your "public" faces that you put on at different times. Name and describe them in each circle. If one of your "selfs," for example, is a caretaker, label or name the circle that and describe how people would know you are in a caretaker mode. Below the line, identify negative parts of self that people may not see. For example, if you have a seductive, self-sabotage, or an exploitative part, again name and describe this in the circle. These are your "dark passengers" that take over your life.

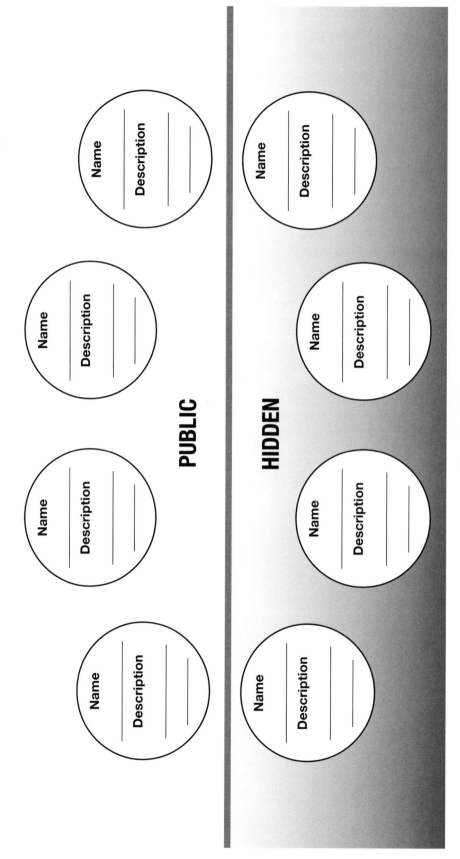

PUBLIC

HIDDEN

Name

Description

Exercise 7.3A

Congruency Check: Five Most Trusted People

In the circles write the names of your most trusted friends. Below the circles estimate what percentage of your "dark side" they know. List your most hidden and shameful secrets. Notice how the hidden selves (your versions of Mr. Hyde) relate to specific secrets. Then think of you and your five most trusted people. How much do these people know of your darkest secrets and the dark passengers that accompany them?

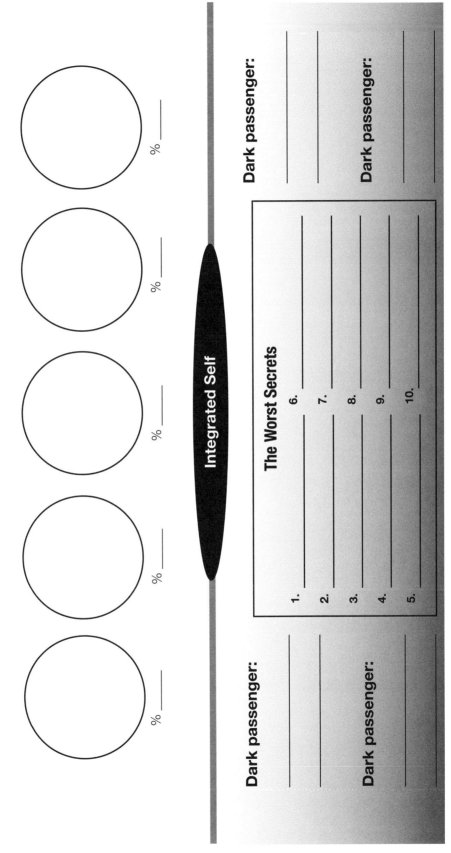

Dark passenger: _____

Dark passenger: _____

Integrated Self

The Worst Secrets

1. _____
2. _____
3. _____
4. _____
5. _____

6. _____
7. _____
8. _____
9. _____
10. _____

Dark passenger: _____

Dark passenger: _____

___ %   ___ %   ___ %   ___ %   ___ %

What secrets do each dark passenger have an interest in? Draw a line from the dark passenger to the secret.

Exercise 7.3B

Fifth Step Updates

List below the names of your most trusted people who do not know one hundred percent of the real you. Provide the percentage. Then record what it is that they do not know. The goal is to understand that you are still in recovery. This does not mean you rush to tell them; rather, you need to think through how to "come clean," so you will need a plan. Some people in your life need to know it all. Get assistance from your therapist and your group. Be aware that they may know things about you that you might not know they know. Or, they may know things about your dark side that you are unaware of at this time. Record what it is they may know that you do not.

First trusted person: _____ _____ **% unknown**

Does not know: _____

_____

_____

May know about me that I do not: _____

_____

_____

_____

Second trusted person: _____ _____ **% unknown**

Does not know: _____

_____

_____

May know about me that I do not: _____

_____

_____

_____

Exercise 7.3C

Fifth Step Updates continued

Third trusted person:_____ _____ **% unknown**

Does not know: _____

_____

_____

May know about me that I do not: _____

_____

_____

Fourth trusted person: _____ _____ **% unknown**

Does not know: _____

_____

_____

May know about me that I do not: _____

_____

_____

Fifth trusted person: _____ _____ **% unknown**

Does not know: _____

_____

_____

May know about me that I do not: _____

_____

_____

Exercise 7.3C

The Fourth and Fifth: The Real Person Showing Up

The design of the original Fifth Step was to share everything with one person. Typically, this person was either a Twelve Step member or a clergy person. In that sense, a Fifth Step was regarded as almost a confessional experience. It was cathartic and could take many hours. A good Fifth Step has evolved and can be shared over many weeks. The principle is to have several people, starting with a sponsor and then others, to know your whole story. In order to "live in consultation" your consultants need to know the worst of it and the details of it. Typically, it starts with a sponsor or a therapist or both, and the transparency grows. If you have many discrepancies on your congruency check, do not rush to fix that. Start with your most trusted people and get them on board first. Ask for their help in who should know what.

The bottom line is that to "kill it," that is the shame core, you strive for transparency. That means people have to know the worst of the worst and stay in your corner. One of the surprises that always happens is: they know elements of your shame core that even you are not conscious of. A new, clearer picture emerges that frees you to be you, not your separate selves that you act out, but your authentic self. The process of sharing is the way out and why patients resist it. The dark passenger's reasons become unmasked. Consider the story of Madge.

Madge was thirty-five years old. She was in treatment for the fifth time for drugs and alcohol. Although slim and attractive, years of hard living aged her. She was a nurse and extremely efficient and competent, but her nursing license was now being held by the state board because she could not stay sober. Members of her family attended two family groups a week. Madge had invited her seventy-two-year-old father to go through treatment with her.

One night it was her turn to "take time" in group and talk about her family. At first she refused to speak. Her silence and her facial expression told us that she was in a struggle with herself. The group members became even more attentive knowing that whatever came out, it was going to be important. Finally, she looked at me, and said, "Pat Carnes, you and your damned secret list." With that, she threw papers that had her secret list on the floor.

The secret list was an early version of the assignment you just did. It was given to addicts in early treatment. It asked them to list all their secrets. No action was required. However, most people found that if they wrote them down, they had a hard time keeping them secret. The whole purpose was to raise awareness that addiction thrives in secrecy. Madge clearly was wrestling with that fact.

Haltingly, the story came out between sobs. Madge had been given the responsibility of nursing her mother in her last days. She died of cancer ten years before, still a relatively young woman. Her death was long and painful, and, for much of it, Madge was her primary caregiver. Madge told the group that at the end her mother was in terrific pain. She begged Madge to give her an overdose of pain killer, so that she could leave in peace. Madge at first resisted. But as the illness became even more painful, her mother's logic made so much sense, Madge gave her mom a dose of morphine that she knew would end her life.

She turned to face her father with a mixture of defiance, anger, and sorrow. She almost choked as she said to him, "Dad, I killed Mom. I murdered my mother and your wife." With the truth out, she crumpled into a fetal-like ball and sobbed with years of pent-up grief, shame, and guilt. The group intuitively knew she needed to express this pain and allowed her to have it. No one rushed to her. No one even spoke as the sobbing ran its course.

Gently, her father took her hand and said, "Honey, it was the right thing to do. She was in so much pain; I would have done the same." He took his daughter into his arms. "I miss her terribly," he added. "It still hurts to think about it. But I have missed you too. I have felt so alone." Father and daughter cried together. The shared sorrow had a different tone. They were the transforming tears of reconciliation.

Madge now has more than thirty years of recovery. To this day she counts the revealing of the secret as the day she started true recovery. Her father has died but their relationship made his death a grace-filled experience. Her best day was when she killed the secret.

Sometimes the secret becomes public but no less transformative. The story of Fred and Anne speaks to the level of "letting go" that people need to have in order to be clear about who they are. It requires both endurance and a willingness to risk oneself. Fred was a very popular clergyman who gave stirring sermons and was noted for his compassion and help to others. His charisma made him very attractive to women. Unfortunately, he also had a secret life of sexual acting out that was clearly addictive. Women in his congregation became part of his conquest scenarios. Eventually, one came forward. When the others heard, there was a firestorm. The church board relieved him of his pastoral responsibilities and the denomination withdrew his faculties. Fred went to treatment.

Anne enjoyed her work as a mother and a pastor's wife. When the storm came, she was deeply hurt by her husband's behavior. She also received backlash from people in the church. She thought that she had many friends and was deeply cared for by so many. Yet when Fred's issues became public, her support system disappeared, which added to the wounds. She deeply resented the hypocrisy of people who were her confidants and companions when she was married to a popular pastor. Her "friends" were now remote and unavailable as she tried to sort out her next steps. She wondered if everything was a sham—church, God, her husband, men, and women.

While Fred was in treatment, Anne found a therapist. With the therapist's help she prepared for family week. Family week was like a roller coaster. She started to see her husband's addiction and plight clearly, and she began to remember her love for him in between surges of resentment. More importantly, she recognized how bankrupt her own emotional life was to end up so isolated and alone. Anne had almost been in a life of make-believe. She started the painful journey of looking at her own family, her roles with men, and her excessive caretaking. She had surrendered to the addictive compulsive attachment that set her up to rely on people she helped. With the help of her therapist and her Twelve Step groups she started to disinter her dream.

One of the many facets of figuring out how Anne lost herself was the realization that she wanted to be a pastor herself. As part of her own self-realization Anne went to seminary, earned a master's degree in divinity, and was ordained. Fred was also making progress and invited her to join Recovering Couples Anonymous (RCA) with him. They worked hard in therapy and Twelve Step work. Fred was given pastoral faculties again. As a couple, they started talking to congregations about recovery and what they had been through. They were able to tell the whole story from the outset. One of those congregations asked them back and interviewed them as co-pastors for their church. They opted for pastors who were real and knew suffering. They have now served in that role for more than a decade.

Pain motivates us to the deep examination of how we lose ourselves in our secrets. Yet when we speak the truth, we take on a new authority. For Fred and Anne, the process brought them to understand the level of change they needed in order to stay together. The crisis pulled things apart. Both had to look at the darkest corners of themselves. The resulting healing helped to define who they were separately and together. The recommitment created a new level of relationship they would never have obtained otherwise.

Becoming more transparent can then ripple through a whole family. Fred and Anne decided to do a recommitment ceremony. Almost four years of recovery work and two years in RCA had brought them to a deeper commitment than either had ever known. They had radically changed their lives. They certainly were different from when they first exchanged wedding vows, and a world apart from the turmoil filled early days of recovery. They invited friends and family who had supported them along the way. Fred and Anne each asked a friend to say something, and then they shared their new statements of covenant between them. They also asked their three children to say something.

Anne's friend Michelle told the story of Sir Gawain and the old hag. Sir Gawain had agreed to marry the old hag in order to help his friend Sir Lancelot. When he met the old hag she appeared as a beautiful, striking woman. The old hag asked how Sir Gawain reacted to her appearance. He admitted how attractive he found her. The old hag then said, "Then you shall have a choice. You can have me like this for half of each day. I can be like this during the day at court and with your friends, and then I will be an old hag who you shall sleep with at night. Or you can sleep with me as you see me now, and your consort during the day will be an old woman. What is your choice?" Gawain's response was immediate: "That should be your decision." The old hag responded by saying, "Then I shall be beautiful all the time, for you have given me dominion over myself!"

This generated many responses from the group. People spoke about how important it is to learn that giving up control over another leads to a deeper relationship. This is a hard-won lesson that recovery together teaches.

Perhaps the most moving part of the whole process came from Kim, their thirteen-year-old daughter. She spoke about how much she learned by watching her parents work through their recoveries. Then in a halting, hesitant, and soft voice she shared one more secret. In the last days before her mom and dad entered treatment, the fighting was so bad she could not bear it. Her older siblings could get out of the house because they could drive or get friends to drive. She was trapped. One particularly bad night she crawled out of her bedroom window onto the roof and prayed to God to find a new family. She doubted that God would ever help her, and she considered just jumping. Her confession was heart breaking. Tears were the only punctuation to the silence. The legacy of dysfunction and control was apparent to all.

Fred and Anne, after holding their children, turned to each other and said their commitment promises. They then turned to each of their children and made a commitment about how they would work separately and together to be better parents. When they were finished, there were no dry eyes in the room.

The lesson is simple. When you go through something as profound as recovery, it is important to mark the progress in some way. It is important to have witnesses and important to make your commitments and lessons public. A ceremony that involves those who are most dear deepens the resolve. This does not mean you have declared your life as problem free. Rather, in a conscious way, you are marking the progress, sharing the meaning of it, and involving the key people who have brought you to this point. You do not get to this point without the initial transparency. In that lies what recovery programs refer to as a "new freedom."

The Five Paths Out of the Shame Core (The Black Hole Experience)

To summarize, it is important to review the ways our shame evolved and how we perpetuate it. The initial impetus came from our family, but we incorporated rules and habits into our own repertoire of survival. Here are the five key ways we preserved our core of shame:

- **Dishonesty.** In our families we learned to present as reality that which we knew was not true. We were asked to deny our limitations, desires, and mistakes in the interest of family image management. We traded our humanness for family peace. This was one of the first of our bargains with chaos. For our limitations we needed help, for our desires we needed support of our dreams, and for our mistakes we needed acceptance. Instead we kept the peace. We began to have a secret life and compartmentalize our issues. Eventually we convinced ourselves that was "normal." Our fear of abandonment, fear of being alone, and our sense of unworthiness justified behavior that added to our loss of self. Entitlement sealed our early bargains with chaos.
- **Expectations.** We listened to the voices of family, culture, and religion which denied our internal realities. Unrealistic beliefs about ourselves formed around our

unacceptability. Standards of acceptance were beyond our reach. This made the opinions of others the arbiters of how we viewed ourselves. As a result, our own experience of intimacy and sexual desire became more remote. The worst was we believed in the judgments of others and wove them into the stories of our lives. We tried daydreams and obsessions to escape, but we really only believed the judgments. Our beliefs were so strong that we expected others to make up the deficits in ourselves. They were the only ones who could make us whole. In truth, we were born adequate and whole and deserved to be nurtured as such.

- **Ideals.** Consequently, we measured ourselves by unrealistic expectations and unreachable goals that validated our critics. We focused on our inadequacies rather than on our accomplishments and progress. Mistakes were indictments versus testimonies to our learning and risking. Our ideals flowed from the notions of success of others but really were about fantasies of power and importance. The original dreams, those life-rewarding visions of achievement in which we could thrive, were mired and obscured by the expectations of others.

- **Promises.** Our promises were not reliable commitments; they were often various forms of seduction so people would not leave us alone. We promised more than we could do, overstating what was true. Often the result was our own over-extension, crises built on over commitment, unfinished work, or, worse, unsuitable or even unworthy projects. Rather than acknowledge our humanness when things did not go well, we blamed others for our own doings. We covered it all in the righteousness of toxic talk, gossip, triangulation, and slander. That is where people go when they cannot live up to their own promises.

- **Self-disintegration.** We tried to be what others wanted. The footings of our core beliefs were our perceptions of our own unworthiness, unlovability, lack of value, and abandonment. Worse, when no one was there to denigrate us, we created our own attacks on the self. Our feelings of shamefulness caused us to repeat dysfunctional scripts, either to defend ourselves or to preserve an identity we did not feel.

Joseph Campbell spoke of the space between the inside of a person reflecting on the dark side, and the nature of the self and the necessity of relating to others and the world. He called it the "seat of the soul," which was the intermediary between the turmoil of the inside and the demands of the outside. His was a very similar conclusion to Carl Jung's notion that the most "spiritual place" is between being faithful and true to oneself, and being faithful and true to others. Both men made the case that the "sorting out" process of an examined life meant that the inside turmoil must have help from the outside to make sense. Sharing the story with others is the portal to the insight. The great stories, myths, and spiritual traditions are ways we access collected human wisdom to help inform us of our own narrative. Modern neuroscience tells us this sharing and story reconstruction is one of the most direct, proven ways to create new neural circuitry in our brains.

There are five paths that will preserve you in being able to be sturdy in that spiritual space. Ironically, they are the mirror images of what kept you stuck in the shame. To preserve your own "seat of the soul":

- **Honesty.** Jung said that the greatest gift one can give to children and to partners is to acknowledge your struggles and challenges. Now you know that pretending does not work. Twelve-Step people use the words "rigorous honesty," which means an end to secrets, private deals no one knows about, and omissions about things people do not to need to know. You want your witnesses to be credible to help you. To be credible they must be witnesses to the truth. Thus, to be honest means that trusted people get the whole story. The revelation of the story is the essence of the Fifth Step ethic. Authenticity about your life and circumstances requires dropping the stage appearances, assorted scripts, and costumes, and living in your own narrative. Finally, one must have clarity about intention and investment in relationships.

- **Boundaries.** In that spiritual space between self and the world, a series of barriers exist that preserve the integrity of that space. We call them boundaries. They are filters which assist in what gets through and what does not. From the inside, trust your personal discernments that do not offer short cuts. That way, you forestall potential bargains with chaos. Like the movie *Godzilla*, kill potential monsters while they are little. Boundaries depend on articulating a personal voice that is clear about bottom line decisions and non-negotiables. This works best when there has been a reliable review of scripts, stories, judgments, beliefs, and dreams for validity. This is ongoing work that is organized by the Inner Observer, who does not take things personally. In essence, that is what a Fourth Step is. When boundaries exist and an honest inventory is complete, you will not make assumptions, nor take things personally either.

- **Vision.** Vision is the core path because it emanates from what really matters. Its parameters are determined by being at your best (zone, flow, excellence). Vision works best with a defined mission built on your unique abilities, passion, and meaning. With a working mission in place, mistakes are part of learning (and being imperfect). Mistakes add clarity and focus to your life. Plus, mistakes help you measure progress. Use your vision to make goals that are specific and measurable. You have to have a plan.

- **Commitments.** The whole journey is a measure of commitment. The ordeal of completing this Recovery Zone work, for example, is that you decided you were not satisfied with being well enough to get by. You chose the work of a road less traveled, to be truly at your best. Therefore, when you make commitments, make them achievable so they can be honorable. For yourself, you have learned that in order to survive great efforts, you must have methods for keeping balance while you meet the challenge. With others, it matters that you keep your word impeccable about yourself and about them. Taking responsibility for your actions includes prompt admission of mistakes because it honors the commitment to the relationship. In addition, it shows you know that you own the problem and will fix it. Do not overlook errors or omit them. Not making amends is another shortcut that the dark passenger will make in a bargain and add weight to your shame core. You might term the latter "convenient" recovery. True commitments are not convenient. Just like truth.

- **Self-Integration.** Always ask first, "How do I come to my own assistance?" It is the most critical internal dialogue we have. Have strategies for transforming negativity and bad experiences into meaning and value. Create affirmations that you can recall in difficult moments and empowering metaphors to sort out the internal chaos. Remember the "seat of the soul" is where we make things true. Thus, it is here that the internal constellations of sub personalities join to help you. If you dialogue with them, you will be amazed at the assistance you get. Note that we always make our most trouble when we do not accept our own limitations. Discretion, humility, and the acceptance of limits are not only attractive, they are signs of healthy shame because they show discretion. Bargains with chaos depend upon wanting to ignore the simple realities of our limitations. The Greeks called ignoring human limits "hubris" or pride, which was the tragic flaw that would always undermine the heroic effort.

These five paths comprise a recipe for resilience and staying out of the shame core. **Figure 7.1** summarizes and contrasts the paths.

Five Paths *Into* Shame: The Black Hole Revisited

Dishonesty	Expectations	Ideals	Promises	Self-disintegration
■ Presenting reality of life which is not true ■ Denial of limitations, desires and mistakes ■ Image management ■ Compartmentalizing, secrets ■ Indicating care and level of relationship which is not there ■ Secret life is normal ■ Entitlement justifies deception	■ Voices of family, culture, and religion ■ Unrealistic beliefs about self, others, and sex ■ Expecting dreams and fantasies to be fulfilled by others ■ Judgments and stories told to self ■ Expecting childhood deficits to be met by others	■ Measuring self by unrealistic or unreachable goals ■ Focusing on the undone versus accomplishments ■ Perfectionism and rigidity ■ Mistakes are indictments ■ Ideals are success-based versus achievement-based and usually determined by others	■ Promising, implying, or stating more than is true ■ Crisis on over-commitments, unfinished work, and non-sustainable projects ■ Unresolved relationships and issues ■ Not keeping one's "word" and blaming others for failure ■ Toxic talk including gossip, triangulation, and slander	■ Core beliefs around worth and value ■ Affect rooted in humiliations, defectiveness, and flaws ■ Attack on the self by the self ■ Shame-bound affect and needs resulting in dysfunctional scripts (defending an identity) ■ Behavior based on unrecognized split of "selves"

Five Paths *Out of* the Shame Core: Creating Resilience

Honesty	Boundaries	Vision	Commitments	Self-integration
■ Sharing of struggles and difficulties ■ End to secrets, private deals, and omissions ■ Ongoing consultation with others who know the "whole story" (5th step ethic) ■ Authenticity about life and circumstances ■ Clarity about intention and investment in relationships	■ Trusting personal discernment ■ Articulating personal "voice" ■ Reviewing scripts, stories, judgments, beliefs, dreams for validity ■ Clarity about bottom lines and non-negotiables ■ Avoid personal reactions and taking things personally	■ Use ideals to reach goals that are specific and measurable ■ Measure by progress and not the unfinished ■ Mistakes are part of learning (learning to be imperfect) ■ Defined mission built on your unique abilities, passion, and meaning ■ Parameters determined by being at your best (zone, flow, excellence)	■ Achievable commitments which are honored ■ Impeccability of your word about self and about others ■ Methods for keeping balance and productivity ■ Responsibility for behaviors including amends-making, intention (don't make assumptions, and omission of errors) ■ Knowing ownership of problems	■ Discretion, humility, and the acceptance of limitations ■ Consistently coming to your own assistance ■ Strategies for transforming negativity ■ Create affirmations and empowering metaphors ■ Inner constellation of sub-personalities becoming explicit and integrated

Figure 7.1

Healthy Shame: Respecting Your Abilities

Mihaly Csikszentmihalyi tells a great story about his early years in Europe after World War II. He was struck by the gloom and desperation of post-war Europeans. One night he was in Zurich and so broke that he had no money to do anything. The only free event was a lecture on flying saucers, so he went. The lecturer said that he was not there to talk about aliens. Rather, he wanted people to understand why obsessions like this occur. The lecturer spoke about the trauma of war and how people would obsess about unrealities like flying saucers rather than face the darkness within. The speaker was Carl Jung, who continued to be connected with Bill W. and the early AA people. The lecture inspired Csikszentmihalyi to research what brought people happiness, building on Jung's insight that you had to sort through what was meaningful and make that the focus of your life work. Happiness ensues when a person is good at what he or she does, feels that his or her activities are important, and focuses so that he or she improves his or her skills. Moreover, these activities do not have to be noble prize-winning efforts. They only have to be about what is important to a person, giving one a sense of accomplishment and required focus. Csikszentmihalyi called this *flow*.

The story of these two giants in psychological thought and the confluence of their thinking helps us make sense of shame. Shame builds on feelings of inadequacy and beliefs in insufficiency. In recovery, we must focus on those things that give meaning and purpose to the self. Otherwise, obsession rules. An important part of our internal work is seeing when we have been at our best. We call this "Mission Reclamation." As you do your mission reclamation project, remember that it does not have to be perfect at the end of this chapter. In fact, by continuing in this series you will be refining it for some time. Now is the time to give yourself the freedom to articulate your mission in different ways.

My wife will take a block of wood and see something beautiful within. She then starts the process of liberation by chiseling out the pieces until what remains is a thing of beauty. When she liberates the beauty, almost always there is a message implicit. They call this the artist's statement. The band I traveled with had a similar metaphor. The song is about a sculptor named Max. (The song really was about therapist Max Haskett who creates beautiful carvings that are symbolic of the points of therapy). In the song Max is asked why he carves the wood, and his response is that he is "chiselin' out the soul."[12] In a Fourth and Fifth Step, you are chiseling out your soul. A primary tool is the mission statement. And like all "soulish" work, you have to continue to reshape it until the liberation of the truth is complete.

Mission Reclamation – Part 1

Part of recovery is to determine the mission you were given and what parts of that you accept or reject. The more important sequel is to reclaim your own voice without all the programming which obscured your true spiritual mission (how to be) and operational mission (what to do). Start this "mission reclamation" by completing the following project. Reflect on your best moments and answer the following key questions:

What has mattered the most to you?
(meaningful, motivating, passionate about—made life worth living)

1. _____

2. _____

3. _____

4. _____

5. _____

6. _____

7. _____

8. _____

9. _____

10. _____

What are your unique abilities?
(strengths special to you)

1. _____

2. _____

3. _____

4. _____

5. _____

6. _____

7. _____

8. _____

9. _____

10. _____

Exercise 7.4A

Mission Reclamation – Part 2

Addiction has been compared to craving the state of ecstasy or trying to "drink God" from a bottle. Yet, if you think over your life you have had "ecstatic" moments when you experienced deep joy, felt one with the world, and the experience was worth the effort (had meaning). This part of mission reclamation helps to focus on those moments in your life so that you might define what "flow" or zone is for you. Start by identifying moments of ecstasy and true happiness in which you felt joy, felt connected, and felt meaningful. Identify those times as a child, as an adolescent, as an adult, and those moments in the past year. Then identify what they all have in common. This will take some thought for you to complete. Then summarize what you must have to be in the zone. Identify areas of being in the zone, you need to bring back in your life.

Moments of ecstasy:
(joy, oneness, meaning)

In childhood
_____
_____

In adolescence
_____
_____

In adulthood
_____
_____

In past year
_____
_____

Common features:

1. _____
2. _____
3. _____
4. _____
5. _____
6. _____
7. _____
8. _____
9. _____
10. _____
11. _____
12. _____
13. _____
14. _____
15. _____

For flow to be in my life, I must have zone:

1. _____
2. _____
3. _____
4. _____
5. _____

Zone areas to bring back in my life:

_____
_____
_____
_____

Exercise 7.4B

Mission Reclamation – Part 3

Reviewing part one, list seven words that would describe your "original" child. These are descriptive words which people would use to characterize how you are and to underline your strengths. (For example, use words such as witty, tenacious, wise, or peaceful.)

Seven words to describe you: **Best three:**

1. _____   1. _____

2. _____   2. _____

3. _____   3. _____

4. _____

5. _____

6. _____

7. _____

Now pick out three words which are the best descriptions and list them under the "best three." Go back to part one and identify seven activities which give you the most meaning in life.

Seven most meaningful activities: **Best three:**

1. _____   1. _____

2. _____   2. _____

3. _____   3. _____

4. _____

5. _____

6. _____

7. _____

As above, select the three activities which most represent what you are called to do in life.

Exercise 7.4C

Mission Reclamation – Part 4

Now it is time to draft your spiritual and operational missions. Remember, this is a draft. You will refine them as you move through this process and as your recovery deepens. Start with a spiritual mission statement.

Write a statement using the three best descriptions you identified in Part 3. This statement is about how your original child was meant to be.

My spiritual mission is to be ...

_____

_____

_____

_____

_____

Then, operationalize your mission by writing a statement of what you feel called to do. Use the best three activities identified in the previous section. Think of the two statements as connected, such as, you were meant to be _____ in order to do _____.

My operational mission is to do ...

_____

_____

_____

_____

_____

Key questions: How do these statements compare to the mission given to you by your family and culture? How much of your life currently reflects your mission statements? How could you be more congruent in these statements?

_____

_____

_____

_____

_____

Exercise 7.4D

© Copyright P.J. Carnes, 2009

Chapter 8 **Suffering and Loss**

Much of life is about loss. Every decision you make involves selecting one option and letting others go. We assume that when we get a job or buy a house we will be there indefinitely. Yet the average person moves every three years and has at least eight different employers over a lifetime. We all have had opportunities that we passed on, later realizing what we could've had. Sometimes we have loved people and given up too early. Or they gave up on us. Misunderstandings that end relationships create a myriad of sorrows. Sometimes even the most minor of events is tinged with regret. There are moments when I get sad just turning in my rental car. But then, I have a thing for cars.

From small things to very large events, the truth of Buddha's observation is proven: Suffering is clinging to that which changes.

We teach our children to be independent, and then they go and practice what they were taught. When they choose to exercise this independence, miss holidays or special occasions, parents feel an acute awareness of loss. The parent realizes that being together as a family is much less important to the child. I did not appreciate the inevitability of the difference in perspectives until my children had other priorities and my parents were gone. I realized how often I ducked out on their family events.

As parents, we say that children are "ours" but, in truth children are but "guests" in our lives. We rarely grasp that notion when children are young. For myself, my twelve years of single parenting was incredibly stressful. Yet I count that period as one of the best epochs of my life because of my constant contact with the children I love. Today I am so proud of each of them and what they have done. Yet I have this secret sorrow most of us parents have. I miss them terribly. It is the inevitable sorrow of loving them yet allowing them to have lives of their own.

To love someone usually means to not choose others. There are probably many people we could be partners with. We learn also that monogamy works best, but we may encounter people who we could or even do love. Yet the discipline of a "partnered struggle" is critical to our social context and our personal development. Having a successful, long-term, sexual relationship is one of our great tests as humans. Not to have experienced that is a great sadness. Sometimes to experience it is an even greater sadness. Either way, we have to say "no" and thereby pass on what could have been. Those that pursue the fantasy of having life fixed by the right person are perhaps ironically those who experience the most suffering.

Aging is the worst because it is subtle in how it creeps up on you. I have experienced this with myself, my friends, my family, my elders, and my patients. Suddenly it dawns on you that parts of your body have shifted. Reversing the migration of body mass to its original spots becomes a lifelong struggle. Of greater significance is when you notice the loss of balance, sight, or hearing even with help. Despite a constant and rigorous exercise regimen, you cannot do at fifty what you did at twenty. It is terrible to realize that a loving partner's abilities are eroding. The very worst is when you finally admit that the decline has changed that person to the extent, that although physically functional, he or she is no longer present.

Death has the advantage of finality and a moment to which to attach the pain. Nobody prepares you for the death of a parent. Even the death of a parent from whom you are estranged is filled with sorrow. As your life progresses, you start to lose your friends as well. A great irony is revealed when close friends die—but you have not seen them in many years. The problem is that one can only maintain a limited number of active relationships at one time. When you hear of their death you are stricken and fault yourself for not having contacted them. The truth is, contacting them was probably not realistic, but your care for them is real. That pain clarifies the importance of who is in your life.

Sometimes grief happens in bunches. I remember holding my dying mother's hand as it became cold. The sorrow was searing to me, because she was so much a part of my life in her last years. I had tried so hard to make the most of our remaining time. Yet within days of her passing, I realized that there was so much more to talk about. For a week I was in a fugue finding it hard to work or do much of anything. Then eight days after she died, the wife of one of my closest friends called early one morning. She said, "Richard got up to get the baby and did not come back. I just found him face down in the carpet. He is dead." How could this be? It seemed like I was just his best man in his wedding. He was fifty-one.

Then I heard that a former colleague and therapist, was dying of cancer at the age of forty-six, she had been a sex addict, and she and I had appeared on the Oprah show to discuss the topic. I went to see her in the hospice. Even in our visit together, she got tired and said she needed to stop. In my discomfort I joked, "You mean even when you are dying you have to have boundaries?" She gave me this huge smile, and said, "Patrick, boundaries go to the very end."

Almost simultaneously a case manager whose breast cancer had been in remission became very ill again. She was a retired military officer who was known for her toughness and her huge heart. I loved working with her because I could count on her to face the difficult issues. When she was a few months from death she bluntly told me, "I am dying and you are avoiding talking to me about it." We talked. I will never forget going to her funeral and her thirteen-year-old daughter singing to her mother, *Will You Remember Me?*" I know I will.

From the day my mother died, ten friends died in the next twelve weeks. I had to accept death as a companion in my life. In fact that is the purpose of this whole soliloquy of sorrow. A cycle exists which is based on impermanence. That is why there is no human security (Chapter 6 opens with this line). There are seasons, creative rhythms, and the inevitability of passing time. Our very biology depends on consuming other forms of life. Our immunological system is a battle field of organisms; hopefully, our white blood cells win and toxic pathogens lose. Deeply acknowledging this cycle of life and death is where growth and creativity reside. The portal is pain, and our task is to surrender.

One of the great Greek stories illustrates this path. Daedelus was a builder, architect, and construction agent in his time. A monster called the Minotaur was loose and the king of Minos asked Daedelus to build a structure to capture this monster which was wreaking havoc across the island. Daedelus and his son Icarus built a giant labyrinth. When the king asked whether the labyrinth would contain the monster, Daedelus said with pride, "Nothing will get out of there." The King read that statement as a challenge and decided to test the labyrinth by tossing Daedelus and his son in the trap. They had the problem of being trapped by their own construction—along with the Minotaur in the labyrinth.

To escape the labyrinth, the monster, and the island, Daedelus conceived of a plan to make wings out of feathers and wax. He told Icarus they could make it to the mainland, but he warned his son that he must stay close to the water. If he flew higher the sun would melt the wax and he would plunge to his death. The wings worked and they flew toward the mainland. Icarus loved flying and could not resist the temptation to fly higher. Unfortunately, the wax melted as his father had forecast. Daedelus watched his son fall into the sea helpless to do anything to save him. He flew on alone to the mainland.

The Greeks were smart about grief. Just as centuries ago, one of the most difficult losses is the loss of one's own child. Daedelus had witnessed the worst loss possible. The story goes on to describe how he handled the pain of the death of his son. When he reached the mainland, he resolved that the death would not be meaningless. He poured his energy into making beautiful, useful buildings for his countrymen. Rather than dwell on the unfairness of the king, he transformed his mourning into clarity of purpose. He even built a temple for Apollo, the sun god. His best building honored that which hurt him the most (the sun having melted the wax on his son's wings).

The pattern is the same in all the great stories. No hero avoids loss. The utilization of loss to persevere and to overcome obstacles is the essence of courage. Loss provides clarity of purpose and releases new energy and creativity. Going back to the introduction of the book, we suggested that the heroic journey and the recovery journey share the same path and principles. (See **Figure 8.1**) After the ordeal, the great story is the transformation of the hero. The person who has done the work is more substantial, has more depth, and is "more" to be reckoned with. The most obvious features of heroes are their new confidence in marshalling their abilities and new found talents.

Stages: The Heroic Journey

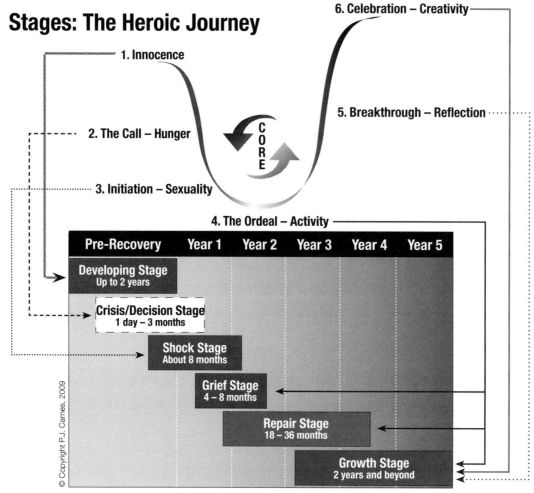

The Course of Recovery Over Time

Figure 8.1

The same is true for the recovery journey. As the cycles of loss, both big and small, weave their way through one's life, the essential task is to lean into the challenge. More specifically, that means to lean into all the feelings, including sorrow. Very often the bargain with chaos was, in part, to not have the feelings. Addictions, as we have come to know them, are maladaptive responses to stress and trauma. The bargain was to avoid the pain. Anger, fear, and shame are the easiest emotions to identify. The toughest emotion to face (and why it is almost always the last to be identified) is sorrow.

When recovering people tell their story, often a gateway event emerges that is hard to describe without tears. But once the tears flow, the others come as an emotional cascade. Here are some examples:

- A forty-two-year-old man tells of his life as a farm boy. He had raised a young bull which took first place at the fair. The animal and the boy had high trust for one another. He would wile away summer afternoons lying between the front legs of this giant animal. In retrospect, he realized that this was the only real affection he could remember in his alcoholic family. Then the day came when the truck pulled up from the meat cutting plant. His parents had sold the bull and never told the boy he was losing his pet. He remembers the look of the animal's eyes as he was pulled away from the sobbing boy.

■ The fifty-year-old codependent told of the Christmas morning when she set six little suit cases by the door in preparation for her "ex" to pick up the kids. At that moment it hit her that she was going to be alone on Christmas, having taken care of everyone (including the "ex") but herself. She thought it would not matter and that she needed a break. Turns out it did matter a great deal as she faced all the accumulated losses that led up to that fateful morning. She never dreamed she would be the one alone on Christmas.

■ The thirty-year-old graduate student addicted to cocaine and sex reported a moment that was life changing for him. He had heard a rumor that his father was not really his biological father. So he went to the man who he always thought was his father and asked for the truth. The man who raised him told him that he was not his biological son, but he had made a promise to cover up the truth for his mother. There were two losses involved here. First, he did not know his real father. Second, he found out that his mother was not the woman he thought he knew.

■ The twenty-one-year-old woman had a prescription drug problem that started with stealing her parents' medication at the age of twelve. It was easy to do, going back and forth between houses. No one could track her drug use or her boyfriends. Her golden retriever died about a month before her mom left her dad. She was in the seventh grade. She recalled the dog's patience with her. She would sit on the floor and tell him of her unhappiness and loneliness. He always welcomed her. Between sobs she confessed to thinking he died intentionally because he did not want to see what was coming. This grief session was held during family week so all the family members were present including her siblings. One by one they all started talking about the dog but each then went deeper into other losses that had been much too difficult to express. The great irony is this wonderful dog was still helping the family express the pain of fractured relationships and addiction.

Bargains with chaos are never durable. Sooner or later the pain surfaces. The sweet voice of escape can no longer cover the sounds of our losses.

Four Sorrows Sequence

M. Scott Peck, M.D., opened his classic book, *The Road Less Traveled*, with the sentence, "Life is difficult." This book argues for a more conscious life through therapy and spiritual practice. As we have noted, the "examined life" requires focus and determination. Furthermore, surrendering to the recovery process can show us that suffering has meaning, and we must focus on what really matters.

Developing skills for coping with loss and pain are essential for a healthy life. These skills are even more critical for the recovering person. Often times the implicit brain (that section of our brain that directs behavior without our knowledge) makes decisions on the basis of pain. That pain is beyond the awareness (our explicit brain) of addicts and codependents. From this we have the phenomenon of the "hijacked brain." The hijacked brain plans to do one thing important but ends up doing something else. With compulsive behavior, that something else is called "addiction" or "codependency."

The following story illustrates what I mean. A psychiatrist was treating a woman who had significant brain damage from an accident. She had no idea who she was or what her life had been like. The part of her brain that was damaged affected her memory. She also had no short-term memory and so she could not remember the previous day. She was only aware of the present. Each morning her doctor shook her hand and interviewed her, and each morning she seemed to have never met him before. As an experiment one morning he put a tack in his hand. When they shook hands she was pricked by the tack. Then he interviewed as before. The next morning when the doctor extended his hand in greeting, she refused to shake hands. Part of her brain remembered the pain. This story illustrates the role of "implicit" memory. In short, the woman altered her behavior but did not remember why.

So it is with all of us. Our implicit brain manages much of our life beyond our awareness. It is the automatic pilot where we no longer think about how to tie our shoes, drive a car, or even when to breathe. This part of us also operates on the basis of life experience. Hurts are incorporated into decision-making, often without any examination or reflection. The reason we end up in the same situations over and over again without intending to is because of this embedded decision-making process. Our brains become hijacked. We systematically need to review our lives so that we may examine the sources of sorrow. We resist this when we ask why we need to "dredge up the past." The answer lies in our inexplicable behavior that we will continue until we address the pain. We must overcome our resistance because our pain can be a great ally in providing resilience, wisdom, and compassion. Or, unexamined pain that is not grieved and not integrated into our explicit selves adds to the probability that our brain is being hijacked.

Addictive and coaddictive obsession is a "repression mechanism." These behaviors are maladaptive ways of coping with stress that draw upon earlier traumas for their strength. As long as obsession rules, the brain does not have to feel the current suffering as well as the wellspring of earlier unresolved hurts. Unresolved pain is one of the primary sources of power for compulsive behavior. We have already learned from our own "stressmakers," that when someone is traumatized and there is a new stressor, the body pumps hormones for intense activity that untraumatized people do not experience. Addiction is really a solution to accumulated, unresolved suffering. Similarly, codependent obsession and behavior serve the same function.

Earlier, we pointed out that for both addicts and codependents *starting* recovery is comparatively easy. *Staying* in recovery is the problem. As things improve, the old hurts start to seep out and demand to be acknowledged. This "flooding of feelings" usually occurs in the second six months. When the feelings that have been on the shelf for years finally hit, relapse can often occur. Also health declines. Recovering people at this stage have more sickness, more visits to the doctor, more emergency room visits, and more accidents. Emerging pain clearly burdens our bodies until it is addressed. Thus, many of us are resistant to the "dredging up of the past." Yet, to release ourselves from the bondage of addiction we must systematically understand how life has stuck us with tacks, driving our "irrational" behavior.

Thus, there are four sorrows in recovery. The first is from change and loss. Our parents and relatives die. We change careers, companies, and locations. The woods we played in as kids have now been developed into a neighborhood with houses every hundred feet. Divorces occur. Children grow up and move away. We lose track of dear friends. As we age we lose the physical capabilities we had as young people. There are moments of great happiness or meaning that we will never be able to recreate. These losses are inevitable, yet the sadness is no less genuine.

The second sorrow is about abuse and betrayal. Trusted people have hurt us. Sometimes abuse occurs without intention to hurt. Examples would be parents who had no idea of how to raise children, due to their own confusing childhoods. Or they had significant mental health or addiction issues themselves, causing them to neglect us or act in ways that were hurtful. Or they simply made mistakes that had bad results. The pain is still real. Betrayal happened when trusted persons exploited their relationship with us. They used us or betrayed our trust. The pain here stems from intentionality. We were hurt by someone to whom we thought our relationship mattered. Yet we were not protected or even insulated from harm. They took advantage of us through seduction, deceit, or abuse of power. This happens for adults as well as children. Betrayal has no age limits. Intention does add sorrow because of the breach of trust. By corroding our capacity to trust, these people compromise our ability to be fully ourselves.

The third sorrow is about chaos. These losses are due to events beyond our control. These are not the inevitable losses of change but rather of catastrophe. Think of accidents, disease, war, and natural disasters like tornadoes, hurricanes, and lightning. Economic shifts which result in bankruptcies, business failures, and recessions. No one expects the drunk driver who hits our spouse, the burglar who takes a treasured family heirloom, or the disease which takes our child. The ancient Jewish mystical tradition of the Kabbalah uses the word *Satan* for chaos. This *Satan* is different than the Christian concept of a fallen angel whose task is to tempt us. Rather, this *Satan* is the inexplicable chaos with no rhyme or reason which tests us. Remember how we have talked about how the brain naturally tries to make order of the world. When we cannot make order, then we must find meaning in the suffering. Chaos takes loss to an exponential level because it seems so purposeless. It is chaos which really tests us with the question of, Why do bad things happen to very well meaning people?

The final sorrow is about addictive illness. Both addicts and codependents have paid prices for their behavior. The very gateway to recovery is pain that we could no longer live with. Consequences helped us to accept our illness. We often catalog these consequences as part of our First Step: the financial costs, divorces, legal problems, business failures, and lost time. The list seems endless when we start. Yet, often we leave them at the gate with our First Step. As part of our inventory of sorrow we must revisit them again. Our purpose is not to feel sorry for ourselves. Rather than self-pity we must translate our pain into clarity so we understand what matters, self-knowledge so we do not repeat mistakes, and resilience so we reclaim our strength. Our very power comes from having integrated what has made us profoundly sad. Failure to do this inventory leaves us vulnerable to relapse or finding other ways to obliterate our feelings. When we began the ordeal, we described the universal description of "waking from the dream" as central to the recovery process.

This work is essential in doing the Fourth and Fifth Steps which ask us to look at our interior world and take action about it. We have to make friends with our sorrows. We start with a timeline which provides an important perspective on what we now have to do.

Four Sorrows Timeline

In this exercise, you're going to create a timeline from birth to the present. On the line above the top of the worksheet record your current age. Place ages along the timeline so you know approximately where to put things. For example use each decade or every five years depending on your age. An example has been provided so that you can see how the worksheet is designed. Then under each domain of sorrow list the events which are a source of sadness, pain, and grief in your life. If you wish to use a larger sheet of paper, feel free to do so. Take time to do this task. If it feels overwhelming, get support so that you can complete it. Let your group and therapist know that you are doing this task now in case you need support as you do this work.

Current Age _____

Age	First Sorrow: Change and Loss	Second Sorrow: Abuse and Betrayal	Third Sorrow: Chaos	Fourth Sorrow: Addiction/ Codependence
7-8	Parents divorced, father moves away	Molested by oldest sister		
25	Lost job	Partner cheating		String of bad/abusive relationships to mask pain

Exercise 8.1

© Copyright P.J. Carnes, 2009

Transforming Suffering into Meaning

Sorrow and its critical lens in deepening and clarifying the meaning of life are core elements in psychotherapy. Viktor Frankl, one of the earliest pioneers of psychotherapy, described this as the transformation of suffering into meaning. As a concentration camp survivor, he noted that the people who survived were the ones who held on to purpose in their lives. Even in the midst of the very worst experiences known in contemporary times, they found something for which to live. Thus, resilience is the core human skill and the primary teaching of psychotherapy. Resilience is central to the notion of *recovery*. Ultimately the test is to turn bad into good. Or to use a recovery phrase, "nothing is wasted" meaning that no matter how awful something was, there is something to learn. Most often, that "something awful" is a doorway to a greater good. Remember, most heroes did not want to be tested.

Some of our oldest stories are about the link between sorrow and resilience. When the Greeks told the story of Daedelus, whose son Icarus died in front of him, they knew that loss of a child was one of humankind's most sorrowful experiences. Yet, Daedelus was able to use his grief to create buildings and monuments, which added to the well-being of all humans. The very soul of recovery is this type of resilience. Yet, the question remains, how do you transform suffering into meaning?

Consider *The Religion*, the epic novel of Dr. Tim Willocks, one of those rare authors who does many things well. As a psychiatrist, he specializes in addiction medicine. As a novelist, he tells great tales from the Middle Ages when Christianity and Islam were in mortal combat. His novel, *The Religion*, is an extraordinary journey into this world. He writes about Tannhauser, a key figure in the story who, at the end of his life, has to contemplate his losses in a brutal world. In many ways he captures the critical spirit of resilience. One has to wonder if it is the novelist or the psychiatrist who speaks:

> In these mountains far from everywhere, Tannhauser came to understand that sadness was the thread that wove his life into a single piece, and that in this there was no reason for regret, much less surrender. And this his father taught him: that in spite of sadness, in spite of loss without measure, life beckoned yet, like a billet of base iron awaiting transformation. Since Tannhauser had last raised a fire in that pale stone temple, where his father brought things into being that had not been before, emperors and popes had fallen and the lines on the maps had been changed. Flags had been brandished and armies had marched and multitudes had killed and died for their tribes and their gods. But the Earth yet turned, for the Spheres danced to a music of their own, and the Cosmos was indifferent to the vanity and genius of Men. The human spirit eternal, if such a thing there was, was here, in an old man with his hammer and his hearth, and with a woman and fine children whom he loved.

If sorrow is the affect that helps us to knit together our life in a meaningful way, grief is not without its pitfalls. It, in fact, is one of the principal themes of J. K. Rowling's *Harry Potter* novels. We learn in the final novel the key to much of the mystery of Harry's adventures. Lord Voldemort is the villainous wizard who, among many other misdeeds, killed Harry Potter's parents. We finally understand in *The Deathly Hallows* that Voldemort compartmentalized himself as a way to cope with his original family losses. As long as the split parts of himself continued to exist, so would his evil. (Remember our work in the previous chapter on compartmentalization!) When asked whether the splits could be healed, Rowling, in speaking through the character of Hermione Granger, answers that, yes, they could be. Yet, one of the key factors was that healing could only come with taking responsibility for one self. This was especially true if those losses were connected to behavior that harmed others. There must be remorse and Hermione says, "You've got to really feel what you have done…. The pain of it can destroy you." Addicts and codependents know that lesson. Compartmentalization was the strategy many of us used to keep suffering at bay.

Modern neural science confirms the truth of our great stories. We know that anger, fear, shame, and sorrow are woven into our unconscious processes of our addictions. Grief is perhaps our greatest and most potent activator of our more destructive selves. Remember the source of the word *grief* is a medieval word meaning to *grip*—as opposed to *let go*. We now are learning how grief also is a primary way to access the brain's reward centers. Holding on to that which has changed is part of our efforts to escape our realities.

In many ways these fundamental truths have emerged in all the programs of recovery. Perhaps one of the most eloquent comes from Co-Dependents Anonymous which refers to the "deep sadness." In fact, the fellowship observes, "Our sadness and loss bring us here." Al-Anon echoes the sentiment but also reminds us that as "feelings of sadness and grief surfaced, other feelings bubbled up as well." Debtors Anonymous notes, "… we were hurting from many losses." Sex Addicts Anonymous is even more concrete, "We would use sexual fantasy to deal with emotions and situations that we didn't want to face." As Willocks observed in his character, Tannhauser, sadness is the "thread that makes a single piece." In *Alcoholics Anonymous*, Bill W. wrote, "We find it helpful to list the losses we've experienced in our childhood and adult life. We allow ourselves to grieve." To make grieving effective we must first search for patterns in our pain.

Patterns of Pain

No one ever sat us down and taught us about grief and sadness. There was no course in handling suffering. The closest thing we have is grief groups for when divorce or death occurs. Therapy also is after the fact. Many indigenous peoples did prepare for suffering. They used what is called an initiation rite. The assumption of the initiation rite is that life will present you with challenges and pain. So the rite will create an experience in which the participant experiences pain. As part of that, elders teach the spiritual skills, the physical skills, and the psychological skills necessary to face adversity. Author Michael J. Meade tells us that the closest thing we have in our culture to the initiation rite is military boot camp. Boot camp provides challenges and pain, but it is not the whole process. After all, master sergeants in the Marine Corps are not known for their spiritual direction. Most cultures have had elaborate rituals to support all significant passages and changes in life. These rituals were like a curriculum in which resided the collective wisdom of the people in how to cope.

Our culture does not provide us with good rituals of passage. For example, we do not deal well with death and loss. Phillippe Aries wrote a famous history of death and dying called *The Hour of Our Death*. In it he notes how in earlier times, all the way back to the Greeks and Romans, most people knew they were soon to die. They would talk about it with friends and family. The exception was people who died suddenly of accidental causes. Native Americans had a similar attitude captured in the phrase "I heard the owl call my name." This meant they knew their time was coming and it was time to talk.

Aries points to a shift in history which occurred with the rise of science. In the seventeenth century we reversed how we talked of death. The conversation about impending death became neglected and the focus was on death from chaos. That trend has deepened until the present day where we can know our neighbor next door is dying and never address them about it. But we will talk endlessly about the media accounts of those whose deaths are sudden. We have turned the process on its head as science has opened the possibility of postponing death. Our funerals and our grieving have little support compared to earlier times and other cultures.

Think about your experience with pain. Did anyone attempt to help you cope with pain and loss? What was the advice that you received? How have you coped over time with your hurts? One way to organize your thoughts is to go back to your timeline and notice if there are any patterns. Are there any themes in terms of how you were hurt? What messages were you given? How did you cope? On the next page you will be asked to reflect on these patterns in each domain of sorrow.

Patterns of Pain: Reflections on Loss

Review each of the four sorrows you have documented. Record below themes that appear, who helped you, what advice you were given, and what your coping strategies were. Note the commonalities that appear across the sorrows by underlining themes, people, advice, and coping strategies that keep appearing. The fact that people helped, that advice was given, or that you coped, does not necessarily mean you were given healthy help. Rather your purpose is to summarize what happened thus far—healthy or not—in your grieving. Finally, note with the perspective you have now, what you have learned.

1. Change and Loss

Common Themes: _____

_____

_____

_____

_____

_____

Advice Received: _____

_____

_____

_____

_____

_____

Coping Strategies Used: _____

_____

_____

_____

_____

_____

New Perspectives: _____

_____

_____

_____

_____

_____

Exercise 8.2

Patterns of Pain: Reflections on Loss continued

2. Abuse and Betrayal

Common Themes: _____

_____

_____

_____

_____

_____

Advice Received: _____

_____

_____

_____

_____

_____

Coping Strategies Used: _____

_____

_____

_____

_____

_____

New Perspectives: _____

_____

_____

_____

_____

_____

Exercise 8.2

Patterns of Pain: Reflections on Loss continued

3. Chaos

Common Themes:_____

_____

_____

_____

_____

_____

Advice Received: _____

_____

_____

_____

_____

_____

Coping Strategies Used: _____

_____

_____

_____

_____

_____

New Perspectives:_____

_____

_____

_____

_____

_____

Exercise 8.2

Patterns of Pain: Reflections on Loss continued

4. Addiction/Codependence

Common Themes:_____
_____
_____
_____
_____
_____

Advice Received: _____
_____
_____
_____
_____
_____

Coping Strategies Used: _____
_____
_____
_____
_____
_____

New Perspectives:_____
_____
_____
_____
_____
_____

Exercise 8.2

Unsaid and Undone

After completing your timeline and looking for patterns you will be filled with feelings. Emotional flooding is the phrase that is used to describe being overwhelmed with feelings. Our task now is to help bring these feelings to resolution and order. We will never eliminate them. We must acknowledge and express them. To integrate them into our resilience we must bring them to some form of resolution. We have to create our own rituals and expressions around the painful transitions in our life. Most of us have catching up to do in expressing and working through our pain.

A helpful way to organize this work is to make a list of the unsaid and the undone. Review again the events recorded in your timeline. Make a list of things you wished you had said and a list of things you wished you had done. On the following pages are worksheets to help you organize how you now perceive what you needed to say and do. As you do these worksheets know that it is normal to feel regret and to have unfinished business and unsaid conversations. It is also normal for recovering people who have lived in obsession and escape to have much of their pain unexpressed. Our job is to get as much of it done as possible. The spirit of the Serenity Prayer applies here. There is much we can do something about, and much we cannot. The importance is knowing and accepting the difference. And allowing and expressing the appropriate feelings that flow from realizing how much we have lost.

Sorrow: The Unsaid

List below the conversations in which you recognize you have not said what you wanted (use an additional sheet if necessary):

Person	Unsaid
Example: Mother	How much I appreciated her willingness to listen even when it was painful for her to hear.
1.	
2.	
3.	
4.	
5.	
6.	
7.	
8.	
9.	
10.	
11.	
12.	
13.	
14.	
15.	

Exercise 8.3

Sorrow: The Unfinished

List below those tasks or steps you now recognize as something you wanted to do in response to your sorrow (use an additional sheet if necessary).

Task or Step Description
Example A: I said I would invite my siblings to distribute Uncle John's ashes, but have not.
Example B: I wanted to visit my Aunt before she dies but have not.
1.
2.
3.
4.
5.
6.
7.
8.
9.
10.
11.
12.
13.
14.
15.

Exercise 8.4

Owning Sadness and Responsibility

By completing our focus worksheets the bulk of our work is done. One of the easiest ways to express the unsaid is to write a letter to individuals based on your unsaid list. You then could read the letter in your group or to your therapist or go to a gravesite or some place of significance in your history with that person. Read your letter there. The importance is that you publicly own your sadness. For that we need witnesses and coaches to help us say adequately what is on our list to be finished. Again the feelings will not go away but they can be transformed. We will have done all that we can.

Often, when words fail us we use symbols. We can express our pain in creative acts, symbols, and metaphors. We can write music and poetry. We can incorporate a symbol into what we wear or create something as a statement to our experience. For example, we built a wall with all the names of those lost in Vietnam. Individuals create symbols of their loss to remind them and keep the important explicit. In other words, do something to take your pain out of the realm of your autopilot. Not all of us can write a symphony or run a marathon as a statement of our loss, yet each of us can do something.

When it comes to creative acts, expressing feelings and doing something become blurred. Creating something might be all that we can do about a past situation. However, most of us realize that there are things that we can still do to make it right. In abuse situations, for example, if there was a failure of nurturing, we could do something extraordinary to nurture ourselves. If we were robbed of an education, we can return to school. If we were battered as children, we might volunteer or give money to agencies that help abused children. If we lost a lot to addiction, we can sponsor others seeking help or get involved in fellowship service.

With understanding our pain comes responsibility. Suffering is what calls us to become better people. The undone list naturally leads us to actions we know we must now take. We know too much to leave things as they are. Our internal guidance systems are fundamentally altered. Self-pity, bitterness, and repression kept us in our old compulsive ways. Acknowledging our pain brings relief but also new responsibilities. As C.S. Lewis put it years ago when his beloved wife died six months into their marriage, "Pain is what God gave us to grow up."

Make concrete your resolve to clean up the unresolved in your life. On the next page, list ten of the most important action steps you can take to register, recognize, or resolve sorrows in your life. Like Daedelus, ask yourself, How can suffering launch your creativity and your commitment to live in the zone?

The Core Realities of Recovery

Immersion in our feelings transforms us. It gives us a readiness to do the deeper work to reengineer our lives. Pain has provided new awareness, skills, and principles by which to do that work. Recovering people use the term *willingness* which basically means that we have accepted

Ten Action Steps to Utilize My Grief

Record below ten action steps that will help you access your feelings, sorrow, or associated feelings. These should be actions that will also bring creativity, resolution, or purpose to your life. Set a date to complete these ten action steps.

Action Step No: 1

Date Completed:_____

Action Step No: 2

Date Completed:_____

Action Step No: 3

Date Completed:_____

Action Step No: 4

Date Completed:_____

Action Step No: 5

Date Completed:_____

Action Step No: 6

Date Completed:_____

Action Step No: 7

Date Completed:_____

Action Step No: 8

Date Completed:_____

Action Step No: 9

Date Completed:_____

Action Step No: 10

Date Completed:_____

Exercise 8.5

that bargains with chaos did not work and that we were no longer willing to trade off our souls and future. So "we became willing" to do the work. We saw that "half measures" would gain us nothing. We understood that mere details would require our deep attention and focus. We saw that people with successful recoveries would have peace, purpose, and joy.

Most importantly, there appeared in each of them a deep resolve never to return to the old patterns. Even in this, there is grief over the loss of the addictions. The sweet voice of escape was like an old reliable friend who always did what was promised. Euphoric recall brings to mind some of the best times, the best drinks, and the best escapades. Yet, the surrender of recovery means that one remembers that the best dramas relied on fear and danger, lies and deception. The best times cost us our integrity and our relationships. So the pain, when felt deeply, creates commitment to the sobriety imperative of giving up the old life. We accept core realities that can bring peace, creativity, and a call to a higher destiny. The following core realities have been the essential themes of learning from the ordeal:

Challenge. From the beginning when we accepted that we had to make choices, we learned we could not duck challenge. In fact, early in the book we discovered that the brain craves challenge and is built to solve problems. It is the refining process that helps us to become better people. Challenge summons forth the courage we need to face the inevitable difficulties. We also learn that, in order to respond to the call, we must know what matters. We must avoid the seduction of drama and shortcuts.

Legitimate Suffering. In order to know what matters and keep our focus on the important, we have to rely on our emotional intelligence. Carl Jung used the term "legitimate suffering." In every life, there will be pain. Jung further taught that unacknowledged pain was a sure path to obsession. Knowing the difference between drama and loss is key to emotional intelligence and is the way we actualize the Serenity Prayer. We ask for wisdom to know the difference between that which we can change and that which we cannot change. We must acknowledge real sorrow and make it explicit so it does not affect our resolve. Yet, we no longer invest in needless suffering, we pick our battles, and we learn from our challenges.

Zone of Excellence. The ability to know what matters helps us stay in that cluster of abilities and purposes in which we thrive. No sobriety can survive without the active pursuit of that "sweet spot" where our brains are challenged in ways that are synchronous with our unique selves. Our job now is to have clarity about those challenges, and our emotional intelligence will help us avoid going back to the old ways. That is what is so important about the phrase, "How it was then and how it is now." In Chapter 2 we contrasted the difference between Alan Alda's joy at performing at his peak as an actor and Bill W's being an actor to cover up his behavior. One was congruent and the other was compartmentalized. For all of us, the goal now is to experience all the ways to be most truly oneself.

Taking Responsibility. In every chapter, the bottom line has been coming to your own assistance. Blaming others and living in "grievance" or grief always adds to the rationales for bargaining with chaos. Taking responsibility is the direct path that the Serenity Prayer describes. Mental health starts with a firm grip on the obvious and deepens when we own our mistakes and appreciate our limitations.

Currency. The essential way to accept responsibility for self resides in the recovery concept of "getting current." Getting current means that you have done all you can to make things right with self and others. The spirit of this existential reality appears throughout all Twelve Step literature. When wrong, promptly "admitting it" is about keeping current. Developing a support network who knows what is happening to you at all times is keeping current. Steps Four through Nine are about repairing relationships and keeping them in repair. The Serenity Prayer is the bottom line about taking action in all things you can take action on. From a mental health perspective this makes so much sense. Imagine your brain is like a computer. When you load so many applications sooner or later the machine will slow down and even crash. Similarly, your brain, when current, extends its "bandwidth" so you can be more conscious in your life.

In effect there is a logic to these core realities: **There will always be challenges, and suffering will concurrently result. Humans can thrive in this environment, if they focus on being their best and on what matters to them. Since life is difficult, the bottom lines of mental health are to take responsibility and to get current.** With these realities in mind, it is now time to reengineer your life.

The problem, now that we understand these core realities, is to implement our understandings into life. This implementation requires a new arrangement within yourself, a contract that changes everything.

Chapter 9 **Restructuring the Relationship with Self**

My wife is a pragmatic woman. She had noticed that the silverware drawer was quite some distance from the dishwasher. By swapping it with the pot holder/towel drawer, we could unload the silverware right from the dishwasher into the drawer without taking a step. Plus pot holders were now close to the stove and much more convenient. I thought the move was brilliant, and I marveled at how I had not noticed that we were making extra work for ourselves. Knowing this, however, did not stop me the next morning from going to the old drawer looking for the spoons. I would ask myself, "Who moved the spoons?" Then I remembered that Suzie had this idea, that I had thought it was a great one, and that they were now by the dishwasher. Also, I was somehow angry about the change, thinking she was always "moving stuff."

For the two years that we remained in that house, I still sometimes went to the old drawer and asked who moved the spoons. Note that it is a decision I participated in and agreed was a great idea. I knew where the spoons were. There was no secret kitchen cabal to drive me crazy. Yet why, first thing in the morning, would I head for the wrong drawer? Years of routinely going to that drawer were wired into my neural circuitry. All of our brains rewire to do things automatically in order to free up our focus for things that need our attention. The brain always works for unconscious competence. In learning a language, fluency occurs when we no longer have to worry about vocabulary, structure, or pronunciation. For language to work best, it becomes automatic. We simply do it. Similarly, we can drive or ride a bike. As we have noted, the automaticity of the brain means we do not think about almost three billion decisions a second.

We all have a spoon drawer story. Yet the most important feature of the story is this: knowing something is better does not automatically change the behavior. Change requires focus and attention, as well as great effort. Great achievement, whether as an athlete, an actor, or a surgeon, takes thousands of hours (usually the threshold is about ten thousand hours) to build the integrated neural circuitry of success. To absorb and become competent in a language takes thousands of hours. To become a pilot or even a safe driver of a car means hours of experience. Our lives build on accumulated decisions which become systematically streamlined so we can go on to other challenges. In reality, our brains consist of a series of "add-ons" to which we may have not given much thought.

When the add-ons become an addiction (the ultimate in reward center rewiring), we now have a brain disease. Like any organ that malfunctions (loss of reality), it is a medical problem. It can happen to anyone and does. An interesting exercise is to add up all the alcoholics, drug addicts, compulsive eaters, sex addicts, compulsive debtors, and their codependent loved ones; you have involved a large part of contemporary culture in the United States and other developed countries.

So, who moved the spoons? You did. Recovery becomes like a new language we have to master, and addiction is neural wiring we have to understand and "rework." Simply recognizing, "life would be better if we made deep changes," will not do it. Our lives are a tapestry of countless decisions which have an accumulated force of their own.

You are at a critical juncture. Early recovery has so much pain attached to it that people are motivated to deal with what is in front of them. After the white water of the initial chaos, there is usually a great deal of awareness and most of us have to make changes. Yet the accumulated power of old decisions starts to reassert itself. Thoughts like these occur:

- If I just stop the visible behaviors, that will take the pressure off.
- If I stopped drinking, I could at least have sex, food or (fill in the blank) _____.
- Therapy and meetings take up so much time. Plus, I do regular meditation, so I don't have a life.
- I have had to do all the work, and yet my family has not changed—so why bother?
- Everything in recovery has started with me. I am tired of being the person who initiates, carries the ball, and does the work.
- I met a man (woman) who seems to be really healthy; it is time to reset my life (the relationship version of the geographic cure).
- The financial costs are too high—treatment, therapy, and lost time. (It is interesting how people in their delusion can afford their addictions but not their treatment.)
- I just need some down time.
- I just need some rewards.
- It is better than it used to be.

All types of rationales emerge. The old bargains reassert themselves. As denial creeps in, some simply settle for improvement and others relapse. The real question which is seldom asked is: Do you want to be well enough to get by or do you want to be at your best? Now is when "good enough" can seem like a good answer. Yet, when the early pioneers characterized the illness as "cunning and baffling," it came out of their experience that "good enough" only lasted so long. Once the illness is there, it will reassert the old process.

Those who experience the dark night of the soul know the truth that "half measures" avail nothing. They now know too much. Yet how to take all this awareness and redesign your life seems overwhelming even if the motivation is there. This chapter is designed to help springboard you forward into that process. To start wc must first resurrect how the original bargains with chaos were made. That understanding will lay a foundation for the next phase of your Recovery Zone work.

Bargains with Chaos

Bargains with chaos always start with an impulse or choice. And always the goal has good in it. At the core of these choices is a payoff or reward (the good part). These rewards are tracked by your brain. It becomes a bargain with chaos when there is a tradeoff in which there is a price being paid for the impulse. But the initial choice is about somehow feeling better or happier. It is extremely important to note that the original choices were made in your own interest.

Born in denial and purpose, these bargains have a logic to them. "I can stop if I want to." This acting on impulse is only temporary or not serious or intolerable. So when chaos occurs, the effort is to preserve the bargain and contain the chaos. But what starts in denial must move to delusion, which is a loss of contact with reality. Wishful thinking morphs into the reliance on your ability to clean up the messes—or chaos—rather than admit the insanity of a pattern of bad choices. What started as a choice now has a force of its own. The original sense of choice to pursue a certain kind of rewarding activity becomes a prison, and we no longer have a choice. The dark side of impulsivity is compulsivity. We now have a mental health problem. The brain reworked your neural circuitry (to be helpful) in a powerful way. The reward centers have allied with delusion, family enablers, and obsession to run the show. Until the addict and codependent admit to the bargains, no change occurs. Just chaos.

In courtship, such bargains are made when obvious problems are overlooked because of the thrill of romance and the power of the moment. The tradeoff is planning to "fix" them later rather than interfere with the ecstasy of the powerful feelings of "destiny." Consider the early use of cocaine as a way to perform work quickly and with greater precision. The plan is always to cut down or stop later when the crisis subsides. Yet another crisis moves in and chaos assumes command. Similarly, many use food as a comfort or reward in stressful times, yet, as we know, we carry our Stressmaker within. Addiction is like a mafia character who relentlessly collects exorbitant interest fees which escalated with each extension of the deal. For addicts and codependents, chaos is the enforcer which adds to the future burden.

An alcoholic can mortgage her soul because under the influence she could be what she wanted to be—sexy, at ease, funny, confident, and competent. At the time she wanted to be at her best, and the results were temporarily worth it. She bargained for the moment and put off the challenge of being at her best under her own power (which of course involved pain and anxiety). Instead of facing chaos on her own terms, she traded. Instead of leaning into the challenge, she mortgaged her soul. With chaos, the accumulated challenges become overwhelming.

The codependent overlooking the obvious to pursue closeness and intimacy is no different than the cocaine or food addict. Intimacy, success, coping, and self-expression are most worthy goals and signify the core desire to be at your best. Successful recovery hinges on recognizing your original desire to be at your best. This core recognition becomes a critical context to understanding how chaos got its leverage on you. It provides clarity on how to get the original you back.

So let us examine this process with more depth. Consider a fourteen-year-old learning to smoke. We say learning because initially cigarettes do not taste good. Yet in a group it can be a sign of acceptance and looking cool. Nicotine, once in the brain, does amazing things. It reduces anxiety and is what neuroscientists call "anziolitic" (numbing your emotions). Also, nicotine can stay in the brain of an adolescent for up to thirty days. The effect continues and the kid feels on top of things. Nicotine also stimulates the brain to be able to multi-task, and it enhances the ability to remember things. When the nicotine starts to wear off in three weeks, the kid has another cigarette. Addiction is far from the adolescent's mind. After all, his last cigarette was weeks ago. What seems innocent is not. Here are the bargains made:

- Smokers can dispatch uncomfortable feelings to the recycle bin so they are not distracting. However, having got this far in the Recovery Zone you already know it is a recycle bin which means the feelings will be back.
- Smoking will ramp up the ability to remember and handle multiple tasks under the influence. However, nicotine steadily erodes memory and multitasking abilities. What smoking gives in the moment is taken away in the future. In fact, studies of executives of equal ability have shown that smokers are less effective in remembering and coping with multiple tasks.
- Smokers pay dearly for the temporary stimulation it provides, because smoking has been proven to contribute to a host of chronic, serious illnesses.

Chaos, the enforcer, compounds the life costs because addicts cannot stop. Progressively, they lose contact with reality. Note that addiction always compounds the costs. The sex addict who sought sexual stimulation and exploration ends where having "normal" sex does not work. The compulsive debtor who makes a sound decision about a mortgage initially enhances the quality of his life, but when second mortgages and credit cards pile up, he may face decades of payments or insolvency. Both the sex addict and the debtor now obsess about their behavior and its costs. The obsession and the costs add to the rewiring process.

There is a certain logic to it all. **Figure 9.1** summarizes the logic. Addiction is really an accumulation of decisions, impulses, and choices that become hard wired. The brain creates an "operating system" similar in function to what happens in a computer. This system consists of rules that govern choices and run in the background. The user is mostly unaware of it. The system evolves with various add-ons tucked in. No one starts off with the goal of becoming addicted. In fact, many say that they promised themselves it would not happen to them. However, this is no longer about who moved the spoons. Rather, addiction affects the person's ability to function and have consistent contact with reality.

By doing the anatomy of the addiction/codependency process and following the logic of how the bargains got made, we learn important insights about how the brain works. We also learn how we can change it. To start, we need to go back to how these bargains started, which often takes us back to our adolescence or earlier.

We need to think about the original choices. When recovering people complete a First Step, implicit is the surrender to addiction reality. A bad bargain was made. Lists of powerlessness demonstrate that addicts no longer choose consistently in their best interests. Addiction and codependency were in control. Our unmanageability was proven in our inability to stop the bargain. Doing these lists is critical to admitting the bargain was a bad one.

A critical aspect of that Step is to note what your original desires were when you made the early choices. Usually it was to experience an improved life or to cope with challenge or to be at your best in some way. In other words, that original impulse was not bad. In fact, those impulses can tell you a lot about the original true self. In that sense it is part of being able to disinter the dream. The following Addiction Bargain Worksheet will help you with perspective on your early choices. The worksheet asks that you label a specific addiction and list your original desires, needs, wants, or dreams that went into your first choices. The worksheet then helps you identify the early tradeoffs which were rewired with the potent reward systems of the brain. So you create a synopsis of how addiction's extortion works. After completing the scenario, the worksheet asks you to reexamine the original motivation. Most people find validation in the original choices. The original impulses, in fact, can tell you much about the original self and even about the zone in which you are at your best.

The Logic of a Bargain with Chaos

1 Choice

The bargain starts with a choice to be better, happier, more tolerable, or more rewarding. Often times this initial choice simply is an impulse or maybe even an experiment.

2 Tradeoff

Almost always, there is a shortcut or temporary reward which appears to have little or no immediate impact. Indulging the impulse is worth whatever consequence might occur. The bargain is, "If I do this now, I will deal with problems later."

3 Denial

Usually important realities are overlooked, dismissed, or postponed. Belief one can control the impulse leads to secretive or hidden behavior. "No one knows" erodes transparency and integrity issues so bargains can be made.

4 Impulsivity

Our brain circuitry becomes altered as we choose behaviors that make us feel good. The behavior becomes repetitive or habitual.

5 Compulsivity

The brain rewires itself so our behavior is no longer an option and requires sustained, more, or riskier behavior to meet the created need. The brain adjusts to maintain a level of stimulation, reward, or stress (what is termed a set point). Compulsivity is the dark side of impulsivity which uses obsession as a catalyst.

6 Obsession

Preoccupation becomes a principal factor in maintaining the brain circuitry at the level required. Obsession intensifies delusion and thought errors which makes costs and consequences tolerable. The addiction threshold is passed.

7 Costs

Losses compound in unexpected ways, and the only solution is to do more of the behavior. The bargain is embedded in the neural circuitry of the brain's reward systems. The resulting behavior becomes like a bad loan with interest so high that the only way out is to borrow more which preserves, but magnifies the initial tradeoff.

Figure 9.1

Addiction Bargain Worksheet

Addiction Type _____

Beginning Choices:
List what you wanted, needed, desired, or dreamed

1.
2.
3.
4.
5.
6.
7.
8.
9.
10.

Validation:
Circle numbers of choices which had valid, good reasons

Early Tradeoffs:
List what you risked, overlooked, or ignored

Reclamation of Self:
What do your early choices reveal about the original self?

1.
2.
3.
4.
5.

Contribution to the Zone:
What of your original self would contribute to you being at your best?

1.
2.
3.
4.
5.

Ultimate Bargain:
What of yourself did you give up?

Costs to You End

© Copyright P.J. Carnes, 2009

Exercise 9.1

Restructuring the Relationship with Self

The question remains about how to undo the bargain. The answer is you need to create a new one. As in moving the spoon drawer, you can improve how things work by making a new arrangement. This arrangement takes some concentration, however, to make it part of your brain's circuitry, and in this case, it requires a new agreement with yourself. We term this *restructuring the relationship with self*. From the very beginning of this book we have used the phrase *coming to your own assistance*. We have worked to help you knit together the scattered parts of yourself into a more coherent sense of self that you could trust.

In the original research, we found that when people sorted through their painful feelings, a deep resolve emerged to make things different. All the assumptions that have been incorporated into your decision-making processes are now examined. These assumptions are about men, women, family, sex, money, work, relationships—all aspects of being human are questioned. The most important of these is the relationship with yourself. A new agreement or covenant has to emerge that can be honored. In the hero's journey, the metals of the self are reblended and a new person emerges. The hero reflects and integrates his or her experience. In therapy, we call this a "paradigm shift" because the patient now views the world differently. See **Figure 9.2** to picture where this fits in the recovery process.

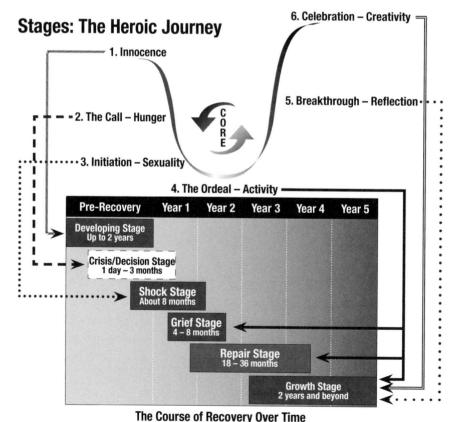

The Course of Recovery Over Time

Figure 9.2

Core to this change is the covenant with yourself. You decide that from here on out you will make decisions in a different way and you keep the agreement. In effect, recovery means moving from unconscious bargains with chaos to a new covenant with self. The logic of the process remains (the brain has not changed its desire to make things better for you). Only now, as opposed to add-ons and inherited rules, you start moving your internal spoon drawers to make things work better. Like my spoon drawer story, there will be lapses in which you go through some of the old motions but then you remember you were part of the decision-making team. The flow of the logic is the same, but now you are conscious of how choices become integrated into your life:

- **Choice.** Choices are made with an intention based on what your call and life purposes are. You have a compass built on the emerging congruency with your own spirit and feelings as well as the call of the vision you have for your life. The original choices that brought you to your addiction become part of that clarity.

- **Challenge.** Fundamental to mental health is the premise that there will always be challenge. To stay healthy means the tradeoffs of the "easier, softer" way are replaced with motivation and commitment. Resilience and a deep desire to be in the Recovery Zone will bring you joy and rewards.

- **Reality.** M. Scott Peck in *The Road Less Traveled* observed that in an examined life, "mental health is a dedication to reality at all costs." Central to that realism is the acceptance of your own personal limits. The Greeks saw hubris or "pride," as the tragic flaw of heroes and heroines who saw themselves above the rules. Seeing yourself as an "exception" leads to tradeoff rationales and unsustainable bargains. Ernest Becker in *The Denial of Death* made a similar observation that the insight of the Greeks is core to the origin of all mental health and addiction issues: the acceptance of limits of which the ultimate limit is death.[13]

- **Intentionality.** Understanding that the brain will streamline our choices into automatic behaviors means selecting positive behaviors, goals, and living premises. Life will never be perfect, but as Csikszentmihalyi observes, those who take on the lifelong challenge of making their lives better do have a much happier life.

- **Mindfulness.** Cultivating a sense of mindfulness helps create that inner observer that tracks the traffic of the brain, expands options, keeps the inner compass intact, and helps to still the mind.

- **Focus.** Focus is the daily process of implementing changes, goals, and rewards based on the clarity of what is important. Focus serves to implement the self and builds trust with the self by honoring agreements.

- **Benefits.** Researchers describe how implementation of these strategies raise the brain's capacity for "transpirational functioning," which means that the brain functions so much better that it actually evolves to a new level. Joy as well as other feelings are easily accessed, and personal congruency is maintained. New levels of spiritual consciousness are achieved.

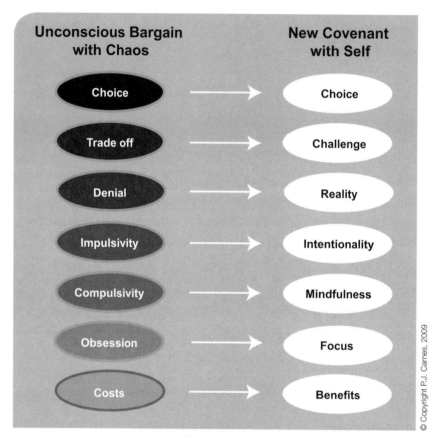

Figure 9.3

Author Henri Nouwen describes this shift in the relationship with self as literally a conversion from "loneliness to solitude." Most of us recognize that in the pre-recovery days, being alone was intolerable. Yet, to hear your true voice requires the capacity to sit with yourself, to go beyond tolerating your feelings to discernment, and to develop a consistent vision for your life. Those who achieve much report the ability to enjoy being in their own presence. Yet many of us filled our lives with distractions, only felt okay when engaged with others, and had to keep busy. A week, a day, or an evening alone could be unbearable. Yet, when you have a solid relationship with yourself, such times are treasured. Here is how Nouwen describes this transition:

> Loneliness is painful; solitude is peaceful. Loneliness makes us cling to others in desperation; solitude allows us to respect others in their uniqueness and create community.

Nouwen says the relationship with self is built on trust. When the self learns that it is trustworthy, a major shift occurs. In the past, commitments and promises to self may have been elastic or easily abandoned. This half commitment can erode motivation, cripple a vision for one's life, and lead to despair. Consistently coming to your own assistance builds a life momentum. If you become available to yourself, you become much more available to others. As you become available to others, you become more available to a Higher Power. Tapping into the larger energies of the universe releases more of who you are. So there is a cycle of trust that is self-reinforcing which sustains new internal arrangements.

In any relationship, making your agreements explicit is clarifying and, in fact, spiritual. Wedding vows are an example of written promises, with witnesses who have special meaning. In having a relationship with self we are not talking about the narcissist's illusion. Rather, it is important to have an agreement and accountability with the self—with witnesses and meaningful rituals.

Making a workable agreement with yourself involves five core strategies. Embedded in each are principles which will make the agreement with yourself concrete. These will become building blocks to a new operating system which is conscious, which is designed for change and growth, and which accepts imperfection.

Core Strategy One: Build Resilience

Aristotle observed that without courage, no other virtue was possible. We have noted how being willing to face problems is one of life's great tasks. Failures of courage are how the tradeoffs get made in addiction, because addictive intensity takes the place of courage. It is like Styrofoam in that it takes up space, can hold some things, and has certain insulating qualities. At best it is a temporary solution and definitely not for white water rapids situations. Life, after all, simply is filled with white water rapids. More than that, your brain is built to thrive in challenge. Therefore we cannot duck challenges. The only solution is to build resilience for the inevitable and necessary challenges.

Resilience is core to recovery. The key principle is learning to cope with difficulties, which teaches us important lessons. Our mistakes, our disasters, and our challenges expand our conscious awareness. When challenges emerge, we know that we have faced similar issues in the past. Harry Potter is a story of repeated challenge. In each segment of the story he went back to earlier times when he faced difficulty. Part of his ability to keep his focus and courage was reminding himself he had faced unfathomable challenges and grew from the experience.[14] The essence of resilience is learning from the challenges. Your operating agreement with yourself needs to reflect your learning from your ordeal. The Lifelong Learning Inventory will help you to collect your basic learnings so you can integrate resilience into your new covenant.

Lifelong Learning Inventory – Part 1

The following worksheet is designed to help you summarize the greatest lessons you have learned. These lessons are critical to be integrated into your new covenant. Start by listing those moments that at the time appeared to be your greatest disabilities. Then list the positive outcomes these defining moments had in your life. Finally, write up the "lessons learned" as if they were rules to live by. For example, if you learned how perseverance was the factor in making things work out, you would write, "Perseverance is key." Or, if disaster was an opportunity, you would write, "Look for the opportunity when it seems all is lost."

Worst Disasters	Positive Outcomes	Lessons Learned
1.		
2.		
3.		
4.		
5.		
6.		
7.		
8.		
9.		
10.		

Exercise 9.2A

Lifelong Learning Inventory – Part 2

When disasters occur, one of the greatest challenges is to "let go." Reflect on the disasters you have listed and specify what was the most difficult to let go of:

1. _____
2. _____
3. _____
4. _____
5. _____
6. _____
7. _____
8. _____
9. _____
10. _____

Is there any commonality in this list? If so, record below what most likely you will have trouble letting go of in the future:

1. _____
2. _____
3. _____
4. _____
5. _____

Very Critical: List below the lessons most important for you to integrate into your life. You can have as few or as many as you wish:

1. _____
2. _____
3. _____
4. _____
5. _____
6. _____
7. _____
8. _____

Exercise 9.2B

Core Strategy Two: Utilize Feelings

Our emotional intelligence is critical for knowing if we are in synch with ourselves. Identifying our feelings and knowing how they inform us help us to be congruent. To make a new covenant with the self is to acknowledge the "affective work" you have done so far. The great irony is that you live in a culture which not does not acknowledge addiction, it does not acknowledge the role of feelings. The word "affect" actually comes from Baruch Spinoza, the seventeenth century mathematician and philosopher. While he was widely recognized for his achievements in various branches of science, many did not realize the significance of his speculations on the role of feelings as being a "way of knowing."[15] Even today we are reluctant to teach about emotional intelligence. The Twelve Step process, however, makes feelings an integral part of the curriculum of recovery. Even the early pioneers recognized the potency of accessing feelings. Today we know that toxic feelings perpetuate the addictive process and activate the powerful reward centers which interfere with normal brain function.

No amount of therapy or treatment will erase the legacy of pain. Each of us will continue to have issues that will come up. We can become expert at handling them so they do not take us down toxic paths. Each of us, however, will have issues that will remain on the table. By now each of us knows most of them. Part of an operating agreement is to identify these issues as old visitors who may show up again. Part of building trust with self is our ability not to be seduced by the old grievances and affective delusions. Our family and support network should have them on the radar as well, which is another good reason to make them explicit. The next exercise, "Issues Always on the Table," will assist you in gathering, naming, and recording these visitors.

Issues Always on the Table

No amount of therapy will erase all of our issues. However, we will recognize them when they come up because there will be incongruency or the potential of it, and your feelings will tell you.

Issues Always on the Table	Potential Incongruencies	Feelings Present

For your operating agreement to be effective, record what particular areas are important for you in which to remain congruent. Write them as decision rules, "I will spend time only ..." or, "I will not jeopardize ..." Basically there are guidelines to your choice making which will help you keep congruency in focus:

1. _____

2. _____

3. _____

4. _____

5. _____

Exercise 9.3

Core Strategy Three: Internal Observer

In the story of Daedelus and his son Icarus, Icarus ignored his father's warning that flying too close to the sun would melt the wax on their wings. In the original story, Daedelus also warned Icarus that flying too low would water log his feathers. The same is true of our challenge. As Csikszentmihalyi pointed out too much challenge is as much a disaster as not enough challenge. There is an area in between which is functional for us. We learn from our heroes and heroines that when we are *called* to extraordinary effort, there is always the risk of losing our dreams (cowardice). There is also the danger of self-destruction and recklessness. We who have heard the call of recovery wrestle with both.

Staying in the window of functional and courageous (motivated) behavior can only happen if there is a part of our brain that monitors our progress. Throughout this book we have referred to this aspect of self as the "inner observer." It is a cultivated activity of the brain to track how the system is working and to reflect on the brain's function. Scientists who have researched "wisdom" regard this function as the epitome of resilience. Trauma researchers note the critical role of having a part of ourselves detached sufficiently so we don't over-react. Neuroscience researchers have long documented the importance of mindfulness to mental health. Every religious tradition has spoken to the importance of "quieting the mind." From a recovery perspective the strategy of observing the self as a daily process was profoundly recognized when Hazelden published the *Twenty-Four Hours a Day* book. Today a wealth of resources builds on that tradition.

Having the observer on board means you also must have the parameters of what your zone is. There are four central factors to consider. The essence of zone behavior stems from:

- Those activities that make you very happy
- Those activities that give you meaning
- Those activities that give you the sense of being most truly yourself
- Those activities that you are good at or have the ability to become good at

Exercise 9.4 is a graphic representation of the overlap of these four areas as consisting of your core zone of recovery. On this worksheet, identify the five best activities in each category (for example, the five activities in which you feel most like yourself or the five most meaning-filled activities).

The Core Zone

Abilities

1. _____
2. _____
3. _____
4. _____
5. _____

Original Self

1. _____
2. _____
3. _____
4. _____
5. _____

1. _____
2. _____
3. _____
4. _____
5. _____

Happiness

1. _____
2. _____
3. _____
4. _____
5. _____

Meaning

1. _____
2. _____
3. _____
4. _____
5. _____

Exercise 9.4

Like Daedelus, you need to specify where you should not be. Start with the five most important aspects of your sobriety imperative out of Chapter 3. These are specifics which put your recovery in jeopardy. Then take from your list of "Issues Always on the Table" the five items that are most likely to derail you. Then it is simple to list the things you simply dread—activities you are not good at, have no desire to become accomplished at, and avoid (and probably always will). Finally, be honest with yourself about five limitations you do have. They can be physical, emotional, or behavioral. These also are not likely to change. Together, the overlapping categories can regenerate the Black Hole of addictive use.

Exercise 9.5 shows in concept how the Core Zone dimensions and the Black Hole activities can be summarized. Do the worksheet on page 253 where you can think through the core issues that put you at risk. Obviously you could make much more elaborate lists. The effort here is to synthesize them into a succinct set of guidelines to be incorporated into your written new covenant.

The Black Hole

Sobriety Imperative

1.
2.
3.
4.
5.

Limitations

1.
2.
3.
4.
5.

1.
2.
3.
4.
5.

Issues Always On Table

1.
2.
3.
4.
5.

Dreaded Activities

1.
2.
3.
4.
5.

Exercise 9.5

Core Strategy Four: Mission

Authors Joseph Campbell and Bill Moyers observe that the difference between a celebrity and a hero is "that one lives only for self while the other acts to redeem society." None of the above makes sense without purpose. There is little reason to have resilience, or be congruent, or be at your best unless it serves others. Focus is impossible to develop without a sense of purpose. Psychologists make the distinction between being successful versus achievement oriented. Those who are happy, who have the determination to develop competence, and who have peace are those whose efforts draw strength from their meaning.

Throughout this book we have used Viktor Frankl's phrase of transforming suffering into meaning, which is in essence the heroic journey. The hallmark of successful recovery is service within the Twelve Step fellowship. In **Exercise 9.6** we identify the various activities you have labored through in order to provide perspective on that mission. As you see you have accomplished much of that work already. As you read the chapters you were encouraged to enter the various versions of mission statements that emerged. In previous pages you have written down your work, so in some ways you knew this was coming.

Developing the statement is critical to your new covenant. Writing and rewriting that statement will be a clarifying exercise. Moreover, it becomes the touchstone for your focus in life. Most addicts lost their dreams to obsession. To harness the brain's power to make things happen requires focus. For focus you have to know your mission. But you will not become your true and best self if your efforts do not reside in a well-articulated purpose.

So complete the Mission Consolidation worksheet. Please be aware that it does not have to be perfect. More opportunities to work with issues around meaning and focus will come. Take it as far as you can now.

Mission Consolidation

In this book, you have worked to define your mission. Review the various ways you have looked at purpose in your life, using the exercises from the pages listed. Summarize each in the spaces provided. Then synthesize all of the categories into a concise statement of two to three sentences about your purpose in life.

Recovery Zone Optimums p. 44	1	Anger & Mission p. 133	2	Trauma Egg p. 149	3
Hero Map: Courage p. 163	4	Your Place in Family p. 177	5	Mission Reclamation p. 207-210	6

Exercise 9.6

Core Strategy Five: Intimacy

Malcolm Gladwell's book, *Outliers*, discusses the factors most important to successful achievement. At the top of the list was attachment. In fact, he makes the case that participating and belonging to a loving community is perhaps the strongest factor in longevity that medicine can measure. Further he argues that people of great achievement seemed to always have people in their lives who were advocates as well as accountability partners.

Addiction in many ways can be defined as an intimacy or attachment disorder. Failure to bond seems to be a central factor in the genesis of addictive behavior. Addicts and codependents understand that resistance to help from others led to further self-deception. Throughout the ordeal we used the phrase that it was important to "live in consultation." We are smarter and more effective together than separately. In many exercises you were encouraged to share with your therapists, sponsors, and groups. Recovery and the Twelve Step process is essentially a bonding experience built around the telling of stories. Neuroscience tells us that the most critical catalyst to brain change is relationship growth, and that the most strategic way to encourage synaptic growth is story telling.

In your experience so far you have developed relationships in which you have been helped. Now is the time to harness some of that relational power for you to get to the next level. For some people, these are individuals who are part of a regular group or program. Others have emerged just out of therapy, Twelve Step work, or friendship. In order to complete this process and prepare for the next process, we invite you to convene them together. Think of them as your own personal board of directors. They can be the same group you selected for this role in considering your Fourth and Fifth Steps, on page 110.

By bringing them together, you will create a crucible in which to examine your covenant work and your decision table. Not only does each have a perspective, but they can pool their knowledge of you. Yes, you will be more vulnerable, but those who have done this work agree, you will get so much more by asking them to gather on your behalf. What follows, in **Exercise 9.7** is a Board Selection Process to help you think through whom you want.

Board Solution Process

Throughout this book, you have been asked to share your work with key people who know you well. A helpful process is to form them as a group or "board" to discuss major decisions in your life. Our purpose is to assemble them for an in depth discussion of your decision table as it now becomes revised (in the next section). Who are the people who have proven themselves good consultants to you? List them below and what you value most about them. Try to put eight people on your list (some may not have time to meet with you).

Key Consultants	Helpful Qualities
1.	
2.	
3.	
4.	
5.	
6.	
7.	
8.	

Exercise 9.7

Sometimes a group just decides to do this as part of the group work. Or your therapist may ask that you do it as part of your therapy. Always remember you have the option of asking people to meet on your behalf to review the work you have done. In fact, a number of fellowships actually structure groups in that fashion.[16] To live in consultation, it will serve you well to be more explicit.

Next, you will find instructions for your operating agreement in which you will write a letter of agreement with yourself (your new covenant). When you complete that task, it will be time to revise your decision table. By this time your perspective will have changed so that revisions will be timely. In effect, you will be able to use the decision table tool all the time as a way to think about your life. This decision table, however, will have the benefit of your new covenant. Plus, we have added two new scales to evaluate the decisions on your table. Your therapist may assign different versions, either in print or online formats.

Having completed both the covenant work and the decision table, convene your board. Provide them with copies of your work so they can discuss it with you. Record their reactions so you can make revisions. **Figure 9.4** below summarizes the core strategies and core principles for this process.

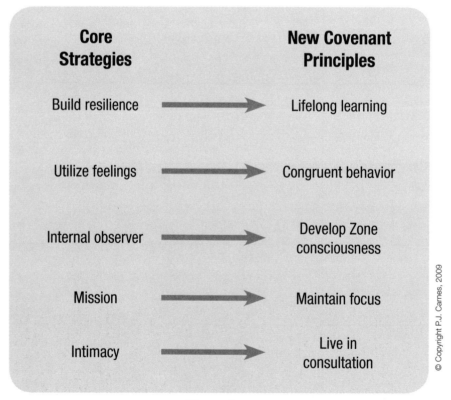

Figure 9.4

Key Concepts of Recovery Zone

Five Life Tasks	Bargains with Chaos	Core Decision Essentials	Core Barriers	Core Abilities	Core Paths	Core Realities	Core Strategies	New Covenant Principles
Courage	Living with unresolved	Must decide	Addictive intensity	To create safely	Boundaries	Challenge	Build resilience	Lifelong learning
Pain	Affect intolerance	Unknown outcomes	Toxic feelings	To focus on purpose	Commitment	Legitimate suffering	Utilize feelings	Congruent behavior
Call	Loss of dreams	Must commit	Destructive narratives	To risk	Vision	Zone of Excellence	Internal observer	Develop Zone consciousnes
Self	Traded off future	Come to own assistance	Entitlement	To trust oneself	Self-integration	Take responsibility	Mission	Maintain focus
Relationships	Resistence to help	Accept help from others	Self-deception	To have witnesses	Honesty	Currency	Intimacy	Live in consultation

Figure 9.5

The New Covenant

In relapse prevention, a successful device is to write a letter to yourself to read when you feel like a slip is possible. The letter is written when you are "sane" and sober as an appeal to yourself when you are tempted to slip back into the insanity of addiction. Many people are sober today because of this kind of letter. I know people who had their letters laminated with small type so they could carry it with them. This letter builds on that premise. Writing becomes a clarifying tool and implements the premise of coming to your own assistance. It fits in the tradition of what we call the "core dialogues" which are really internal conversations made explicit.

In this letter, write an agreement with yourself about how you will conduct your life. Incorporate your most important learnings, your issues, your core zone behaviors, and your mission definition. Make it as personal as you wish. We have provided space here to write the document. You may, however, wish to have a more extended document that is reproducible in various formats. Use this space to develop notes to write the letter and actually complete it in another format. Many have found the "notes to outside format" actually works best.

Your Notes for Your Relapse Prevention Letter

Revisiting Your Decision Table

After all this work, it is time to revisit your Decision Table; however, this version is a bit different. You may relate back to the Decision Table that you completed in Chapter 1, on page 27. You can add new decisions that have become a priority in your life or describe new decisions that have become a priority in your life. You may wish to complete a new table and you may need additional worksheets which are available from recoveryzone.com or your therapist.

Identify five decisions you wish to work on. Use a separate worksheet for each decision. Record your best description of the decision on the table. Then rank the issue in the five categories:

- **Courage.** How ready you are to face this decision
- **Importance.** What the impact would be for improving your life
- **Recovery.** How significant this decision would be to improve or preserve your recovery
- **Zone Behavior.** How critical this decision is in your ability to stay in your best zone of well being
- **True Self.** How congruent this decision is with your new operating statement

Use a scale of one to five, with one being low and five being high. For each decision, list specific steps you need to take to implement this choice.

After completing the worksheets, compute a total for each worksheet by adding all five scores. Enter that number in the box labeled "rank score." You can the arrange the worksheets in order of importance.

Convene a board meeting. Have everyone read your new operating statement (new covenant letter). After discussing their reactions, present the five issues in order of priority. (We have provided space for you to take notes.) By having this meeting, you will be laying the ground work for the next stage, the external tasks. Your board now has the background to help you implement a vision for your life.

The Decision Table: Focus Worksheets

Describe a key decision that has become a priority in your life. Then rank the decision on a scale from one (low) to five (high) in five categories: **Courage**—How ready you are to face this decision. **Importance**—What the impact would be for improving your life. **Recovery**—How significant this decision would be to improve or preserve your recovery. **Zone Behavior**—How critical this decision is in your ability to stay in your best zone of well being. **True to Self**—How congruent this decision is with your new operating statement. Afterward, note steps that you will need to take to implement the decision. Keep in mind that some of your decisions will be a multi-step process. Finally, consult your "Board" or group of most trusted persons about your decision(s) and take notes.

Your best description of the decision to be made.

Courage Index	Importance	Adds to Recovery	Increases Zone Behavior	True to Self	Rank Score
1 2 3 4 5	1 2 3 4 5	1 2 3 4 5	1 2 3 4 5	1 2 3 4 5	

Rank 1–5   1 = Low   5 = High

Steps to take to implement decision	Board Notes

Exercise 9.8

© Copyright P.J. Carnes, 2009

The Decision Table: Focus Worksheets

Describe a key decision that has become a priority in your life. Then rank the decision on a scale from one (low) to five (high) in five categories: **Courage**—How ready you are to face this decision. **Importance**—What the impact would be for improving your life. **Recovery**—How significant this decision would be to improve or preserve your recovery. **Zone Behavior**—How critical this decision is in your ability to stay in your best zone of well being. **True to Self**—How congruent this decision is with your new operating statement. Afterward, note steps that you will need to take to implement the decision. Keep in mind that some of your decisions will be a multi-step process. Finally, consult your "Board" or group of most trusted persons about your decision(s) and take notes.

Your best description of the decision to be made.

Courage Index	Importance	Adds to Recovery	Increases Zone Behavior	True to Self	Rank Score
1 2 3 4 5	1 2 3 4 5	1 2 3 4 5	1 2 3 4 5	1 2 3 4 5	

Rank 1–5   1 = Low   5 = High

Steps to take to implement decision

Board Notes

The Decision Table: Focus Worksheets

Describe a key decision that has become a priority in your life. Then rank the decision on a scale from one (low) to five (high) in five categories: **Courage**—How ready you are to face this decision. **Importance**—What the impact would be for improving your life. **Recovery**—How significant this decision would be to improve or preserve your recovery. **Zone Behavior**—How critical this decision is in your ability to stay in your best zone of well being. **True to Self**—How congruent this decision is with your new operating statement. Afterward, note steps that you will need to take to implement the decision. Keep in mind that some of your decisions will be a multi-step process. Finally, consult your "Board" or group of most trusted persons about your decision(s) and take notes.

Your best description of the decision to be made.

Courage Index	Importance	Adds to Recovery	Increases Zone Behavior	True to Self	Rank Score
1 2 3 4 5	1 2 3 4 5	1 2 3 4 5	1 2 3 4 5	1 2 3 4 5	

Rank 1–5   1 = Low   5 = High

Steps to take to implement decision	Board Notes

Exercise 9.8

The Decision Table: Focus Worksheets

Describe a key decision that has become a priority in your life. Then rank the decision on a scale from one (low) to five (high) in five categories: **Courage**—How ready you are to face this decision. **Importance**—What the impact would be for improving your life. **Recovery**—How significant this decision would be to improve or preserve your recovery. **Zone Behavior**—How critical this decision is in your ability to stay in your best zone of well being. **True to Self**—How congruent this decision is with your new operating statement. Afterward, note steps that you will need to take to implement the decision. Keep in mind that some of your decisions will be a mult-step process. Finally, consult your "Board" or group of most trusted persons about your decision(s) and take notes.

Your best description of the decision to be made.

Courage Index	Importance	Adds to Recovery	Increases Zone Behavior	True to Self	Rank Score
1 2 3 4 5	1 2 3 4 5	1 2 3 4 5	1 2 3 4 5	1 2 3 4 5	

Rank 1-5   1 = Low   5 = High

Steps to take to implement decision	Board Notes

Exercise 9.8

The Call Continues ...

This book ends at the point where pain has helped define who you are. To provide perspective, **Figure 9.5** on page 259 summarizes the key concepts of laying down the foundation of living in a zone of recovery. The goal of this book was to systematically help you through the ordeal of the Fourth and Fifth Steps and do the deep work for articulating your life differently. Now the goal is to complete the process, achieve the life breakthrough, and channel the resulting creativity. This is the deep work. It takes longer and more daily attention, but it lightens the burden dramatically. Essentially it is Steps Six through Twelve, and is the repair and growth stages of recovery. After creating the covenant, you must implement it to harvest all the gains. Two new tools are necessary. We call them the Vision Table and the Legacy Table, which you will do in *Recovery Zone: Achieving Balance in Your Life, The External Tasks*. They tap into the most powerful forces known to humans, Vision and Purpose. The following two graphics summarize where you are in the process (**Figure 9.6** and **Figure 9.7**).

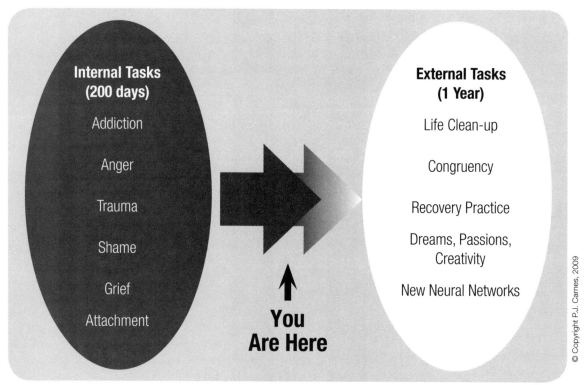

Figure 9.6

Task Centered Architecture of Meaning

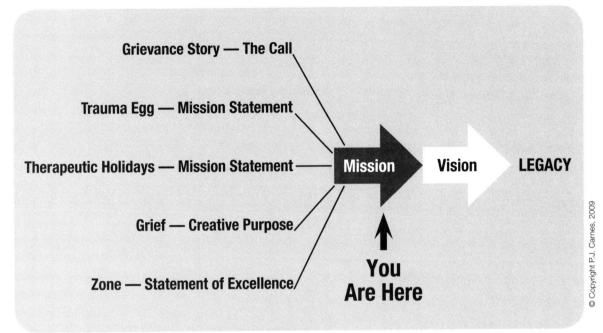

Figure 9.7

Acknowledgments

To Heed the Call Is Not Easy

In the early 1970s, I received a grant to write a conceptual paper on sex addiction. At about fifty pages, it was the beginning of a book that was eventually to be called *Out of the Shadows: Understanding Sexual Addiction*. At the time I was writing from my own experience and watching what was happening to patients who struggled with sexually compulsive behavior. This document circulated for a half dozen years as kind of a therapeutic underground paper. At the time, we simply were not ready to make such a document public. Yet we did workshops, and Twelve Step groups grew with all the miracles of recovery.

I finished my doctorate in psychology in 1980. My first book, which was on family health, also appeared during this time. I shared with some close friends that the time had come to publish a book, based on the early research papers. One of those people was Thomas Correll, who was teaching at Bethel College at the time. He got into sexual issues as a well-published anthropologist. I met him as the author of the state plan for the treatment of sex offenders. I had come to his attention as the recipient of a federal grant from the National Center for Child Abuse and Neglect. Tom was a minister, an anthropologist, and an expert in public policy. Also, he was a great friend.

Shortly after I had discussed with Tom my submission of the manuscript, he called to invite me to a conference on sex offenders. We went together on a lovely spring afternoon in 1981. The keynote speaker came from an Ivy League university who presented a case involving a pedophile who had been treated with an anti-androgen called Depo-Provera. This treatment reduces testosterone (chemical castration) and can have a profound side effect of obesity. The gist of the presentation was a video tape of the patient who was now very obese, speaking of his gratitude for the pills, even though they were making him fat. He would do anything not to do what he was doing.

The video was sad to me because we had treated so many similar cases successfully without resorting to what I saw was a solution for only special situations. The biggest problem was the speaker. Throughout the presentation she made fun of the patient on the video using degrading comments about his weight and character. She saw him as less than human and beyond pathetic (not to mention untreatable beyond the pills).

I could hardly bear it. I walked out and sat by a nearby river. From somewhere deep inside me came this deep pain about how somebody could treat someone so badly. I had struggled with my own sexuality in a much different way but it was still a struggle. I had my weight issues as well, given that I spent most of grad school well in the obesity range. Tom found me and held me as the deep sobs came. After they subsided he said, "I wanted you to see what you would be up against." We talked for some time. Then he respectfully left me to my thoughts. As I sat there I realized that I had run into an extraordinary prejudice against addiction of all types. No matter which addiction or codependency you chose, there are those who would be derisive. No matter what, the world would never be ready until people started talking about it. I decided to submit my manuscript.

Thus, I experienced a call. I did not realize at the time how much complexity was involved if you said there were addictions. You had to prove it. And you had to prove that people could recover. Almost thirty years later, I am deeply involved in implementing our research that there is a measurable path that works. I had no idea what would be asked of me. If I had been able to see, I am not sure at that point I would have committed. Fortunately, God breaks these things up into more digestible pieces.

There also have been many blessings. In my experience they come in the form of people, and Tom Correll certainly was one of them. The many therapists and researchers (almost a thousand at this point) who have participated in the development and training to make these materials a coherent whole are a testimony that those prejudices give way when you have strong, competent people doing therapy. These professionals meet chaos in their offices every day, which takes a toll on them. Yet, they persevere and I am grateful for their perseverance.

I am particularly indebted to the people of the International Institute for Trauma and Addiction Professionals, Recovery Zone, and Gentle Path Press especially Suzanne O'Connor, Marianne Harkin, and Tami VerHelst. Each of them in their own ways have had to have tolerance which go beyond just professional duty. I am very grateful to the board of professionals who have helped so much with certification and implementation. They are too many to list, but especially I am grateful to Bart Mandell, Steve Delugach, and Anne Foster for their board leadership. The staffs of Pine Grove and the Gentle Path program have been extraordinary in tolerating all the extra demands that writing this series has asked of us. One of the great joys in all of this has been the opportunity to work with my daughter, Stefanie Carnes, as a member of that staff. Her efforts to move the task-centered approach into being have been invaluable.

On a personal level, my wife Suzanne is a working sculptor, which means she understands the creative process. To have a mate who understands working with the muses is an asset beyond measure.

Finally, this journey has been made so much better by the members of the band, Voices From AFAR. They are accomplished musicians with careers and heavy travel schedules. Yet, they saw our workshops together as a priority and a way to give back for their recovery. Our efforts to raise money on behalf of the American Foundation for Addiction Research (AFAR) helped me to teach at my best. I have had some of my best moments in public with them. We practiced the principles in this book and the next one (*Recovery Zone: Achieving Balance in Your Life, The External Tasks*). They worked and lived what we were teaching. In that they helped shape so much of my writing and continue to be a great gift to me. So I dedicate this volume to them: Jewelie Hargrove, Porter Howell, Paul Jefferson, Sherie Phillips, Vee Maurice, Boh Cooper, Templeton Thompson, and Stephanie Urbina Jones.

I can truly say of all of you that you knew the difference between being a celebrity and being a hero.

As in all of this, the call was difficult, but the people made it a joy.

Patrick Carnes

The Twelve Steps of Alcoholics Anonymous[1]

1. We admitted we were powerless over alcohol—that our lives had become unmanageable.

2. Came to believe that a Power greater than ourselves could restore us to sanity.

3. Made a decision to turn our will and our lives over to the care of God as *we understood Him*.

4. Made a searching and fearless moral inventory of ourselves.

5. Admitted to God, to ourselves, and to another human being the exact nature of our wrongs.

6. Were entirely ready to have God remove all these defects of character.

7. Humbly asked Him to remove our shortcomings.

8. Made a list of all persons we had harmed, and became willing to make amends to them all.

9. Made direct amends to such people wherever possible, except when to do so would injure them or others.

10. Continued to take personal inventory and when we were wrong promptly admitted it.

11. Sought through prayer and meditation to improve our conscious contact with God a*s we understood Him*, praying only for knowledge of His will for us and the power to carry that out.

12. Having had a spiritual awakening as the result of these steps, we tried to carry this message to alcoholics, and to practice these principles in all our affairs.

[1]The Twelve Steps of AA are taken from *Alcoholics Anonymous*, 3d ed., published by AA World Services, Inc., New York, N.Y., 59-60.

The Twelve Steps of Alcoholics Anonymous Adapted for Sexual Addicts[2]

1. We admitted we were powerless over our sexual addiction—that our lives had become unmanageable.

2. Came to believe a Power greater than ourselves could restore us to sanity.

3. Made a decision to turn our will and our lives over to the care of God, as *we understood Him*.

4. Made a searching and fearless moral inventory of ourselves.

5. Admitted to God, to ourselves, and to another human being the exact nature of our wrongs.

6. Were entirely ready to have God remove all these defects of character.

7. Humbly asked Him to remove our shortcomings.

8. Made a list of all persons we had harmed, and became willing to make amends to them all.

9. Made direct amends to such people wherever possible, except when to do so would injure them or others.

10. Continued to take personal inventory and when we were wrong promptly admitted it.

11. Sought through prayer and meditation to improve our conscious contact with God as *we understood Him*, praying only for knowledge of His will for us and the power to carry that out.

12. Having had a spiritual awakening as the result of these steps, we tried to carry this message to others and to practice these principles in all our affairs.

[2]Adapted from the Twelve Steps of Alcoholics Anonymous.

Appendix B **Tasks One through Thirty**

The tasks on the next pages emerged out of following one thousand sex addicts and their families over seven years. The gist of that process is described in the book, *Don't Call It Love*, and in various professional publications. One of the principal findings was that the addict usually has another addiction besides the sex addiction; in addition, usually the addict was from a family of addicts. The recipe that emerged contributed to the success of people who had multiple issues along with being raised in families with multiple issues. The other finding was the documentation of a process that covered five years; previously, no map existed for both recovering people and their therapists. Thus, we started the agonizing challenge to codify and structure what worked to help therapists be good guides in the process. Building the tasks has been an effort of articulation as well as experimentation.

Today the map is complex because it includes assessments and clinical materials not available in 1991 when we finished the initial work. It includes specific competencies that therapists need; these also were not clear when we started. Because of space limitations, we have included this overview which summarizes the process. We have highlighted the tasks that Recovery Zone I covers as another way for you to understand how the tasks work. This scenario uses sex addicts' first seven tasks to serve as an example. In addition, there are people within the professional community also evolving tasks for chemical dependency, eating disorders, codependency, and financial disorders.

A complete map to the tasks can be found on the recoveryzone.com website. You will also find a checklist for tracking of the task process. Task-centered certified therapists have additional ways to track and chart the tasks. These therapists are listed on the website for the International Institute for Trauma and Addiction Professionals website (iitap.org). They are credentialed either as Certified Sex Addiction Therapists (CSAT) or Certified Multiple Addictions Therapists (CMAT).

The tasks represent the accumulated efforts of many people in both the professional and Twelve Step communities. If you have gotten this far in reading, you probably are now part of this process. When we are finished, our accumulated efforts will leave a legacy of a recovery journey that follows a clearly delineated map.

Tasks 1–30

Recovery Task	Performables	Life Competency
1. Break through denial	■ Creates a problem list ■ Records a secret list ■ Completes list of excuses ■ Completes Consequences Inventory ■ Learns 14 ways to distort reality ■ Inventories 14 distortion strategies in personal life ■ Accountability—Victim Empathy exercise ■ Makes full disclosure to therapist	■ Understands the characteristics of denial and self-delusion ■ Identifies presence of self-delusion in life ■ Knows personal preference patterns of thought distortion ■ Accepts confrontation
2A. Understand the nature of addictive illness	■ Completes assigned readings on sex addiction ■ Learns different ways to define sex addiction ■ Understands addictive system ■ Understands deprivation system ■ Maps out personal addictive system ■ Understands criteria for addictive illness ■ Applies criteria to personal behavior ■ Learns key factors in the genesis of sex addiction	■ Knows information on addictive illness ■ Applies information to personal life
2B. Sexual addiction component	■ Understands sexual modularity ■ Understands sexual hierarchy ■ Knows ten types of behavior ■ Reviews ten types for personal patterns ■ Completes and shares sexual history ■ Completes ideal fantasy list ■ Completes and shares fantasy contamination exercise	■ Understands sexually compulsive patterns ■ Knows specific stories/scenarios of arousal template

Tasks 1-30 continued

Recovery Task	Performables	Life Competency
3. Surrenders to process	■ Understands context of change, grief, commitment ■ Understands existential position on change—essence of recovery ■ Understands principles of anxiety reduction ■ Completes sexual addiction history ■ Completes powerless worksheet ■ Completes unmanageability worksheet ■ Identifies ten worst moments ■ Understands guidelines of step completion ■ Gives first step	■ Acceptance of addiction in life ■ Knows personal limitations ■ Discerns difference between controllable and non-controllable events
4. Limits damage from behavior	■ Understands first and second order change ■ Understands concept of paradigm shift ■ Records provisional beliefs ■ Completes damage control plan ■ Completes a disclosure plan ■ Writes a "turning it over" letter to Higher Power ■ Completes second and third step	■ Integrates self-limitation into personal paradigm ■ Responds to crisis plan fully ■ Uses boundaries at a minimum level ■ Has internal skills for anxiety reduction ■ Develops resolve for change and commitment
5. Establish sobriety	■ Understands sobriety as boundary problem ■ Commits to and completes celibacy contract ■ Writes sobriety statement ■ Understands relapse process ■ Writes relapse plan ■ Establishes a date	■ Uses clearly stated boundaries of sobriety ■ Manages life without dysfunctional sexual behavior

Tasks 1-30 continued

Recovery Task	Performables	Life Competency
6. Ensure physical integrity	■ Learns physical aspects of addiction ■ Completes physical ■ Completes psychiatric assessment ■ Learns neuropathways of addiction ■ Maps personal neuropathway interactions ■ Understands arousal template ■ Maps personal arousal template	■ Understands physical aspects of addiction ■ Identifies neuropathway interaction ■ Identifies dysfunctional arousal patterns
7. Participate in a culture of support	■ Participates in a Twelve Step program ■ Develops relationship with sponsor ■ Completes sponsor debriefing ■ Does service in program ■ Knows signs of a healthy group ■ Has a celebration date	■ Maintains a healthy support system
8. Understand multiple addictions and sobriety	■ Completes assessment of all addictions and deprivations ■ Completes an Addiction Interaction screen and exercises ■ Understands addiction neuropathways ■ Completes a multiple addiction Relapse Prevention Plan ■ Understands "Black Hole" metaphor	■ Capacity to be relapse free from concurrent addictions

Tasks 1-30 continued

Recovery Task	Performables	Life Competency
9. Acknowledge cycles of abuse	■ Completes Stress Index ■ Finishes trauma "egg" process ■ Understands forms of abusive and exploitive behavior ■ Completes life inventory of abuse ■ Has boundary management and anxiety reduction "soothing" skills ■ Has strategies for resentment, forgiveness, and meaning making around abuse events ■ Completes Seventh Step ■ Completes Angel "egg"	■ Identify abuse and exploitation ■ Integrate understanding of abuse into value system ■ Can cope with abusive persons and situations
10. Reduce shame	■ Completes Steps Four and Five ■ Recognizes personal shame ■ Understands shame cycle ■ Identifies carried shame ■ Has specific strategies for interrupting shame ■ Knows boundary-setting strategies ■ Identifies "Gap" issues in life ■ Does Therapeutic Holidays	■ Recognize and manage shame ■ Sets boundaries in shaming systems and situations

Tasks 1-30 continued

Recovery Task	Performables	Life Competency
11. Restructure relationship with self	• Completes eighteen months of individual therapy (sixty-five sessions) • Completes Sixth Step • Understands and states personal limitations • Completes mission statements • Completes Zone Plan	• Have a workable, compassionate relationship with self • Capacity for self-determination and autonomy
12. Grieve losses	• Understands grieving process • Completes timeline of losses • Identifies personal losses • Has strategies for effective sorrow • Understands Twelve Steps as a process to grieve	• Recognize grief • Have skills for grieving
13. Bring closure and resolution, taking responsibility for self	• Completes Steps Eight and Nine • Does couples weekly exercise for ten weeks, if couple • Uses integrity check list for twenty days • Understands importance of closure	• Keeps current on shame, resentment, and relationship issues

Tasks 1-30 continued

Recovery Task	Performables	Life Competency
14. Restore financial viability	■ Understands financial disorders ■ Completes financial disorder assessment ■ Completes financial template process ■ Able to live within financial means ■ Lives within financial recovery plan ■ Financial resilience	■ Maintain financial viability
15. Restore meaningful work	■ Understands dysfunctional, obsessive work patterns ■ Completes work template process ■ Completes work satisfaction survey ■ Establishes meaningful, successful career pattern	■ Have meaningful, successful work
16. Create lifestyle balance	■ Uses Personal Craziness Index for eight weeks ■ Understands rest, renewal, "Sabbath" principles ■ Regular windows of rest ■ Has sources for renewal and competing passions ■ Early Warning System	■ Capacity for balance, harmony, and renewal ■ Uses Negative Experience Transformers ■ Uses Zone principles and plan

Tasks 1-30 continued

Recovery Task	Performables	Life Competency
17. Build supportive personal relationships	■ Attends a therapy group for 175 hours ■ Finds and uses a sponsor ■ Be a sponsor to others ■ Has "best" friends	■ Initiate and sustain enduring life relationships
18. Establish health, exercise, and nutrition patterns	■ Has weekly aerobic exercise program ■ Remains in appropriate weight range for age and height ■ Completes Recovery Zone physical assessment process	■ Stays physically fit
19. Develop a spiritual life	■ Finds and uses a spiritual director or mentor ■ Joins a spiritual community ■ Attends Twelve Step meetings ■ Completes Spiritual Genogram ■ Develops Spiritual Timeline ■ Completes Medicine Bag and shares with family members: Brings five items that give them strength to share with family ■ Interviews three to five people who have different perspective on spirituality than own ■ Sets aside quiet time daily for meditation and reflection ■ Understands different meditation techniques	■ Has on-going spiritual practice ■ Knows divergent methods for preserving "conscious contact" ■ Participation in supportive spiritual communities ■ Seeks and gives spiritual direction

Tasks 1-30 continued

Recovery Task	Performables	Life Competency
20. Commit to recovery for each family member	▪ Family members enter a recovery program for themselves ▪ Each family member completes Step One with a sponsor ▪ Understands Twelve Steps as a family process ▪ Completes a Powerlessness & Unmanageability Inventory ▪ Attends six meetings with Al-Anon, Co-da, S-Anon, or ACOA ▪ Completes drawing exercise: how family was, how family is, how family would like to be ▪ Writes a Family Mission Statement with goals and tasks to accomplish ▪ Children design and plan Weekly Fun Time for family	▪ Take responsibility for self ▪ Understands and accepts impact of addiction disorders ▪ Uses Twelve Step principles to handle anxiety and to redirect family processes ▪ Capacity for fun and spontaneity
21. Resolve original conflicts/wounds	▪ Participates in therapy specific to family-of-origin or trauma issues ▪ Understands core beliefs about self ▪ Creates list of specific events, behaviors, and attitudes that interfered with development of self ▪ Summarizes the impact into a list of "character defects" ▪ Relates these defects to the addicts/co-addicts core beliefs and the nature of shame and trauma ▪ Completes a Family Conflict Genogram ▪ Completes Voices in My Head exercise ▪ Identifies voices outside the family that activate the shame or old trauma triggers ▪ Specify how those voices create dysfunctional responses and feelings ▪ Learns the six steps in creating positive affirmations ▪ Reframes the old voices with reframed affirmations ▪ Use dolphin guided imagery to expand affirmation ▪ Completes draft of a Covenant with Self	▪ Identify and manage recurring dysfunctional patterns ▪ Has realistic sense of personal limitations ▪ Has skills to transform negative messages of remembered experience ▪ Has an internal covenant which replaces old beliefs

Tasks 1-30 continued

Recovery Task	Performables	Life Competency
22. Alter dysfunctional family relationships	<ul><li>Completes Boundary Setting exercise to establish non-negotiables for relationship</li><li>Family members explore disconnects in family communication by completing Johari Window exercise</li><li>Family members learn importance of disclosure by examining the impact of dishonesty in the family</li><li>Family learns six rules of boundary setting and writes out personal boundary lists</li><li>Family members write a bottom-line "non-negotiable" list</li><li>Family members use "rules of disclosure" to create a disclosure list</li><li>Discloses to primary partner and members of family as appropriate</li><li>Completes draft two of a "Covenant with Self" based on new knowledge and non-negotiables</li></ul>	<ul><li>Remain true to self in the presence of dysfunction or stress</li><li>Becomes a direct, appropriate communicator</li><li>Has clear, appropriate boundaries with self and others</li><li>Breaks self-limiting family rules and roles</li></ul>
23. Resolve issues with children	<ul><li>Understands guidelines for disclosure and does age-appropriate disclosure</li><li>Shares secrets and makes amends to children when appropriate</li><li>Asks for feedback from other adults who have been actively involved with children</li><li>Completes Children Raising Children exercise</li><li>Shares exercise as a Family</li><li>Children attend regular meetings with a therapist</li><li>Couple writes a Unified Communication Agreement</li></ul>	<ul><li>Resolve conflict in dependent relationships</li><li>Learns to negotiate covenant with dependents and honors communications</li><li>Understands limitations in power situations</li></ul>

Tasks 1-30 continued

Recovery Task	Performables	Life Competency
24. Resolve issues with extended family	<ul><li>Shares secrets and make amends to extended family when appropriate</li><li>Understands the five tasks of family-of-origin work</li><li>Defines a family of choice</li><li>Defines qualities of a safe person and sees if anyone in Genogram meets criteria</li><li>Reviews basics of grieving and completes an unfinished and unsaid list</li><li>Uses letter writing and role playing to resolve issues with family members who have died or who are unwilling to participate in recovery process</li></ul>	<ul><li>Resolve conflict in interdependent relationships</li><li>Creates personal intimate support community</li><li>Knows key information about patterns in extended family</li><li>Brings closure to personal issues</li></ul>
25. Work through differentiation	<ul><li>Understands rules for fair fighting</li><li>Writes a Fair Fight Contract</li><li>Understands guidelines for having difficult conversations</li><li>Completes Difficult Conversations History</li><li>Identifies conflict issues, including non-negotiables, triggers, and coping styles</li><li>Lists unresolved difficult conversations and creates a resolution plan</li></ul>	<ul><li>Sustain intimacy without loss of self</li><li>Develops difficult conversation skills</li><li>Ability to establish effective boundaries</li><li>Utilizes Fair Fight principles</li><li>Understands importance of closure</li></ul>

Tasks 1-30 continued

Recovery Task	Performables	Life Competency
26. Succeed in intimacy	■ Understands the Twelve prerequisites for intimacy and completes self-assessment ■ Completes Circle of Intimacy Assessment: plots circles, identifies people in circles, identifies what is missing in circles, identifies what couples would like circles to look like ■ Shares circle with significant persons and discusses what it means to be intimate ■ Completes a minimum of one hundred hours in therapy with one therapist ■ Completes one hundred and seventy-five hours in some type of group therapy ■ Attends regular base or home Twelve Step group	■ Be vulnerable and intimate ■ Creates a personal support network ■ Sustains a "primary" relationship ■ Recognizes relationship priorities
27. Commit/recommit to primary relationship	■ Shares Definition of Commitment: "What commitment means to you?" "How has the meaning of commitment changed over time?" ■ Identifies current priorities in couple's life: where time is spent ■ Completes Primary Relationship exercise: "What's kept you from success in your primary relationship?" "Identify losses and feelings associated with losses" ■ Completes IMAGO exercise ■ Identify Dreams in Recovery and Honoring Those Dreams (Gottman's work) ■ Completes Intimacy-abled and Intimacy-Disabled exercise using the 12 Pre-requests of Intimacy to rate where they see themselves and where they think others see them ■ Completes the Commitment Renewal Process: individually, as a couple, with a couple sponsor, and with a therapist ■ Couple creates and performs a Ritual of Recommitment	■ Capacity to maintain and renew committed relationship ■ Understands obstacles to having primary intimacy ■ Integrates intimacy knowledge with recovery principles ■ Understands and honors key relationships ■ Integrates commitments

Recovery Task	Performables	Life Competency
28. Explore coupleship recovery	■ Attends Twelve Step meetings for couples regularly ■ Understands the problems of compulsive attachments ■ Reviews Chapter 5 principles ■ Understands differences between steps done as individual and steps done as couple ■ Completes a Couples First Step over dynamics of addictive/codependent relationships ■ Understands concept of couple shame ■ Completes and processes couple shame exercise as part of couple's Fifth Step ■ Completes Internal Commitment Audit	■ Knows Twelve Step couples processes, language, and strategies ■ Supports therapeutically couples Twelve Step work ■ Assists with key concepts around couples First Step and couple shame ■ Maintains resources for Twelve Step couples work
29. Restore healthy sexuality	■ Writes a sex plan and keeps it updated ■ Understands the twelve dimensions of human sexuality and how they become the map to one's sexual self ■ Associates the Twelve Step Recovery Principles with the Dimensions of Sexual Health ■ Completes Sexuality Genogram ■ Completes Sexuality Timeline ■ Develops plan for sexual health ■ Identifies Sexual Development Events—Lists five events that have shaped positive sexual development and five that have done harm ■ Understands concept of "emotional intercourse" ■ Understands connection of individual recovery to larger cultural and life issues	■ Knows dimensions of healthy sexuality ■ Uses Twelve Step principles to focus on sexual health ■ Integrates sexual self-knowledge into sexual practice ■ Conscious sexuality relates to larger society and culture

Tasks 1-30 continued

Recovery Task	Performables	Life Competency
30. Involve family members in therapy	■ Family members attend together a structured family therapy program ■ Family members attend two or more family therapy days ■ Shares story with family ■ Shares Genogram with family members, therapist, and support group ■ Completes Accountability Exercise and shares with family, facilitated by therapist ■ Completes timeline of how addict has abused/offended family members ■ Completes Family Impact Sharing exercise ■ Complete Interpersonal Amends & Affirmations ■ Complete Family Affirmations with family and therapist	■ Capacity to ask for help ■ Take responsibility for personal behaviors ■ Connects story to learning and mentoring ■ Ability to risk being vulnerable

Appendix C **Notes**

Chapter 1

[1] It is events like this that convinced me over the years that we humans communicate on a level seldom understood. Somehow this man knew that his woman was about to become unavailable. He waited, literally, until the last second. I think that we form deeper bonds than we know and tap into the connection only when we have to or are in crisis. Test that out for yourself by asking about times you knew something about someone you had a connection with—which turned out to be true. Yet, no one had told you. There was absolutely no way you could have known about it. Some would call it intuition. I believe in that. Intuition is our brain working behind our awareness. It puts patterns and facts together so we know without knowing. But I am talking about the level of connection that physicists talk about when they say that molecules have a lasting relationship upon encountering one another. Our bonds are deeper than we understand. As every relationship continues, it changes how you relate to others. That knowledge makes you more careful with any encounter, let alone serious relationships. Carl Whittaker was right when he said that there is no such thing as divorce, we just add marriages. Bonds persist no matter what our decisions are or how serious the relationship.

[2] I found parenting to be the biggest challenge in my life. One factor was the amazing people I was given to parent, as this story illustrates. I have no idea how my daughter figured out Paulette's dilemma. Nor does she remember now. I do know that my children have often had a clearer perception of my life than I have. That did not diminish the battle implicit in having to share with them my perceptions of theirs.

[3] See Joseph Campbell, *The Hero With A Thousand Faces*. I have long been fascinated with Campbell's analysis of the profile of becoming a hero and the stories of people's recovery. In recovery fellowships people start by sharing how it was then and how it is now. I am convinced it is the same profile and the same process. It is the part that therapists cannot share and why fellowships continue to grow – and which the professional community often does not understand. In the middle ages these stories were around a character called "everyman" or "Jedermann." The recovery community is truly the forum for the "everyman" of our time.

[4] I highly recommend reading books by Charles L. Whitfield, M.D., and John Bradshaw. They write about how certain life experiences can lead into addiction.

Chapter 1 continued

[5] *Permission to Be Precious* by Pia Mellody (CD) can be purchased from her website at www.piamellody.com

Chapter 6

[6] One of the great ironies about this quote is that it precedes his more profound treatments of the leap of faith necessary and at a time when his own mother was ill. The piece is prescient for his later work and reflects his observations about attachment, which probably given her illness are autobiographical.

[7] Miller's observation really came from a book by science fiction author Robert A. Heinlein called *Stranger in a Strange Land*. This book was an international bestseller precisely when Miller was formulating some of her most important writing. The "fair witness" character was a social role in which the person took no sides and reported only what happened.

[8] The data on the impact of trauma on the brain is quite extensive. Dan Siegel's book *The Developing Mind* is one of the best maps.

[9] To start this journey, see Dr. Bruce Perry's 1994 article, "Post-Traumatic Stress Disorders in Children," www.child-trauma.org.

[10] See the article, "The Compulsion to Repeat the Trauma," by Bessel A. van der Kolk, M.D., *Psychiatric Clinics of North America*, 1989. ·

Chapter 7

[11] I encourage readers to read about shame in John Bradshaw's *Healing the Shame that Binds You*.

[12] Voices from AFAR has a recording of these songs and a meditation series on CD featuring Dr. Carnes, *Spiritual Skill Set: Discernment Part 1*, *Spiritual Skill Set Resilience Part 2*, available through Gentle Path Press (www.gentlepath.com).

Chapter 9

[13] *The Road Less Traveled,* by M. Scott Peck, M.D., and *The Denial of Death,* by Ernest Becker, should be required reading for all recovering people, because they use mythology so elegantly. They have been primary reading for so many in recovery, and they point to the "reality" of reality.

[14] For a great description of courage see *If Harry Potter Ran General Electric: Leadership Wisdom from the World of the Wizards,* by Tom Morris.

[15] Antonio Damasio's *Looking for Spinoza* is a guide not only to his role but to the brain mechanisms involved.

[16] Debtors Anonymous leads in this style of sub-meetings, but other groups make suggestions around this in their literature as well.

Chapter 1

Covey, S. (2004). *The 7 habits of highly effective people*. New York: Free Press.

Hope for Today. (2007). Virginia Beach, VA: Al-Anon Family Group Headquarters.

Kurtz, E. (1991). *Not God: A history of Alcoholics Anonymous*. Center City, MN: Hazelden.

Kurtz, E. & Ketcham, K. (1992). *The spirituality of imperfection: Storytelling and the search for meaning*. New York: Bantam.

Tolkien, J.R.R. (1982). *The fellowship of the ring*. New York: Houghton Mifflin Harcourt Publishing Company.

Chapter 2

Adult children of alcoholics. (2006). New York: Alcoholics Anonymous World Services, Inc.

Alda, A. (2007). *Things I overheard while talking to myself*. New York: Random House.

Alcoholics Anonymous: Big book. (2002). New York: Alcoholics Anonymous World Services, Inc.

Borchert, W. G. (2005). *The Lois Wilson story: When love is not enough*. Center City, MN: Hazelden

Clifton, L. (2000). *Blessing the boats: New and selected poems 1988-2000*. Rochester, NY: BOA Editions, Ltd.

Csikszentmihalyi, M. (1990). *Flow: The psychology of optimal experience*. New York: HarperPerennial.

Wolfe, T. (2008). *The bonfire of the vanities: a novel*. New York: Picador.

Chapter 3

BMC Evolutionary Biology (2008, June 10). Is ADHD An Advantage For Nomadic Tribesmen? *ScienceDaily*. Retrieved July 30, 2009, from http://www.sciencedaily.com/releases/2008/06/080609195604.htm

Carnes, P. J., Murray, R. E., & Charpentier, L. Handbook of Multiple Addictions. In R. Coombs (Ed.), *Addiction Interaction Disorder: Chapter 2*. Hoboken, NJ: Wiley.

Cozolino, L. (2006). The neuroscience of human relationships: Attachment and the developing social brain. New York: Norton.

Di Chiara, G., & Imperato, A. (1988). Drugs abused by humans preferentially increase synaptic dopamine concentrations in the mesolimbic system of freely moving rats. *Proceedings of the National Academy of Sciences of the United States of America, 85,* 5274-5278.

Miller, A. (1997). *Drama of the gifted child: The search for true self.* New York: Basic Books.

Nestler, E. J., & Malenka, R. C. (2004). The addicted brain. *Scientific America,* p. 78-85.

Schmidt, L. G., & Smolka, M. N. (2007). Results from two pharmacotherapy trials show alcoholic smokers were more severely alcohol dependent but less prone to relapse than alcoholic non-smokers. *Alcohol & Alcoholism, 42*(3), 241-246.

Teicher, M. A., Anderson, S. L., Polcari, A., Anderson, C. M., Navalta, C. A., & Kim, D. M. (2003). The neurobiological consequences of early stress and childhood maltreatment. *Neuroscience and Biobehavioral Reviews, 27,* 33-44.

Chapter 4

Chopra, D. (2007). *Buddha: A story of enlightenment.* New York: HarperCollins.

Coelho, P. (1998). *The alchemist.* New York: HarperCollins.

Cozolino, L. (2002). *The neuroscience of psychotherapy: Building and rebuilding the human brain.* New York: Norton.

Frankl, V. E. (2008). *Man's search for meaning* (Kindle Edi.). UK: Ailax Merchandise.

Lewis, C.S. (2001). *The problem of pain.* New York: HarperOne.

Plato. *Book VII of the republic: The allegory of the cave.*

Payne, W.L. (1983/1986). A study of emotion: developing emotional intelligence; self integration; relating to fear, pain and desire. *Dissertation Abstracts International, 47,* 203A.

Ruiz, D. M. (1997). *The four agreements: A practical guide to personal freedom, a Toltec wisdom book.* San Rafael, CA: Amber-Allen Publishing.

Chapter 5

Alcoholics Anonymous: Big book. (2002). New York: Alcoholics Anonymous World Services, Inc.

Lucas, G., Kurtz, G., & McCallum, R. (Producers) & Kershner, I. (Director). (1980). *Star wars episode V: The empire strikes back* [Motion picture]. United States of America: 20th Century Fox.

Lucas, G., & McCallum, R. (Producers) & Lucas, G. (Director). (2005). *Star wars episode III: Revenge of the Sith* [Motion picture]. United States of America: 20th Century Fox.

Seuss, Dr. (1957). *How the Grinch stole Christmas!* New York: Random House.

Rowling, J. K. (2007). *Harry Potter and the deathly hallows.* New York: Arthur A. Levine Books.

Chapter 6

Alcoholics Anonymous: Big book. (2002). New York: Alcoholics Anonymous World Services, Inc.

Cozolino, L. (2004). *The making of a therapist: A practical guide for the inner journey*. New York: W. W. Norton & Co.

Heinlein, R.A. (1991). *Stranger in a strange land*. New York: Ace Trade Books.

Kierkegaard, S. (2008). *Purity of heart is to will one thing*. New York: HarperOne.

Miller, A. (1997). *Drama of the gifted child: The search for true self*. New York: Basic Books.

Morris, T. (2006). *If Harry Potter ran General Electric: Leadership wisdom from the world of the wizards*. New York: Currency.

Siegel, D. J. (2001). *The developing mind: How relationships and the brain interact to shape who we are*. New York: Guilford Press.

Chapter 7

Brown, S. & Free, W. (Producers). Balnicke, J. & Kennard, D. (Directors). (2007). *The hero's journey* [DVD]. United States of America: Acacia Productions, LTD.

Clifton, L. (2000). *Blessing the boats: New and selected poems 1988-2000*. Rochester, NY: BOA Editions, Ltd.

Kaufman, G. (1980). Shame: The power of caring. Cambridge, MA: Schenkman.

Lewis, C. S. (1973). *The great divorce*. New York: HarperOne.

Ted Conference L.L.C. (Producer). (2008). *Mihaly Csikszentmihalyi on flow* [Video Podcast]. Retrieved June 6, 2009, from: http://www.ted.com/talks/lang/eng/ mihaly_csikszentmihalyi_on_flow.html

Ruiz, D. M. (1997). *The four agreements: A practical guide to personal freedom, a Toltec wisdom book*. San Rafael, CA: Amber-Allen Publishing.

Stevenson, R. L. (2003). *The strange case of Dr. Jekyll and Mr. Hyde: And other tales of terror*. (Revised Ed.) New York: Penguin Classics.

Weinstein, B., & Weinstein, H. (Producers) & Chelsom, P. (Director). (2004). *Shall we dance?* [Motion Picture]. United States of America: Miramax Films.

Thompson, T., Gay, S., & Howell, P. (2006). *Chiselin' Out My Soul*. [Recorded by Voices from AFAR]. On Voices from AFAR [CD]. Nashville, Tennessee: Voices from AFAR, LLC.

Chapter 8

Alcoholics Anonymous: Big book. (2002). New York: Alcoholics Anonymous World Services, Inc.

Aries, P. (2008). *The hour of our death*. New York: Vintage.

Co-dependents Anonymous. (1995). Dallas, TX: CoDA Resource Publishing.

Debtors Anonymous. (1999). *A currency of hope*. Needham, MA: General Service Board of Trustees, Inc.

From survival to recovery: growing up in an alcoholic home. (1994). Virginia Beach, VA: Al-Anon Family Group Headquarters, Inc.

Peck, M.S. (1978). *The road less traveled: A new psychology of love, traditional values and spiritual growth*. New York: Touchstone Publishing, L.L.C.

Rowling, J. K. (2007). *Harry Potter and the deathly hallows*. New York: Arthur A. Levine Books.

Sex Addicts Anonymous. (2005). Houston, TX: International Service Organization of SAA, Inc.

Willocks, T. (2008). *The religion*. New York: Tor Books.

Chapter 9

Becker, E. (1973). *The denial of death*. New York: Free Press.

Campbell, J., & Moyers, B. (1991). *The power of myth*. Harpswell, ME: Anchor.

Cozolino, L. (2006). *The neuroscience of human relationships: Attachment and the developing social brain*. New York: Norton.

Damasio, A. (2003). *Looking for Spinoza: Joy, sorrow, and the feeling brain*. New York: Harcourt.

Gladwell, M. (2008). *Outliers: The story of success*. New York: Little, Brown and Company.

Morris, T. (2006). *If Harry Potter ran General Electric: Leadership wisdom from the world of the wizards*. New York: Broadway Business.

Nouwen, H. J. M. (1997). *Bread for the journey*. London, England: Darton, Longman & Todd Ltd.

Peck, M.S. (1978). *The road less traveled: A new psychology of love, traditional values and spiritual growth*. New York: Touchstone Publishing, L.L.C.

Siegel, D. J. (2007). *Neurobiology: Unlocking the mind to promote well-being. Counselor: The magazine for addiction professionals*, 8 (1), 12-19.

Twenty-four hours a day. (1992). Center City, MN: Hazelden.

Appendix E **Contact Information**

Two recovery-supporting websites can be accessed at www.sexhelp.com and www.recoveryzone.com.

For general or purchasing information regarding our publications, please visit www.sexhelp.com or www.gentlepath.com or call us 1-800-708-1796 (US Toll-Free).

For information on both inpatient and outpatient treatment services, contact us at 1-800-708-1796 (US Toll-Free). The staff there will match your needs with the appropriate services.

For more information about Dr. Patrick Carnes and his speaking engagements, access his website at www.sexhelpworkshops.com.

For information on training for counselors and other helping professionals, call the International Institute for Trauma and Addiction Professionals (IITAP) at 1-866-575-6853 (US Toll-Free) or access them via the Internet at www.iitap.com.

Appendix F **Resource Guide**

The following is a list of recovery fellowships that may be helpful to you in your particular situation.

Adult Children of Alcoholics
310-534-1815
www.adultchildren.org

Alateen (ages 12–17)
800-356-9996
www.al-anon-alateen.org

Al-Anon
800-344-2666
www.al-anon.org

Alcoholics Anonymous
212-870-3400
www.alcoholics-anonymous.org

Co-Dependents Anonymous
602-277-7991
www.codependents.org

Co-Dependents of Sex Addicts
763-537-6904
www.cosa-recovery.org

Cocaine Anonymous
800-347-8998
www.ca.org

CoAnon
520-513-5028
www.co-anon.org

Debtors Anonymous
781-453-2743
www.debtorsanonymous.org

Emotions Anonymous
651-647-9712
www.mtn.org/EA

Families Anonymous
310-815-8010
www.familiesanonymous.org

Gamblers Anonymous
213-386-8789
www.gamblersanonymous.org

Marijuana Anonymous
212-459-4423
www.marijuana-anonymous.org

Narcotics Anonymous
818-773-9999
www.na.org

Nicotine Anonymous
415-750-0328
www.nicotine-anonymous.org

Overeaters Anonymous
505-891-2664
www.oa.org

Recovering Couples Anonymous
781-794-1456
www.recovering-couples.org

Runaway and Suicide Hotline
800-RUN-AWAY
www.1800runaway.org

S-Anon
615-833-3152
www.sanon.org

Sex and Love Addicts Anonymous
www.slaafws.org

Sex Addicts Anonymous
713-869-4902
www.sexaa.org

Sexaholics Anonymous
866-424-8777
www.sa.org

**Sexual Addiction Resources/
Dr. Patrick Carnes**
www.sexhelp.com

Sexual Compulsives Anonymous
310-859-5585
www.sca-recovery.org

**Society for the Advancement of
Sexual Heath**
706-356-7031
www.sash.net

Survivors of Incest Anonymous
410-282-3400
www.siawso.org

Appendix G **Recommended Readings**

Adult Children of Alcoholics

Adult Children of Alcoholics/Dysfunctional Families, Anonymous

It Will Never Happen to Me: Growing Up with Addiction as Youngsters, Adolescents, Adults, Claudia Black

My Dad Loves Me, My Dad Has a Disease: A Child's View: Living with Addiction, Claudia Black

Grandchildren of Alcoholics: Another Generation of Codependency, Ann W. Smith

Adult Children of Alcoholics, Janet G. Woititz

Marriage On The Rocks: Learning to Live with Yourself and an Alcoholic, Janet G. Woititz

Healthy Parenting: How Your Upbringing Influences the Way You Raise Your Children, and What You Can Do to Make It Better for Them, Janet G. Woititz

Codependency

Codependent No More: How to Stop Controlling Others and Start Caring for Yourself, Melody Beattie

Mending a Shattered Heart: A Guide for Partners of Sex Addicts, Stefanie Carnes

Boundaries: Where You End and I Begin, Anne Katherine

Living in the Comfort Zone: The Gift of Boundaries in Relationships, Rokelle Lerner

Facing Codependence: What It Is, Where It Comes from, How It Sabotages Our Lives, Pia Melody & Andrea Miller

The Drama of the Gifted Child: The Search for the True Self, Alice Miller

Is It Love or Is It Addiction?, Brenda Schaeffer

Codependency continued

Choicemaking: For Spirituality Seekers, Co-Dependents and Adult Children,
Sharon Wegscheider-Cruse

Learning To Say No: Establishing Healthy Boundaries, Carle Wills-Brandon

Co-Sex Addiction

Open Hearts: Renewing Relationships with Recovery, Romance & Reality, Patrick Carnes, Mark
Laaser, Deborah Laaser

Healing Together: A Guide to Intimacy and Recovery for Co-Dependent Couples, Wayne Kritsberg

Relationships in Recovery: Healing Strategies for Couples and Families, Emily Marlin

Facing Codependence: What It Is, Where It Comes from, How It Sabotages Our Lives, Pia Mellody

Back from Betrayal, Jennifer Schneider

Rebuilding Trust: For Couples Committed to Recovery, Jennifer Schneider & Burt Schneider

Sex, Lies and Forgiveness, Jennifer Schneider & Burt Schneider

*Women Who Love Sex Addicts: Help for Healing from the Effects of a Relationship With a
Sex Addict,* Douglas Weiss & Donna DeBusk

Family of Origin

It Will Never Happen to Me: Growing Up With Addiction As Youngsters, Adolescents, Adults,
Claudia Black

Changing Course: Healing from Loss, Abandonment and Fear, Claudia Black

Healing the Shame that Binds You, John Bradshaw

Family Secrets: The Path to Self-Acceptance and Reunion, John Bradshaw

The Emotional Incest Syndrome: What to do When a Parent's Love Rules Your Life, Patricia Love

Healing The Child Within: Discovery and Recovery for Adult Children of Dysfunctional Families,
Charles L. Whitfield, M.D.

Men's Issues

When He's Married to Mom: How to Help Mother-Enmeshed Men Open Their Hearts to True Love and Commitment, Kenneth Adams

Longing for Dad: Father Loss and Its Impact, Beth Erickson

The Knight in Rusty Armor, Robert Fisher

Fire in the Belly: On Being a Man, Sam Keen

If Only He Knew: What No Woman Can Resist, Gary Smalley & Norma Smalley

Mission Development

The Artist's Way, Julia Cameron

First Things First, Stephen R. Covey

Money Issues

Money Drunk, Money Sober; 90 Days to Financial Freedom, Mark Bryan & Julia Cameron

A Currency of Hope, Debtors Anonymous

Deadly Odds: Recovery from Compulsive Gambling, Ken Estes & Mike Brubaker

The Financial Wisdom of Ebenezer Scrooge: Five Principles to Transform Your Relationship with Money, Ted Klontz, Rick Kahler, & Brad Klontz

Money and the Meaning of Life, Jacob Needleman

Recovery and Twelve Step

Adult Children of Alcoholics/Dysfunctional Families, Anonymous

Alcoholics Anonymous, Anonymous

Al-Anon Faces Alcoholism, Anonymous

Al-Anon's Twelve Steps and Twelve Traditions, Anonymous

Alateen—A Day at a Time, Anonymous

Alateen—Hope for Children of Alcoholics, Anonymous

Recovery and Twelve Step continued

Codependents Anonymous, Anonymous

Having Had a Spiritual Awakening, Anonymous

Hope for Today, Anonymous

One Day at a Time in Al-Anon, Anonymous

Sex Addicts Anonymous, Anonymous

Sex and Love Addicts Anonymous, Anonymous

The Courage to Change, Anonymous

The Dilemma of the Alcoholic Marriage, Anonymous

Twelve Steps for Overeaters, Anonymous

Twelve-Step Prayer Book, Anonymous

A Gentle Path Through the Twelve Steps: The Classic Guide for All People in the Process of Recovery, Patrick Carnes

A Woman's Way Through the Twelve Steps, Stephanie Covington

Twelve Steps for Adult Children, Veronica Ray

Trust the Process: An Artist's Guide to Letting Go, Shaun McNiff

The Addictive Personality: Understanding the Addictive Process and Compulsive Behavior, Craig Nakken

Sex Addiction

When He's Married to Mom: How to Help Mother-Enmeshed Men Open Their Hearts to True Love and Commitment, Kenneth Adams

A Gentle Path Through the Twelve Steps: The Classic Guide for All People in the Process of Recovery, Patrick Carnes

Contrary to Love: Helping the Sexual Addict, Patrick Carnes

Don't Call It Love: Recovery From Sexual Addiction, Patrick Carnes

Facing the Shadow: Starting Sexual and Relationship Recovery, Patrick Carnes

Out of the Shadows: Understanding Sexual Addiction, Patrick Carnes

Sexual Anorexia: Overcoming Sexual Self-Hatred, Patrick Carnes

The Betrayal Bond: Breaking Free of Exploitive Relationships, Patrick Carnes

Clinical Management of Sex Addiction, Patrick Carnes & Kenneth Adams

In The Shadows of The Net: Breaking Free from Compulsive Online Sexual Behavior, Patrick Carnes, David Delmonico & Elizabeth Griffin

Disclosing Secrets: When, to Whom, and How Much to Reveal, Deborah Corley & Jennifer Schneider

Lonely All The Time: Recognizing, Understanding,and Overcoming Sex Addiction, for Addicts and Co-dependents, Ralph Earle & Gregory Crowe

Women, Sex and Addiction, Charlotte Kasl

Ten Smart Things Gay Men Can Do to Improve Their Lives, Joe Kort

Ready to Heal, Kelly McDaniel

Cybersex Exposed: Simple Fantasy or Obsession?, Jennifer Schneider & Rob Weiss

Cruise Control: Understanding Sex Addiction in Gay Men, Rob Weiss

Untangling the Web: Sex, Porn, and Fantasy Obsession in the Internet Age, Rob Weiss & Jennifer Schneider

Sexual Abuse

Silently Seduced: When Parents Make their Children Partners—Understanding Covert Incest, Kenneth Adams

The Courage to Heal: A Guide for Women Survivors of Child Sexual Abuse, Ellen Bass & Laura Davis

Against Our Will: Men, Women, and Rape, Susan Brownmiller

Abused Boys: The Neglected Victims of Sexual Abuse, Mic Hunter

Victims No Longer: The Classic Guide for Men Recovering from Sexual Child Abuse, Mike Lew

Spirituality and Meditation

Answers in the Heart: Daily Meditations For Men And Women Recovering From Sex Addiction, Anonymous

Days of Healing, Days of Joy, Anonymous

Spirituality and Meditation continued

Food for Thought: Daily Meditations for Dieters and Overeaters, Anonymous

The Courage to Change, Anonymous

Journey to the Heart: Daily Meditations on the Path to Freeing Your Soul, Melody Beattie

The Language of Letting Go, Melody Beattie

Spiritual Skill Set: Pt 1—Discernment, Patrick Carnes & the Voices From Afar

Spiritual Skill Set: Pt 2—Resilience, Patrick Carnes & the Voices From Afar

Each Day a New Beginning: Daily Meditations for Women, Karen Casey

Yesterday's Tomorrow: Recovery Meditations for Hard Cases, Barry B. Longyear

The Spirituality of Imperfection: Storytelling and the Search for Meaning, Ernest Kurtz & Katherine Ketcham

Addiction and Grace: Love and Spirituality in the Healing of Addictions, Gerald G. May

The Four Agreements: A Practical Guide to Personal Freedom, A Toltec Wisdom Book, Don Miguel Ruiz

Serenity Through Meditation (CD), Sue Neufeld-Ellis

Trauma

The Betrayal Bond: Breaking Free of Exploitive Relationships, Patrick Carnes

Heartwounds: The Impact of Unresolved Trauma and Grief on Relationships, Tian Dayton

Trauma and Addiction: Ending the Cycle of Pain Through Emotional Literacy, Tian Dayton

Waking the Tiger: Healing Trauma : The Innate Capacity to Transform Overwhelming Experiences, Peter Levine & Ann Frederick

Women's Issues

Perfect Daughters, Robert Ackerman

Motherless Daughters: The Legacy of Loss, Hope Edelman

Women, Anger & Depression: Strategies for Self Empowerment, Lois Frankel

My Mother/My Self: The Daughter's Search for Identity, Nancy Friday

The Princess Who Believed in Fairy Tales: A Story for Modern Times, Marcia Grad

Women, Sex, and Addiction: A Search for Love and Power, Charlotte Kasl

Father Hunger: Fathers, Daughters, and the Pursuit of Thinness, Margo Maine

Women Who Hurt Themselves: A Book of Hope and Understanding, Dusty Miller

Ready to Heal, Kelly McDaniel

She Has a Secret: Understanding Female Sexual Addiction, Douglas Weiss

Women Who Love Sex Addicts: Help for Healing from the Effects of a Relationship With a Sex Addict, Douglas Weiss & Diane DeBusk